OUR SENECA

OUR SENECA

BY

CLARENCE W. MENDELL

In Tragedies, the Grecians, Sophocles and Euripides, far overmatch our Seneca.
ROGER ASCHAM

ARCHON BOOKS
1968

Copyright, 1941, by Yale University Press
Reprinted 1968 with permission
in an unaltered and unabridged edition

Library of Congress Catalog Card Number: 68-12526
Printed in the United States of America

TO
E. L. M.

PREFACE

SENECAN influence on the early drama of England is a well-recognized fact. J. W. Cunliffe has presented the evidence in *The Influence of Seneca on Elizabethan Drama*. Perhaps the best appreciation of this influence is that of C. F. Tucker Brooke in *The Tudor Drama*. F. L. Lucas, in *Seneca and Elizabethan Tragedy*, has given a brilliant summary of their results. It is no longer a matter of proving or illustrating the influence of Seneca. Coming, as it does, both directly in the English translation as well as in the original Latin text, and at the same time indirectly, through Italian and French imitations, there can be no question of its importance. The present study is intended to indicate more precisely what Seneca actually had to give to English drama, to make easier an understanding of the Senecan contribution by presenting the social and political background of his plays, and to make possible for students of the drama a more just evaluation of the contribution of classical antiquity to the stage of sixteenth-century England. To do this it is essential to analyze the relation of Seneca to his Greek predecessors. The pre-Elizabethans did not differentiate sharply between Sophocles, Euripides, and Seneca, and yet the differences between the Latin and the Greek dramatists are fully as important as their similarities.

An acquaintance with the plays of Seneca, at least in English translation, is assumed throughout. New translations of the *Oedipus* of Sophocles and the *Oedipus* of Seneca are presented here in the hope of making somewhat more evident to the student of English literature the essential qualities of the two plays and, more generally, the fundamental differences between Greek and Roman drama. All translations are my own except the long quotation from Tacitus on page 62 which is taken from the Loeb edition by W. Peterson.

The following dates are presented here for the convenience of the reader. Many of them are necessarily approximate.

B.C. 580 Birth of Thespis.
525–457 Life of Aeschylus.
497–406 Life of Sophocles.
480–406 Life of Euripides.
449–429 Period of Pericles' power.
340–292 Life of Menander.
323 Death of Alexander the Great.
219–202 Rome's great war with Carthage.
254–184 Life of Plautus.
185–159 Life of Terence.
168 Battle of Pydna.
133 Tiberius Gracchus elected Tribune.
44 Julius Caesar assassinated.
28–14 Augustus in power.
A.D. 4–65 Life of Seneca.
1559–1581 Seneca's tragedies translated into English.
1561/2 Presentation of *Ferrex and Porrex*.
1587 Presentation of *The Misfortunes of Arthur*.

CONTENTS

Preface		vii
I.	Oedipus: Sophocles and Seneca	3
II.	The Background of Senecan Tragedy	22
III.	The Prologue	64
IV.	Dramatic Technique	82
V.	Long Speeches	94
VI.	The Shorter Speeches. Dialogue	116
VII.	The Chorus	124
VIII.	Superhuman Element	139
IX.	Philosophic Content	152
X.	Stock Characters	169
XI.	Conclusion	189
Oedipus Tyrannus of Sophocles—Verse Translation		201
Oedipus Rex of Seneca—Verse Translation		251

OUR SENECA

OUR SENECA

CHAPTER I
OEDIPUS: SOPHOCLES AND SENECA

IT is a familiar assumption that the great English drama is somehow the outgrowth of the Greek, that Shakespeare is the child of Euripides. This is a tenable assumption if we substitute the words great-grandchild for child. Yet in that change lies a whole world of difference. Euripides begat Seneca. Yes, but what of the inheritance from the side of the mother? How much of the true spirit of Euripides descended to his Roman son and to what extent was that legacy dominated by the hot Italic blood of the other party to the marriage? Seneca begat Marlowe and Kyd but they too had a mother, a mother not long since set at liberty from the confines of the Church. And Marlowe, shall we say, begat Shakespeare? No doubt of that, I presume, but what once again of the mother? A robust creature with a rather hard sense of reality, with an understanding of the world of her day, with a love of humor that is strangely lacking in the male line, with a poise and balance and withal a soul of poetic beauty and romantic imagination. An Elizabethan wench, in fact, wedded somewhat incongruously to the scion of the house of Cordova. An uneasy union scarcely blessed by holy rites but doubly happy in its fruits.

It is hardly to be wondered at if the great-grandfather's Attic features, either of face or character, are scarcely discernible in the Elizabethan child. It will seem even less wonderful if we stop to realize how much we have studied the later family history, how scantily and superficially the middle reaches of the tree. But enough of genealogical figures.

Like the Elizabethans themselves we have been too ready to accept Seneca as the reflection of Aeschylus and Sophocles and Euripides when in reality he is a copy in a different medium. If we are to understand the effect of the translation of Seneca upon Kyd and Marlowe and Shakespeare we must first know Seneca and what he was endeavoring to do. Let us plunge into the midst of the difficulties without even preliminary caution.

Sophocles wrote a play called *Oedipus*. He presented it before an audience who knew fairly well the story of the hero. His play began with a group of suppliants gathered before the palace. To this group Oedipus speaks:

> My children, ancient Kadmos' newest brood,
> What is this embassy that waits impatient
> Bedecked with suppliant branches? All our town
> Is filled with sound of holy sacrifice
> And paeans too and wailing misery.
> These things, my children, I have deemed it wrong
> To learn from others: I went forth myself,
> I, famed on the lips of all men, Oedipus.
> But tell me, sire—for thou art fit to speak
> For these—in what mood stand ye there? In fear
> Or loyalty? Stony of heart the man
> Who finds no pity for such embassy.

Granting a royal dignity of phrase that sounds perhaps too ponderous to our ears, this is direct and illuminating. The place, the occasion, even the name of the speaker are introduced naturally. In twelve lines we are presented with a situation and know where we are. There were no playbills in Athens and no programs. The lines had to speak for themselves and, in this instance at least, they did so adequately.

Seneca had before him the *Oedipus* of Sophocles when he wrote his play of the same name. In the later drama as in the earlier, Oedipus is the opening speaker:

> Banishing night, the uncertain sun returns,
> The dawn creeps up by squalid clouds oppressed:
> And, with a baleful light of ominous flame,
> It shall behold homes swept by greedy pest
> As day shall show destruction wrought by night.
> Joys any man in power? O treacherous boon,
> What ills with what fair seeming thou dost hide!
> Even as the loftiest peaks—

And so on for upward of ninety lines, bemoaning the pestilence-ridden town, the woes of kings, his own unhappy past, and finally once more the plague, involving all.

Let us take first the most obvious mechanical differences that appear here. Only late in the speech are we given any hint as to the place: the race of Cadmus is mentioned in line 34. The speaker is never named. There is no realistic motivation for the speech: to whom is the speaker addressing this recital of woes and why?

When Oedipus is finally compelled to pause for breath Iokaste interposes a half-dozen lines that turn the stream of oratory into a new direction:

> What avails my lord
> To augment with such complaint these evils sore?
> This is the role of kings methinks, to accept
> Misfortunes, and the more in doubt thy state,
> The while the might of crumbling empire fails,
> With foot more firmly planted brave to stand.
> 'Tis not the hero's part to flee from Fate.

Oedipus responds with a defense of himself and his courage, attested by his bout with the Sphinx. A short interchange of remarks on this theme winds up the scene.

But to return to Sophocles. In answer to the direct question of Oedipus, the old priest describes the pestilence and appeals to the King, as father of his people, to help them in their distress. He, the King, speaks his sympathy and explains that he has sent Kreon to Delphi to obtain advice. The priest spies Kreon returning and on his entry he reports the word of the oracle, bidding the people of Thebes drive out the murderer of their earlier King Laius. Oedipus asks some practical questions which bring out the story of Laius' death and the reasons why it has not been further investigated. Oedipus orders an assembly of the people to hear his proclamation and he and Kreon go within to prepare it.

Further differences between the two prologues emerge clearly. The Sophoclean scene develops the actual situation concretely and rapidly. The background of the play *in fact* is presented without waste of time or words. The Senecan, on the other hand, presents a *color tone* and very little else (with one exception to be considered presently). It paints a background of gloom and horror but it does not advance the story at all commensurably with the time expended.

The exception noted is this: Oedipus does bring into his first long speech something of his earlier history—the oracle that warned him of his destiny to be a parricide, guilty of incest, his earlier home in Corinth with his supposed mother and father, Merope and Polybus. Now these points are not immediately necessary for the development of the story. Sophocles, by reserving them, added greatly to his dramatic effect. Seneca, perhaps in his cleverness, felt that it was unreasonable for Iokaste not to be familiar with them and so felt disinclined to hold them in suspense as did Sophocles. But primarily I think he introduced them at this point because parricide and incest added to the general color of horror that he was trying to paint with the utmost intensity.

Again, the Oedipus of Seneca, to all intents and purposes, pronounces a monologue. To be sure, Iokaste technically saves the situation, but only technically. Dramatically her part is wholly undeveloped in this act and, as a result, Oedipus' part is grievously unmotivated.

Again, the effort of the Roman poet to produce sententious lines is at once apparent. There is rhetoric in Sophocles but it is the rhetoric of a man under a terrific strain. It is in part the result of the poetic form of the drama, in part it comes naturally from the lips of an old and emotional priest. It does not labor and it does not become generic. The Senecan rhetoric has another ring:

> Joys any man in power? O treacherous boon,
> What ills with what fair seeming thou dost hide!

> We have stained heaven with guilt.

> The pest filches the cure.

SOPHOCLES AND SENECA

These are not particularly striking phrases, but they are sententious.

Finally, the Senecan lines as compared with the Sophoclean show, to an alarming extent, a repetition of one idea with varied expression, a piling up of phrase to present a single effect. It will be necessary to quote at length to illustrate this.

> No tender breeze with cooling draught revives
> The hearts that breathe forth flames, no Zephyrs light
> Blow now, but Titan multiplies the fires
> Of burning Dog Star, pressing hard behind
> The Nemean lion. Moisture leaves the rivers,
> Color the grass; Dirce is dry, within
> A tenuous stream Ismenus flows and scarce
> Moistens the shallows with its failing flood.
> Darkened, from heaven Phoebus' sister slips,
> The world ensaddened pales 'neath clouded day.
> No star shines forth in any night serene
> But black and heavy vapor broods o'er earth.
> The counterfeit of hell hath deep disguised
> The strongholds of the gods, the homes on high.
> Ceres, long pregnant, will not bring to birth
> But trembles yellowing on the lofty stalks.
> In withering shoots the sterile harvest dies.

This is by no means all but it will suffice. The method is the cumulative method. There is no restraint, no condensation whatsoever. And yet the old priest of the Sophoclean play presents the pestilence naturally and perhaps more effectively in a few lines:

> For, as thou seest too, our commonwealth
> Labors full sore nor yet avails to lift
> Its head above the billowing surge of death,
> Wasting alike in the rich crops of earth
> And in her grazing herds, while women suffer
> The pangs of barren childbirth. Through her midst
> The fire-bearing god, mad pestilence,
> Hurling his shafts, scourges relentlessly
> Our city till, beneath his hand, the home
> Of Kadmos is made void and Hades black
> With groans and lamentations is enriched.

In Sophocles this is all and it is enough. The lines quoted from Seneca are but a fraction of the whole and less terrible than those that follow, describing the deaths in the city and the fights over earth and fire for the funerals.

But the contrast between diffuse writing and compact is by no means the only difference here. Sophocles is simple as well as brief. The pestilence *is* referred to as a god with fiery shafts passing through the city but even this can hardly be called a figure of speech. It was so familiar as to be almost accepted as a literal description. With such a simple adornment Seneca was not content. Astronomy has to be called in and geography. The show of learning is not oppressive but it is noticeable. The story of the Sphinx is elaborated at the expense of dignity.

Before we leave the prologue I should like to emphasize two more points that are, I suspect, obvious but nonetheless worth some attention. The Sophoclean Oedipus is clearly concerned over the state of affairs but by no means in a panic. He is the efficient king, confident in his position, serene. The Senecan king breathes horror and self-distrust when he begins his speech. No satisfying explanation for this is forthcoming. The pestilence is distressing, but it is not convincing when the pestilence makes the king suddenly cringe in terror of oracles that he is sure he outwitted more than ten years before. It requires an elaborate conceit—enthusiastically developed by Seneca—to explain this situation. Oedipus argues that as he alone is untouched by the pest—a premise obviously untrue—he must be reserved for something worse. For no good reason, then, we start the Senecan play on a note of abysmal gloom and horror. Oedipus is a terror-stricken king who cringes and rants alternately.

The other obvious observation is on the mechanical side. Granted the palace background of the Greek theater and the altar in the orchestra in front, the motivation of Oedipus' entrance is perfectly clear. What is this embassy, he asks, as he steps forth from the palace. The entrance of Kreon later is prepared for elaborately. So too the exits are carefully handled. Oedipus sends off the embassy and announces that he will proceed to carry out the injunctions of Apollo. Aside from an actual statement that he and Kreon are going into the house nothing could be much plainer. The stage is cleared simply and reasonably. Now in Seneca there is no particular reason for Oedipus' presence anywhere when the play begins. Toward the end of the first speech we suspect that he came to the altar to pray for help. When Iokaste breaks in at line 81, it comes as a distinct surprise—in reading the play, of course—and there is no explanation of her presence or any sign of her entrance. No exits are prepared for. Iokaste must leave, for she is not present in the next scene. Oedipus may have remained through the singing of the choral ode that follows although this would be highly unorthodox without some special excuse. No sound motivation is given for the departure of either the King or the Queen.

A word in summary before we leave the prologues. The Greek serves the familiar function of putting the audience *en rapport* with the situation, explaining to them what has happened before the play begins, and making it perfectly clear to them who the characters are and at what stage of the history the play begins. The stories were familiar, it is true, but it was important to tell the audience what form of a particular myth was being used, and what part of it was presumed as antecedent. Exposition was evidently the chief function of the prologos, and hence the aptness of its name. But its function is rather broader than this would indicate. From the prologos we expect to get our conception of one or more of the chief characters as they exist normally before any of the things happen to them that are bound to happen in a tragedy. Sophocles, in the present instance, confines himself largely to a presentation of the chief character, Oedipus, and, as we have seen, does it successfully.

Obviously, to Seneca the prologue was a rather different affair. Almost we are tempted for the first few minutes to think that this is just an unmotivated recitation, a speech before the play begins, to put us in the proper mood and, of course, to let us know incidentally about the pestilence. But then it turns out that Iokaste is there, or else comes on, and we have to admit that the play itself is really under way. So we are forced to assume that this panic-stricken monarch is the man with whom the tragedy is even now beginning. At once there is evident a difference in the kind of interest which the two Oedipuses are capable of arousing. The Sophoclean is sympathetic, a reasonable, dignified, appealing sovereign. The Senecan is a device for arousing horror, and he is only that. We do not see the normal man, if such existed in Seneca's mind; we do not find really a man at all, only the mouthpiece of horror, an eloquent and even a moving exponent of dread, but not a sympathetic hero.

Perhaps we have spent too much time on the first few lines of a single play. But the qualities that appear there are typical. The prologue is followed by the first choral ode, technically called the parodos, which must be left until we consider the choruses as a whole. We skip the parodos, therefore, and plunge into Act II. In Sophocles it opens with a fairly long speech by Oedipus. But this was prepared for in the first act. The people, represented now by the chorus, were to be assembled to listen to the proclamation. They have come and Oedipus, emerging from the palace, finds them praying to the gods for help. He addresses them naturally and gets right to his point:

> Ye pray, and what ye pray for—if straightway
> Ye hearken to my words and give me aid
> Against the pestilence—ye may attain.

Then follows an imprecation against the murderer of Laius, an appeal for information, a curse on those who refuse help, a blessing on such as give it. The chorus leader, after remarking that god ought to have told more—a human criticism not unfamiliar—makes a practical suggestion:

> After lord Phoebus, he who seeth most
> In harmony, our lord Tiresias,
> Might best reward our present questioning.

Oedipus replies that already, at Kreon's suggestion, he has sent for the old seer to help him out. Thus Tiresias' coming is naturally motivated and he comes presently as expected. Several familiar facts about the scene that follows should be recalled to mind. Tiresias did not know why he was summoned. He did know all the facts about the murder of Laius. He is taken unaware by the questions put to him and refuses to answer because of the complications involved in a true answer. The quarrel that follows is reasonable and natural. Oedipus' suspicions of Tiresias are wholly natural, too. Furthermore, Kreon had suggested sending for Tiresias who finally in anger denounces Oedipus. What more logical for the King to conclude than that here is evidence of conspiracy? In other words, we have in this scene the splendid development of a well-knit plot. When Tiresias departs with threats not too thoroughly veiled, the story has advanced far and logically.

Turning now to Seneca. It is perhaps a minor detail that Oedipus appears on stage without any apparent reason. It is not, I think, a minor detail that Kreon's arrival the next minute has not been prepared for in any way. He just happens along like a character in the comedy. And Oedipus, for no reason in the world except the atmosphere of horror already created, shudders at his arrival. But we are doing Seneca something of an injustice. Oedipus explains his terror:

> With dread I tremble fearful whither fate
> May lead, my fluttering heart fails me distraught
> By twin emotions: when ambiguous
> Joys come commingled with calamity
> The uncertain mind, though eager, fears to know.

And then we recall the last line of the first act and realize—as the audience could hardly have done, as no one could be expected to do who did not have a text of the play in which he could look back and reread—that the word that Kreon might bring was what Oedipus had in mind when he said:

> One safety, only one, remains for us:
> If Phoebus show us yet the way to life.

Could anyone who did not have in mind the play of Sophocles understand from those two lines that Oedipus had sent his brother-in-law Kreon to Delphi to inquire of the oracle and to bring back to Thebes the advice of Apollo how best to avert the pestilence? Not, I think, an average theater audience, even at Rome. We must conclude that Seneca was not much interested in the niceties of his technique. One thing that did interest him follows immediately. Kreon, instead of reporting the oracle simply and directly, lays down a background that is worth quoting in full:

> Dull torpor wraps my limbs, my blood congeals;
> For when with suppliant foot at Phoebus' shrine
> I entered, duly raising reverent hands
> In prayer unto the god, an ominous roar
> Burst from Parnassus' twofold citadel
> Snow-clad, and Phoebus' laurel pendant there
> Trembled and shook its leaves, while suddenly
> Castalia's sacred stream stood motionless.
> Straightway the Letoan prophetess began
> To shake her dreadful locks, in frenzy caught
> To receive Apollo. Ere she had reached the cave
> Burst forth these words in more than human voice:

This setting of terror will reappear later, but it is noteworthy here because it is so out of proportion with the situation. This first step in the unfolding of the mystery is already presented with the maximum of intensity. Nothing is left for any situation that requires a higher pitch.

Oedipus has only begun to extract from Kreon by questioning the facts of Laius' murder when, without any motivation whatever, the blind seer Tiresias comes stumbling in with his interpreter Manto. He is not the Tiresias of Sophocles. Although Oedipus assumes that he knows about the oracle from Apollo and that, as Apollo's representative, he can explain it, the surprising fact is at once evident that he has no superhuman knowledge of the facts. He says that he is too old to receive the god directly! He is a priest, interpreter of signs. That he is blind is only a happy excuse for having Manto describe to him all that she sees. It seems, although we have not been forewarned, that a sacrifice is preparing. In all its details, spectacular and physio-

SOPHOCLES AND SENECA

logical, Manto describes it vividly and the priest receives intimations of horror. The scene is long and harrowing and well nigh exhausts even Seneca's vocabulary, but it produces no results so far as the solution of the plot is concerned. It makes use of a hundred lines merely to give another thrill of horror. At the end, Tiresias decides that to find the required answer he must invoke the spirit of Laius and, with Kreon as witness, departs to do so.

Gone is the direct simplicity of the scene in Sophocles. In the Greek play, goaded to speech by the intolerable accusations of the King, Tiresias bursts forth:

> Is't true? I charge thee then from thy decree
> Swerve not, nor from this day forevermore
> Speak unto these or me: thou art the man
> That bringest on this land the curse of guilt.

Sophocles uses four lines in contrast with all the hocus-pocus of Seneca. And the explanation? Surely it lay in the purposes of the two poets: the one developing a dramatic plot, economically, logically, relentlessly; the other delighting in hair-raising recitation.

One thing must be noted in passing, even in so hurried a review of this all-important act, namely, the speech of Sophocles' Oedipus after Tiresias has made his direct charge and Oedipus is overcome by his belief in the treachery of Kreon. The first eleven lines are spoken in exclamation addressed to no one. They seem to represent the germ of the philosophizing monologue that, trained under the instruction of Seneca, passed through an apprenticeship with Kyd and Marlowe, to emerge in such famous passages as "To be or not to be." And they illustrate vividly the difference between Sophocles and Seneca when it comes to the use of sustained exclamation.

> O wealth and power and craft outreaching craft
> Throughout our jealous life. What envious thrust
> Can we be safe from if for this throne's sake
> Whereof by gift I ne'er solicited

> Thebes made me master, if for this my lord
> Kreon the faithful—friend since first I came—
> Secretly plotting seeks to thrust me forth,
> Suborning for his aid this muddling priest
> That knows the wiles of wealth, sees faultlessly
> Where gain is for the getting, yet straightway,
> Sought for his priestcraft, stumbles and is blind.

Even in such reflections as these, where, if anywhere, the generic might be expected, Sophocles remains specific and objective.

With Act III the parallelism of the two plays ceases, for the time being at least. Seneca has his own great scene to inject into the drama, the description by Kreon of the invocation of the dead Laius. It has a clearly defined technique. First, a passage of short speeches in which Oedipus demands to know what Kreon has to report, then an excessively long narrative of the reported event, finally the concluding passage, consisting of the resulting conversation, in this case an altercation, with speeches growing shorter as the emotion rises. The two passages of dialogue are in reality a framework for the narrative which is an entity by itself. It begins with a description of the scene:

> Far from the city walls there lies a grove
> Dark with thick ilex; Dirce's is the spot
> Within a well washed valley. Stately woods
> Are guarded by a cypress and an oak,
> Spreading wide crooked branches dry with age.
> One side consuming time has stripped away,
> The other, tearing loose its rotted roots,
> Leans on its neighbors. Laurel trees are there
> With bitter berries, quivering lindens too
> And Paphian myrtle, ash that presently
> Shall drive its oarage through the unending sea,
> And pines whose branches battle Zephyrus,
> Defying Phoebus. In the very midst
> Rises a mighty tree whose shade widespread
> Covers the lesser woods, with far flung limb.
> Alone it stands defender of the grove;
> Darkling beneath, bereft of Phoebus' light,
> The unmoving waters sense eternal chill,
> A stagnant swamp that rims a sluggish spring.

SOPHOCLES AND SENECA

Then follows the narrative, rapid enough when not from time to time held up for the sake of some gruesome picture.

> Hither the aged priest guided his step
> Nor hesitated, for the spot itself
> Bred night. Into a trench new dug were hurled
> Torches snatched up from funeral pyres.

The narrative itself, compelling and tense, need not detain us except for long enough to note the descriptive pause when hell opens and disgorges its ghastly brood (figures made familiar by repeated descriptions in the works of one Roman poet after another):

> Forth in ranks there leaped
> Full armed the serpent host, the Dircaean line
> Of brothers, harvest of the dragon's teeth;
> Baleful Erinys shrieked and Madness blind,
> Horror and all the hidden brood produced
> In the eternal darkness: Grief that tore
> Her locks, Disease with weary sinking head,
> Old Age that hates itself, uncertain Fear
> And Pestilence, the greedy scourge of Thebes.

Such the serried ranks of Dis but quite different the figures of comparison:

> Straightway like fleecy clouds flitting they come
> To breathe heaven's freedom. Eryx scatters not
> So many falling leaves; innumerable
> They come as flowers on Hybla in the spring
> When gather swarms of bees, more countless they
> Than waves that shatter on the Ionian Sea
> Or birds in winter flying from the wrath
> Of Strymon's bitter cold, cleaving the sky
> To exchange the Arctic snows for the warm Nile.
> So thronged the shades to hear the prophet's voice.

With his unconquerably bad taste, Seneca has culled far and wide these lovely similes regardless of their incongruity. For the shades are Zethos and Amphion with their mother, Agave and Pentheus and finally Laius. Flowers and birds indeed!

The corresponding act in Sophocles, who had no need of or interest in a necromantic exhibition, is occupied with the logical development of the quarrel between Oedipus and Kreon which is finally suspended by the intervention of Iokaste who naturally hears the altercation from within. This is compressed in Seneca into a few lines at the end of the act. It had perforce to be introduced but it is subordinated to the more showy narrative of the scene of exorcism. It is not difficult to understand or explain the procedure of Seneca. The technique is that of the messenger speeches. In Aeschylus much of the story was still under the sway of epic tradition. Sophocles too had speeches by messengers, used to supply parts of the story essential to the plot but ill-suited to presentation because of time or place which could not be varied at will by the dramatist. The messenger was often excited and sometimes timorous. When pacified, he was generally diffuse which was in character, for he was traditionally of the herdsman or common-soldier class. Euripides enjoyed those speeches for themselves and with his interest in minor characters often elaborated them unduly. The herdsman in the *Iphigeneia* is familiar and the similar messenger in the *Bacchae*. Seneca had all this tradition before him as well as the epyllia of Rome and the contemporary fashion in epic poetry. Furthermore, as has been appearing in our present study, he seems to have been thinking of the possibilities of his work from the point of view of recitation rather than acting. Hence the value of these purple patches and the emphasis on the part at the expense of the whole. In just this way did Lucan treat the heroic epic and for similar reasons. The custom of public recitation was already well under way in Persius' time and by Seneca's was rampant.

At this point it is clear that, with his handling of the plot, Sophocles is ready for the inevitable converging of the various threads, for the great crescendo leading to the tragic climax. But what climax can Seneca manage? His greatest bolt has been shot. Oedipus and Iokaste simply happen in on the stage and the latter has begun to furnish her husband with the details that he requires when an old man from Corinth enters pouring out in

SOPHOCLES AND SENECA

rapid-fire conversation the news of Polybus' death and of Oedipus' origin. Just as casually the herdsman Phorbas drifts in to furnish the supplementary information that is necessary. Oedipus and Iokaste withdraw (apparently) and the messengers leave (also presumably). After the briefest possible choral interlude a messenger reports the blinding of Oedipus who appears from within. Iokaste (inexplicably present), after some hesitation as to what part of her anatomy to attack, stabs herself in the womb and dies on the stage. Oedipus simply wanders off, careful not to stumble over his dead wife. The play ends on the same note with which it opened:

> O Fate all violent, dreadful Disease,
> Wasting and Pestilence and direful Grief
> Be ye my guides: such leadership be mine.

It is here in the latter third of the two plays that the differences begin to show their significance most clearly. In the Greek, the unfolding of the tragic truth is gradual, inexorable. The culmination is not hurried at any point. There is something august about the fates of Iokaste and Oedipus even when the messenger for the first time—but perfectly naturally—yields to the temptation to retail gory details. The tragedy has reached a point at which these details are congruous. Sophocles' play proves itself to have been the poised unfolding of an inevitable drama. When Seneca had exhausted his melodrama there was no vitality left in the plot itself and nothing for him to do but to wind up the play as quickly as possible.

In this connection, it is interesting to note that, although Sophocles' play is half as long again as Seneca's, the latter devotes 250 lines to the injected material dealing with the sacrifice and magic, and 299 lines to choruses. Of the remaining 512 lines, 109 comprise Oedipus' opening harangue (except for 6 lines by Iokaste to guide the flow of rhetoric and relieve the monologue) and 64 are spoken by the messenger who has the stage to himself except for the chorus, leaving 339 lines for what may fairly be called dialogue. The most rigid exclusion can hardly reduce the number of lines of dialogue in the Greek play to a thousand. The choral odes occupy 224 lines, leaving some 250 lines for the longer speeches—all of which are actually incorporated in the dialogue. To put it in another way, Sophocles devotes two thirds of his play to rapid and wholly natural dialogue and no fraction to spectacular side shows; Seneca uses less than a third of his for natural dialogue, a quarter for his innovations, and nearly a sixth for two long speeches which he does not properly incorporate into what we should consider realistic dramatic action.

Before leaving the *Oedipus*, there is one more element that cannot be ignored, the choruses. In Sophocles' *Oedipus* the chorus is much reduced from the days of Aeschylus. It takes no very great part in the action and in this regard the Latin chorus differs little from that of Sophocles. But with that exception the two have almost nothing in common. In the Greek play the choruses fill natural pauses in the action. The orchestra has been left unoccupied for reasons entirely logical. This is true in Seneca of the chorus which occupies the time of the invocation of Laius' ghost. It is not wholly true of any other choral ode. These odes do not in general *fill* the pauses, they *make* the breaks between scenes of the play. They have lost what little naturalism was left to the chorus; they have become largely mechanical devices.

The five choral odes of Sophocles, on the other hand, furnish a splendid lyrical comment on the drama as it progresses. Each springs naturally from the dramatic situation of the moment. The first one sings of the disturbing oracle that has come and of the pestilence, turning for help to Athena, Zeus, Apollo, and Dionysus, the special patron of Thebes. The second has for its theme the mystery of the murderer, his unenviable situation, and the conviction that it can hardly be Oedipus. In the third ode the chorus expresses its horror at the attitude of Iokaste toward oracles, shudders at her dangerous sentiments, and voices the more conventional piety. The fourth ode is a burst of joy in anticipation of the discovery that Oedipus is Theban-born, while the last is filled with sympathetic mourning over the tragic turn which the plot finally takes.

Seneca does not, to anything like the same extent, adapt his choruses to the progress of the play. His first ode deals, to be sure, with the horrors of the pestilence and does full justice to the dreadful subject. The second is a hymn to Bacchus. It is noteworthy that the few lines by the Sophoclean chorus invoking the aid of the national hero-god are expanded into a full ode to the joyous wine divinity with all of his conventional attributes and only the most tenuous connection with the immediate situation. The very effort to connect it exposes all the more apparently the total lack of connection: as Tiresias leaves the stage at the end of the preceding act he enjoins the chorus:

> Whilst I explore the hidden depths of Styx,
> Let ring the native song of Bacchus' praise.

The third ode deals with the Cadmeian history. The fourth and fifth are short, treating, one the virtue of moderation, the other the power of Fate, both in the best Stoic manner, wholly un-Greek, the truly Roman product of the first-century philosopher.

Considering the character of the Senecan choruses, it is not surprising to discover their metrical quality. There is very little of the anapestic rhythm so regularly associated with the entrance of the Greek chorus; there is none of the choral quality, the rhythmical accompaniment of the dance of the original dramatic chorus. What we have is a jumble of the simpler meters of the Latin lyric, the meters of Horace and Catullus. This would be curious if we could still believe that Seneca's play was intended for acting: it is not surprising in view of the strong suspicion that he wrote it to be read to a literary audience, a suspicion that will become a certainty when we review the mechanics of Seneca's plays.

Finally the more mechanical side of the dramatic technique, already touched on incidentally, presents a marked contrast in the two plays. At the opening of the Greek drama, Oedipus addresses the suppliants in such a way as to identify both them and himself and to indicate the situation. This is reinforced by the priest who addresses Oedipus perfectly naturally by name.

20   OUR SENECA

Kreon's mission to Delphi is mentioned and his expected return. His entrance is natural and emphatic. At the close of the act Oedipus dismisses the embassy and, while his own exit and that of Kreon are not specifically indicated, they are both wholly obvious. The same is true of Oedipus' return to the stage when he comes forth to make his proclamation and directly addresses the chorus. As this second act progresses, Tiresias' entrance is treated almost exactly like Kreon's in the first act. At the end Tiresias bids Oedipus go within, and the implication of his own departure is clear. And so on through the play. Each entrance and exit is plainly and dramatically prepared and handled. The messenger from Corinth comes in without any preparation, for his visit is that dramatic accident in the affairs of men which brings on the catastrophe, but his identity is carefully disclosed by questions from the chorus.

In the Senecan play almost the opposite conditions prevail. At the opening, the first hint of the speaker's identity is his reference in the eleventh line to his father Polybus. The name of Oedipus does not occur in the play until line 216. Iokaste addresses him as husband at line 81 and in 773 he speaks to her as wife, but her name appears first and only at line 1005. There are only six instances in the play in which entrances are noted; in other cases the characters merely speak and how they appear on the stage is not explained. Of the six instances, two consist of the threadbare device so familiar in comedy, the creaking door, in each case noted by the chorus. (911: *postes sonant, maestus en famulus*, etc. 995: *sonuere fores atque ipse suum / duce non illo molitur iter / luminis orbus*.) The other four are also rather weak dramatically and again resemble in method the practice of comedy which did not much interest itself in niceties of entrance technique. "Who is this," asks Oedipus in line 202, "that comes hurrying toward the palace? Is it Kreon?" "Kreon it is," answers the chorus. Furthermore, this is at the opening of an act and Oedipus himself has had no introduction at all. In line 288, Kreon remarks: "Here in the nick of time comes Tiresias," while, at line 838, it is Oedipus who exclaims: "Behold the old man Phorbas," and, at line 1004, the chorus leader announces the entrance of the Queen: "Behold Iokaste rushing forth in rage." Three of the six cases begin with *en, ecce,* or both and all are crudely mechanical.

The same general contrast appears between the exits of the two plays, although Seneca does more often furnish some announcement of the departure of a character than of his entrance.

To what extent do the other plays modify or confirm our inferences from this one? The answering of this question will at once necessitate a great widening of the field: Seneca had before him not only the plays of Sophocles but those of Aeschylus and Euripides, and he was familiar with other Roman tragedies which we do not possess. It is a question, however, that must be postponed, if the answer is to be of much value, until after a review of the environment that conditioned the two literatures, that of Pericles' Athens and that of Nero's Rome.

CHAPTER II
THE BACKGROUND OF SENECAN TRAGEDY
I

GREEK tragedy, whatever its precise origin, began as a religious ceremonial. This simple fact was in itself all-important in determining the most essential characteristics of the tragedy even after it had departed far from its original choral simplicity. It meant that the plays were always inherently serious, dealing with dignified, important ideas. It meant that they practically never departed from the traditional mythology of the race to find new subject matter. It meant that they were on the whole extremely conservative in form as well, so that, in spite of the rapid development of artistic detail, the fundamental type remained always recognizable. It meant that they remained always something to be sung and acted, never something merely to be read. And perhaps most important of all, though at the same time most difficult precisely to demonstrate, it meant that always the Attic tragedies retained a communal quality, never becoming the precious and artificial amusement of a learned clique. The last two points are closely related and should be considered carefully.

The simple dances from which the tragedy sprang were undoubtedly community affairs. The chorus was large and its performance was a ceremonial matter in which all the folk had an immediate interest. In general it was a single performance for a particular occasion, possibly recurring at long intervals but not something to which the ordinary townsman might go or not as the spirit moved him. It was the business of the community and for the moment all its business. This of course did not continue always to be the case but it was true at the beginning and never did the effect of this all-embracing communal interest completely disappear. Even when Athens had taken to herself the dramatic rituals of the countryside and had formalized them in the Dionysiac precinct by the Acropolis, they still represented a function of the body politic, supported by the city, and participated in by great audiences that comprised a large proportion of the citizens. Aristophanes makes Aeschylus and Euripides agree on the serious public responsibility of playwrights, although they are widely at variance over the nature of the teaching which they should provide. A playwright that misled the populace of Athens or was guilty of sacrilege in his productions might die in far-off exile on the very same principle that demanded the cup of hemlock for Socrates.

The presentation of a play was always a public ceremonial, preceded by the proper sacrifice and surrounded with the proper pageantry, participated in by the public authorities, both civil and religious, and by the sovereign people of the city. Such being the case, the tragedy was never confused with comedy. It remained dignified even when somewhat modernized by its most radical exponent, Euripides, who seemed to the conservative critic to have introduced a dangerous realism into the traditional drama. Such realism as did succeed in getting a precarious foothold accounts for the slight traits of humor that may be found, very rarely, in the tragedies. There is no admixture of comedy, no relaxation of the seriousness of the plays. Furthermore, the same touch of realism is oddly enough responsible for the rhetoric that is supposed to mar the later plays. It is never the sort of specious decoration that one associates with the circus barker or the shilling shocker. It is the rhetoric that was rife in Athens in the late fifth century, the newly formulated art of persuasion, at first a legitimate and useful tool of public life until it was seized upon by professional educators, systematized, commercialized, and shorn of its manhood. But before this process had progressed to any great extent, the drama and the environment that produced it had already come to an end.

For it is hard to think of this Attic tragedy as existing, certainly as continuing to grow, in any community that we know of except that of free Athens. Without fear of any charge of exaggeration or sentimentality, it can safely be said that the Athenians as a people had an extraordinarily high average of intelligence, an unusual endowment of imagination, and an unequaled appreciation of the artistic. At the same time their political tradition welded them into a community, full of antagonisms and petty squabbles, scarcely ever wholly harmonious, but nevertheless a community whose essential integrity was fundamentally more important to the individual than his own immediate interest or hobby. There were of course plenty of exceptions but on the whole the generalization is justified. One has but to remember the institution of ostracism to be convinced. When it ceased to be true the days of free Athens were over.

Now the Rome of 200 B.C. was also a free community in which the individual scarcely existed apart from the state. But it was a community of wholly different individuals. The most outstanding creation of the Athenian was his art, of the Roman his law. Both were great builders; but the Greek built beautiful temples and theaters, the Italian magnificent highways and aqueducts. The Athenian was a trader and diplomat, the Roman a farmer and a fighter. But the Roman, arriving late in the era of Mediterranean civilization and with little enough imagination of his own with which to develop art or literature or philosophy, was by nature acquisitive. He had not, like the Athenian, built an empire by lording it over other communities that fell to him by conquest or chicanery. He had expanded by absorbing his neighbors and their accumulated contribution to civilization, when necessary, shaping these to his own uninspired but effective use.

It was in the course of this process that the Romans met the Greek civilization in the towns of Magna Graecia. Already the great plays of the fifth century had become library treasures. In the first place, centuries had gone by and Greek civilization had certainly not stood still under Alexander and his successors. Also the colonial world was not the same as that of Athens. Third-century Sicily and the Athens of Pericles compared in somewhat the same fashion as modern America and Elizabethan London. But Alexandria had in the meanwhile canonized the old literature and, in the literary world, Aeschylus and Sophocles and Euripides had acquired the dignity of classics along with Homer and Herodotus and Plato. By their side there came to the Romans their real successors, the writers of the New Comedy. They were more nearly contemporary and in a way much more congenial to the Romans who had a rudimentary comedy of their own, a holiday amusement for the crowd. But the élite of Rome went in for absorbing and imitating the Greek classics in the grand manner. And after the epic came at once the drama. The tragedy can never have been very vital to them. Homer had the universal touch. He was not Athenian literature; he was artistically mature but essentially simple and direct and universally appealing. The tragedies were sufficiently universal but they were immeasurably too speculative, too largely intellectual for any but the few at Rome. Their subject matter was an alien mythology that even the most desperate attempts could not identify successfully with the Italic versions and their sophistication was even more alien still. So we find throughout the days of the Roman Republic a sort of hypocritical admiration for the Greek drama, evidenced by not a little imitation, done with no understanding of the real values of the originals but tending, as it moved further from mere translation, toward a superficial imitation of the obvious forms, infused with a spirit and adorned with details that were wholly Italic. These Roman products approached popularity only when they diverged farthest from the essential qualities of the Greek plays and furnished gruesome entertainment for the not too sensitive audience. Ordinarily they were written for the intellectuals alone and it is hard to believe that their interest was wholly ingenuous or keenly enthusiastic.

It must, however, be recognized at once that the Rome of Scipio was by no means the same thing as the Rome of Nero, either in the make-up of the city, its constituent population, or its intellectual atmosphere. Rome, the one-time little trading village by the Tiber side, had become the great metropolitan center of the world, and whatever its tastes, whatever our modern estimate of its moral and esthetic qualities, no one can question the sophistication of the society that produced the Golden House of Nero and the novel of Petronius. The average modern reader has a curious twofold picture of Rome: on the one hand, the city dominated by the noble simplicity of a Cincinnatus, ruled by a senate whose incorruptibility made the visiting oriental marvel in disbelief; on the other hand, a modern Babylon of unimaginable wealth and cruelty and degeneration, the milieu of a Poppaea, the playground of a Nero, and the scene of a continuous slaughter of innocent Christians. The one picture is due to the efficiency of such *laudatores temporis acti* as Livy and Tacitus, to a fond exaggeration of the blessedness of the good old days by an age and a class that had much natural human regret and little historical perspective. The other picture is due to pagan satirists and Christian fanatics. Neither is complete or exact and yet each holds something of the truth. And if the Rome of Cincinnatus was very different from the Athens of Pericles there is an even wider gulf between fifth-century Athens and the city of Nero. It is this last that we must so far as possible understand if we are to have a proper conception of what Seneca's imitation of Attic tragedy really was.

II

"Warning: No one shall show a new senator the way to the senate house." So read an effective lampoon spread through Rome toward the end of the life of Julius Caesar. The adlection of certain Gallic senators was the inspiration of its ironic advice and the significance of such a move on Caesar's part fully justified the tense excitement which it aroused. For had not the senate been the very fortress of Roman nationalism? A century later a more noted Satirist represented Clotho as hesitating to cut the thread of Claudius' life because forsooth there were still a few foreigners to whom he had *not* given Roman citizenship. These "foreigners," however, were Spaniards, Greeks, Gauls, and Britons, dwellers within the provinces of the Roman Empire.

As a matter of fact this process of infiltration was not new; it simply became accelerated during the age of the early Caesars. It had long been under way. The phenomenon has been specially stressed in the field of literature where it is striking enough. Catullus came from Verona, Vergil was born near Mantua, Horace at Venusia, and Martial in Spain; Plautus, Cato, Cicero, the Senecas, Juvenal, practically every great Roman writer came to Rome from without. And the fact that their birthplaces were outside Rome has ever been noted and emphasized. More significant, however, is the fact that they all came to Rome. It was from Rome that books went to the provinces; only late in life could Martial, with his prestige firmly established, send his book from Spain to Rome and even then it was to the Imperial City that the book made its appeal. Rome was as much the real heart of the empire as Paris is the heart of France. And Roman life of the first century was fast becoming cosmopolitan.

Cosmopolitan—it is a word so broad and generous as to encourage a vagueness of definition corresponding with its own utter lack of confining limits. That which has to do with a citizen of the universe, or more practically with a citizen of the world. The world comprises less at one time than at another. *The* world is not of necessity even the whole world as known at a given time. The Roman who felt himself a citizen of the world did not really include either the Parthian or the German in his recognized world. When he claimed that his manhood gave him an interest in everything pertaining to man, he was in reality priding himself on overlooking certain traditional class distinctions, not by any means extending even his curiosity to the races outside the pale.

The cosmopolitanism, then, of the first century extended for all practical purposes only as far as the Roman Empire extended and for that reason seems at first hardly to deserve its name. But the extent and the changed character of the Roman Empire really gave it the right to that name. The narrow nationalism with which it is contrasted was the product of the city-state, expanded to be sure, but still governing and controlling the empire, such as it was, by the direct efforts of the citizens at Rome. The Roman in republican Rome (at least in the early, most nationalistic days) was either a slave, without a claim to consideration of whether his outlook was national or cosmopolitan, or a freedman, working so industriously to earn his living that he did not take time to consider his own outlook very much, or else he was a free citizen whose time and energies and interest were absorbed in the running of the state. Every man of sufficient importance to count was identified in one way or another with some function of government.

But when the empire stretched from the Atlantic to the Euphrates and from the North Sea to the Sahara Desert and comprised countless nationalities, when the fighting was done by a regular paid army, when the government was becoming a huge business carried on by experts, and when the only offices occupied by nonexpert free citizens were almost exclusively social in importance, then the thinking individual ceased to be wrapped up in national problems. He ceased to be a national and to that extent he became cosmopolitan. Cosmopolitan meant therefore "not local," "not intensely national."

This widening of horizon led to a narrowing of conscious interest. With the dominating motive of state interest removed, the individual had naturally to make a personal readjustment. His own life required a new *raison d'être*. He did not exist for the state. For what then did he exist? More and more for himself. For Roman cosmopolitanism never of course jumped at once to any altruistic basis for life. The Stoic doctrines may have rather unwittingly given hints of such a basis; Christianity did less unwittingly offer some suggestions that tended toward it. But these are symptoms of the same individualistic interest just as much as are the courtier and the *nouveau riche*, the Cynic preacher and the Epicurean dilettante.

Everywhere the change came. It is the real difference between the old republic of the days of the Scipios and the new empire in the time of the Caesars. Religion had once been as national, as much a part of the accepted machinery as was the law. It was actively satisfactory so long as the state was the end of all things for all men. The individual and his needs were satisfied by the one dogma of patriotism. But that removed, a new *summum bonum*, one that satisfied the need of the individual man, begins to be a general and evidently a crying need. Politics becomes a profession for the advancement and satisfaction of the individual; business, which never made any great strides so long as the government was the one object of service, now, delivered over to individual initiative, takes on increasingly enormous proportions. The stigma is largely and very naturally removed from participation in trade. The national tone of literature is gone after the Augustan Age. Even epic becomes a rhetorical exercise —no Ennius or Vergil could grow up under the incentive of personal ambition alone.

This was no sudden change. It came slowly, it made its way against constant but ill-fated opposition. But it came resistlessly and it became dominant enough to be obvious in the first century. By that time the change in public and private life was altogether patent. Religion and ethics had replaced ceremonial observances and abstract philosophy. Individualism in all things was the order of the day. The great social change was from a comfortably established caste system which had been gradually created for the best interests of the old state to a society in which individual achievement, be it of one sort or of altogether another, gave each man his place. The old order held its isolated strongholds. Slaves could be held down (for a time) and upstarts could be snubbed (with temporary success); foreigners could be discriminated against and philosophers banished. But the social order in which each man fought for his position or voluntarily withdrew from the struggle, what we mistakenly look upon as the modern order, was beyond any question established.

In a very different sense was Rome as a city cosmopolitan. It had long since taken on the character of the great cities of all times and of all countries. Like Alexandria or London or New York, Rome was a world city. The remnant of the old aristocracy, the first families of Latium were forced in on themselves.

Their exclusive society became almost negligible in the eyes of the great populace. The really important aristocracy to the million or more inhabitants of Rome was comprised of the court on the one hand and the wealthy capitalists on the other. Sometimes these were one and the same, but not always. And this aristocracy was in itself cosmopolitan. A Sejanus or a Tigellinus or a Pallas, senators from Gaul, a princeling favorite from Parthia in training to be a puppet king in his fatherland, a Herod Agrippa; free Romans, freedmen, naturalized foreigners, foreigners that had never been naturalized—all these mingled with each other in the court life and politics of the day. Not birth but power and money were the open sesame to the cosmopolitan aristocracy of the empire.

In the city at large, among the thousands of units that merely went to make up the sum of the Roman population, the mixture was even more conglomerate. "The Orontes emptied into the Tiber"; Greece contributed philosophers and acrobats; Egyptian rites vied with Jewish to make the Roman gods appear as strangers on the seven hills; Gaulish trousers no longer excited comment. Bronzed easterner, fair-haired Saxon, black Ethiopian, Spaniard and Egyptian, Briton and Gaul—they were all at home on the banks of the Tiber whither came grain from Africa and fish from Russia, tin from the British Isles and spices from India. And within Rome but no longer of it, like the Codfish on Beacon Hill, regretfully brooding in a dignified silence, dwelt such of the bluebloods as had not yet succumbed to the fleshpots of Egypt.

The steps that led to these conditions are familiar. The struggle of Rome which transformed her from a little community of peasants by the Tiber side to be the mistress city of the Mediterranean world was for long a defensive struggle. Each successive pushing out of her borders was a desperate necessity. At first she fought for actual existence and the Latin League and the Roman Republic resulted. The Etruscan War, the Latin War, the Samnite Wars were not wars of aggression—Rome had to win them or lose her independent existence, and for many a dark hour the second alternative seemed the more likely outcome.

Rome has always perforce traded outside her own borders for many of the necessities and nearly all of the luxuries of life. The removal of her Etruscan masters only partially opened to her the door of world trade. Her impotence is plainly marked by the two early treaties which forbade her to encroach upon the commercial preserves of Magna Graecia and of Carthage: to sail beyond the bay of Tarentum on the one hand or beyond the bay of Carthage or to Spain on the other. Both of these treaties she abrogated to maintain her economic existence. The wars with Pyrrhus and with Carthage followed. It was Carthage that tore up the scrap of paper that guaranteed to Saguntum her neutrality, and it was Carthage that trampled down that fictitious guaranteed security. But the struggle was bound to come, for there was no way known even then by which two great powers could peacefully share the trade of the western seas. By 200 B.C. the question of supremacy was settled and the course of Roman history began to follow a new current.

With the close of the second war with Carthage Rome controlled the commerce of the western Mediterranean. Her own coasts with their ports of entry were secure. The addition of the provinces Sicily and Spain and the destruction of the naval prestige of Carthage left the comparatively young republic potentially, at least, the strongest single power in the civilized world and thrust her immediately into commercial rivalry with the great powers of the East—with Macedon and Syria, with Rhodes and Pergamum and Egypt. For a country like Italy, dependent in large part for support on her importation of foreign supplies, her agricultural strength ruined by the long Carthaginian occupation, this commercial war could not fail to be intense. Moreover, the defeat of Carthage and the acquisition of Spain had given the Romans a taste of conquest. For the first time they were realizing their own strength and their new feeling of power, not far removed from arrogance, boded ill for the peace of the world. Also it foreshadowed an essential change within the Roman state itself.

Hitherto that state had been a unit. Nationalism was its very life breath. Cincinnatus, whether ploughing or fighting, was but a member of the organism that was Rome. Individual ambition, self-aggrandizement, was treachery and the business of the Roman gentleman was to till the Roman ground, to administer the Roman government, to dispense Roman justice, to fight Roman battles, and to rear a Roman family. It was this solidarity that made of the Roman senate an assemblage of kings. It was this sense of nationalism that made the storybook self-sacrifice of Lucretia or of Decius Mus seem wholly reasonable.

But expansion brought a change. Cato in his blind hatred of the Greeks was fighting something even more fundamental than he knew. When they had introduced their culture they *did* destroy the Rome for which Cato stood, for they and the other outside nations that were brought forcibly under the yoke of Rome put an end to the intense nationalism that had been hers. Rome could and did absorb much, transmuting into Roman stuff elements that were only remotely akin to her own stock. She could attack and conquer one by one the uncivilized tribes of Spain. She could place amongst them Roman colonists till the country became essentially Roman. But when she sought to make Roman the nations of the Orient a new era had already begun. In Greece and in Asia Rome met civilizations far older than her own and statesmen schooled in all the finesse of diplomacy, and she met them without the compelling motive of self-defense. Her object was economic expansion and her immediate problem not the conquest of the East but the establishment, through diplomatic means supported by arms, of a balance of power which should guarantee her commercial security. She might have been at a great disadvantage except for the one all-important fact that we have noted: she brought to the struggle a unified power; she had to deal with a multitude of independent and intensely individualistic states.

The eastern Mediterranean had been made over by the conquests of Alexander and the subsequent shattering of his empire into more than a half-dozen kingdoms and leagues struggling with each other. In Egypt, the Ptolemies were secure; in Syria, Antiochus was king and controlled the trade that came overland from the Far East. The kingdom of Pergamum under Attalus had extended its sway in Asia Minor and was a first-class naval power, mistress of the all-important Dardanelles. Rhodes, the island republic, was her great rival on the sea, dividing with her the commercial supremacy of the eastern Mediterranean. Greece was split between several loosely knit confederacies and many independent towns, all overshadowed by the kingdom of Macedonia under Philip the Fifth.

With this complex of governments Rome had to deal by one means or another. Her commercial needs made isolation impossible. Obviously a barefaced policy of conquest, even had it been desirable, was out of the question. Attack from without was the one conceivable force that could unite the East. Rome was thus led to the conception of a doctrine of foreign policy which was to be her guiding principle for more than two centuries. It was a policy of intermeddling, its purpose to maintain a balance of power. Her care for the future was to see to it that the powers of the eastern Mediterranean should preserve an equilibrium that would prevent any one of them from gaining such power as to threaten Rome's security or to overshadow Rome as the least involved power of the Mediterranean world, the natural umpire in the disputes of the others.

Unquestionably Greece offered to Rome the most inviting opportunity to assert her power as conceived in the new diplomatic doctrine. At no time did the Greek states need much prompting to quarrel with one another, and in 200 B.C. Philip of Macedon was building up what threatened to be a real world power. Already the Greek states were alarmed. So was Attalus of Pergamum and so was the republic of Rhodes. Egypt was aroused because Philip was allied with her neighbor Antiochus, and Antiochus was anxious to extend his territory at the expense of the Ptolemies. It was therefore in response to the expressed desire of many of the eastern nations that Rome took one of the most significant steps in her history and entered into the diplomatic maze of the Hellenic concert, whence she was to emerge after two centuries mistress absolute of the Hellenic world.

The details of these two centuries cannot be here rehearsed. The results are written large for all to read. Intermeddling led to almost constant and almost universally successful fighting, no longer within easy reach of home but nearly always in distant lands. This meant that the citizen of Rome could not return from each year's campaign to farm his land or to conduct elections. It meant the maintenance of permanent armies which led in turn to a division of interests between those who fought as a means of livelihood and those who guided affairs at Rome. It meant the influx of wealth and especially, after the battle of Pydna, of slaves. It meant the gradual breaking down of that great communal interest which had characterized the Romans. It meant the growth of individualism. It meant that wealth and political honors became the prizes of personal ambition. It led to the age of strong men when the crowd followed the personal leadership of the popular politician who wrote patriotic platforms and fought for his own aggrandizement. It led to the offering of a crown to Caesar and to the uncrowned but regal power of Augustus.

For the average citizen the result was of course that he was stripped of his all-absorbing interest in the state of which he was no longer, so far as he could see, an essential and active part and was thrown back on himself as the chief center of his own thought and care. It robbed him of a communal interest and gave him a personal one.

But there was also another and an equally important effect of the years of world conquest. The last two centuries of the old era saw Rome acquire one by one the nations over which she had at first sought to be umpire. By conquest, by compact, by bequest she brought into her empire Greece and Macedon and Thrace, Asia, Syria, and Egypt, all of Gaul and a part of Britain. In all of them she maintained a certain amount of local independence and local character, but in all of them she introduced also a considerable element of Romanization. And always representatives of these nations gravitated to Rome. Sometimes they came perforce as slaves, later, by emancipation, to become part of the free populace of Rome. Occasionally they came as honored visitors to be made much of in the capital city. Sometimes she made them citizens of Rome, flattered by the gift which lured them from their old love to the new. The Eternal City was made easily accessible to the subject peoples and the provinces made just as easily accessible to the Roman official and the Roman trader by the great roads which reduced distances as miraculously in proportion as did the railroads of the nineteenth century. Through the Balkan peninsula, through the center of Asia Minor to Mesopotamia and to Egypt, throughout Italy, Spain, and Gaul the great arteries stretched wherever the armies and the traders blazed a path. From the very beginning of the series of diplomatic wars, a process of infiltration was constantly making Rome the cosmopolitan city of the world.

III

ALONG with this development of a foreign policy which of necessity changed substantially the character of Rome went naturally a progressive change in her constitution and in her home policies. But the thread of Roman politics is not so broken as historical nomenclature would indicate. Through kingdom and republic, and even into the empire, the underlying conception of government was the same, obscured from time to time by causes temporary and personal, interpreted in various ways by the politician, the statesman, the plain citizen, or the usurper, but essentially the same when it finally slipped through the nerveless fingers of Romulus Augustulus as it had been when held in the firm grip of Romulus, son of Mars. For the Roman was tenacious of ideas, just as tenacious as he was of territory or of trade. He could and did modify and adapt the forms of his government or his religion or his society, but by his pliability in details of form he preserved intact the broad essentials of content.

The kingdom of Rome was based on the Roman conception of *imperium*.[1] This conception was entirely at variance with the

---

1. The theory of imperium presented here is not the conventional one which makes the Roman king the great chieftain whose absolute powers are progressively curtailed. The present theory is, I believe, consistent with the evidence.

principle behind the oriental monarchies which made the king the despotic master and virtual owner of his subjects. The Roman king had divine sanction but no divine right. His power was not his own but was that of the Roman citizens, the imperium. A group of people banded together have more than the sum of their individual powers. Their union creates a plussage of power and the word "imperium" stands for the sum of their individual powers with the addition of this plussage. The imperium originates with the individual members of the group but, being an entity greater than the total of their individual powers, it must be exercised not by the members singly but through a representative.

In the days of the early kingdom the imperium was entrusted absolutely and for life to the rex, chosen by the people and given the sanction of religious endorsement by the consultation of the omens. It is true that he had a power comparable to that which the paterfamilias had over his own household. The authority of each was limited by custom and by a council of advisers—in the family, the council of kinsmen, in the state, the council of elders, the senate. But the authority of the rex was not his inherently by natural right. His was a delegated power, the imperium of the Roman people.

The change from kingdom to republic was a change in the manner of delegation. The kingdom was an institution based on imperium delegated permanently to one man and limited by custom; the republic was an institution based on imperium delegated temporarily to more than one man and limited by law. The people took back into their own hands to a very large degree the power which originated with them. The kingdom had been the result of a loose amalgamation for the purpose of self-protection and it served well so long as the rex observed the limitations set by tradition. Once these were ignored, however, the kingdom lost its essential characteristic and became, potentially at least, no different from an oriental despotism. The temptation to ignore restrictions must have been increasingly great as the interests of the young state expanded and the relative importance of each individual in its body politic became gradually less, until finally a non-Latin line of kings imposed by the conquering Etruscans threatened the very basic principle on which the kingdom rested.

The great advance made by this new type of monarchical government, the real strength that it had acquired in the course of time is shown by the fact that the change from kingdom to republic took probably a century in the accomplishing. It began in a revolution and ended in a constitution. The act of violence which, according to very untrustworthy tradition, removed the alien kings who had betrayed the Roman ideal, was followed by years of legal construction tending toward the new definition of that ideal.

The imperium was now to be properly safeguarded. To this end provision was made not only for annual tenure of office but for joint tenure of office by two or more magistrates, for additional functions granted to the assemblies who now became the elective bodies in place of the senate of elders, and finally for the publication of the laws under which the imperium must be administered. With limitation of authority went also a removal of restrictions guarding the personnel of the magistracies. The offices were no longer open only to the few families conversant with governmental and religious red tape. Since a magistrate held his position for one year only it was less dangerous to elect men of no proven political worth, while at the same time the expansion of Rome was already bringing to the front men of the people who could make heard their claim to administer the people's power. The tribunate of the plebs was the first step. The use of the army as a voting assembly marks the same tendency. In 449 the laws were published and the most powerful blow struck at the privileged class who had tried, almost successfully, to arrogate to themselves the imperium of Rome.

Democracy was not attained, however, by this change from kingdom to republic. A decisive blow had been struck at what then and always appeared to the Roman the most dangerous threat against his boasted liberty. The monarchy was dead. But the ghost of monarchy was an uneasy spirit and continued to walk from time to time throughout the history of the Roman Republic till the fear of its shadow caused the death of Julius Caesar. Nevertheless, for the time being the king terror had been removed and yet there still existed in the republic another force, one that was increasing rather than diminishing and which was destined in the course of time to assume the role of opponent to the forces of democracy. This was the senate. Composed of all ex-magistrates who had exercised a share of the imperium, it was the one permanent organ of government in the new regime. Originally it had elected the chief magistrate and had acted as his advisory council but, while it still served in the latter capacity for the consuls, the elections were placed in the hands of the assemblies. In the assemblies, however, no debate was allowed and the fact of continuity joined with political experience and the right of discussion led to a constantly growing natural power for the senate.

Meanwhile the struggle for an amalgamation of the classes proceeded, resulting after nearly a century in the opening of all offices to all citizens. The first plebeian consul was elected in 367. Eighty years later the long political struggle ended in the triumph of the plebeian assembly who had at last won the right to legislate for all the people. So far as the constitutional theory of government was concerned the Roman democracy had acquired the control of the imperium.

This whole change was a natural and healthy growth. It marks the vigorous age of Rome during which the Roman citizen took and administered the power that was rightfully his. It is noteworthy that his inherent sense of discipline, his inborn respect for the imperium saved these two centuries and more of political struggle from the stain of violence and revolution. They mark the period during which Rome gained control over Italy from Ariminum to Rhegium. The subsequent expansion beyond the seas nourished the germs of oligarchy and of absolutism already latent in the government. To understand how this was so it is necessary to glance at the situation in the year 280.

On paper, the government of Rome consisted of the magistrates elected by the people, temporary and to a large extent purely administrative; of the senate, consisting principally of ex-magistrates, permanent, with growing prestige, exercising the privilege of debate but having no functions other than advisory, neither the power to elect nor the right to legislate; of the assemblies, the ultimate source of authority, electing and legislating without debate and acting as judges in cases of appeal from the magistrates. Such in brief was the machinery of government on paper.

In the reality of actual procedure matters stood very differently. The assemblies did, to be sure, legislate and elect, but the magistrates called the assemblies at their own discretion, presided over and largely controlled the elections, and prepared all bills on which the assemblies voted without discussion. With the large increase in the numbers of voters and, more especially, as a result of the fact that all voting must be done at Rome, whither the Italian citizens were likely to come only under pressure of some special crisis, and, finally, because of the frequently highhanded methods of the magistrates, the real authority of the assemblies was much less than it appeared to be on the surface. Nor were the magistrates the greatest power. Before they took any action they consulted the senate. Here was a permanent body of experts within which the temporary magistrate was soon to take his place, a body in whose meetings full discussion was customary and whose advice came inevitably to assume the force of a law. In theory, the senate endorsed all actions of the assemblies; in reality it exercised full legislative power. The senate, oligarchic in nature, tended to become the conservative, reactionary body; the assemblies, made up constantly of less and less vitally interested individuals, tended to become the tools of clever leaders.

It has already been observed that the overseas campaigns produced permanent armies and separated the fighting class from the business and governing classes. The deeper significance of the situation appears when the pressure of necessity is removed by the defeat of Carthage. The imminent danger from an invading enemy had given unity of purpose to Rome and the semi-subject peoples of Italy. But the fear of conquest was gone. Furthermore, fifteen years of hostile occupation had largely ruined the productive districts of Italy. After Hannibal's withdrawal, most of the arable land was put to pasture, for cattle and sheep raising required fewer men than farming, and Sicily could furnish the grain that was the mainstay of Roman life, while the defeated foe was yielding tribute to meet the national bills.

The indemnity paid by Carthage was soon replaced by greater riches won in the East. Slaves especially came in huge numbers as the reward of victories. The senate, with native shrewdness, made common cause with the capitalist until the new aristocracy of senators and knights became a firmly entrenched oligarchy separated by an ever-widening breach from the great mass of common people—small businessmen, freedmen, laborers, and unemployed. No direct taxation was imposed on citizens after 167, a fact demoralizing alike to rich and poor. The spread of external power necessarily led to the still further concentration of actual control in the hands of the only permanent organ of government, the senate, and the senate was no longer free from the control of the vested interests. The result was a class government which lacked responsibility and had no real representative character. The senate which had once appeared to the overawed Cineas as an assembly of kings, was growing constantly more autocratic and reactionary, the proletariat more motley, less independent, and more readily handled by any leader, good or bad, who could win their confidence for schemes of betterment or gain their support, active or quiescent, by fair means or foul. Between senate and demagogues, the imperium bade fair to elude the people who had won it back from the kings.

A period of bitter political fights, not without bloodshed, followed from 133 to 88, marked by ineffectual attempts at reform, succeeded perforce by the violent dictation of reform by one strong leader after another. Marius the stupid democrat, Sulla the brilliant cold-blooded aristocrat, and Pompey the natural but uninspired successor of Sulla, all imposed for the time being their schemes of government on a people no longer capable of handling its own affairs. It is no surprise to find politics of a familiar modern type resulting. The ring that has been dignified by the title of first triumvirate was nothing but a coalition of political bosses making common cause to gain their individual ends. Pompey contributed his vast prestige, Caesar his brains, while Crassus furnished the campaign funds and a superb political organization. The split amongst the leaders precipitated the great civil war between Pompey and Caesar which at last brought out clearly the fundamental issue between government by the aristocratic senate and government by an individual rightly or wrongly looked on as a representative of the people.

The successive acts of Caesar have little relation to the provisions of the constitution. He nominated officials in his own right, made new colonies, gave $1,000 apiece to his soldiers and $20 apiece to all citizens and, in an omnibus bill of the most imperial character, provided for roads, traffic, corn doles, municipal regulation, everything. It matters little that he had his laws endorsed by a servile assembly. The "permanent dictatorship" was the logical conclusion and was as much an assumption of regal power as would have been the acceptance of the crown which Antony offered him. By the time of his murder in 44 B.C. it was clear to all thinking men that either the imperium was a lost ideal or the government of Rome must be reorganized along the lines of a limited monarchy.

Augustus interpreted and gave form to the changes that had been developing for at least a hundred years. Under Caesar, over 300,000 citizens in Rome had been receiving government doles of corn, and if bread and the circus were not yet the sole interests of the Roman populace, at least free bread was their chief one. They were quite ready to submit to any form of government not too violently imposed which should give them peace and a living. The investments of the senatorial and business classes and the subsistence of the proletariat demanded a strong hand. Augustus thoroughly and yet diplomatically established a new constitution, a constitution that made Rome "an absolute monarchy disguised under the forms of a commonwealth."

To quote Augustus' own words: "In my sixth and seventh consulships when I had extinguished the flames of civil war, having by general consent become possessed of the sole direction of affairs, I transferred the republic from my own power to the control of the senate and people of Rome. For which good service on my part I was by decree of the senate called by the name of Augustus. . . . After that time I took precedence of all in authority, but of power I had nothing more than those who were my colleagues in the several offices."

Such was his plausible presentation of the case. In reality he held a combination of powers which seems to give the lie to his protestations. During the years of violent adjustment the control of an army had been the key to power and the command of the army was still to be the guarantee of imperial position. With permanent proconsular imperium the emperor was commander-in-chief of the armies. But beyond that he held permanent consular power with the right to initiate legislation, and, by virtue of the tribunician power, he could veto any action which he disapproved; finally, as censor, he controlled the only other organ of government left with any show of power—the senate. The cycle was complete. The imperium which had been violently taken from the kings was restored to the emperors.

And yet the protestations of Augustus were not altogether empty words. We have seen how the senate, by becoming the representative of oligarchy and of class privilege in general, had proven false to the true conception of imperium. It is hardly indeed probable that the people of Rome had a much truer notion of that imperium but, rightly or wrongly appreciated, it belonged to them and, while they drifted helplessly in the stormy waters, Augustus was their representative for better or for worse. He did stand for the imperium and he stood for it against its worst enemy, the reactionary senate. This senate still contained the best elements, the finest individual minds in the republic, but it had ceased to be the defender of the true faith and could bring no just complaint when the people looked to the house of Caesar to administer its rightful power.

Clearly the equilibrium established by Augustus was none too stable. He had flattered the senate and deferred to them sufficiently to smooth their ruffled plumage; he had retained something of the hero worship which an adoring public had poured at the feet of his popular uncle; and he had backed wholeheartedly the businessman on whom more than on any other class depended the future of Rome. All of these groups welcomed peace and prosperity so heartily as to overlook for the moment the fact that one man was in reality administering the imperium. That he was doing so was not only the fact but it was the one possible solution of the situation, as the commercial class clearly saw. For, instead of ruling a small city-state, the emperors were to administer the Mediterranean world. The early conception of that imperium in which every citizen shared and for which he was ready to work or to fight was scarcely possible in such a world where commercial interests were after all supreme. It is not to be wondered at if the emperors looked upon the state as their personal business with the easy acquiescence of the citizen body. The senate became a conservative balance wheel which as a rule produced more sound than balance; the proletariat had to be kept happy by creature appeals; but the commercial class cared not who governed Rome or on what theory so long as that ruling power guaranteed peace and security under which they could ply their trade.

Such a guarantee the emperors could best give. It required the building up of a businesslike and efficient government in place of the wasteful, amateur system which, under the republic, had given the provincials ample ground for complaint. It meant, on the other hand, the final elimination of the man on the street from any real participation in the actual government. He must now have felt himself to be a very unimportant unit in the organism of state. The government of the future was to be a business carried on by experts while the average citizen was to become primarily interested in his own life with only a passing curiosity toward the big news of the day.

The reigns of the Julian–Claudian emperors saw the development of these two tendencies. Augustus, with a clear comprehension of the general longing for peace, established the fixed policy of limiting the expansion of the empire. From now on the borders were to be the Rhine, the Danube, the Tigris–Euphrates, the deserts, and the Atlantic Ocean. Strong armies were stationed where the borders were most threatened and where the armies were, the emperor was supreme. The other provinces were left to the senate to administer. Taxation of provincials was gradually systematized, old abuses removed, trade encouraged, and always the government was more and more centralized.

The emperor at first had much of the routine work done by freedmen in his employ, consulting a group of intimates among the senators when he needed advice. Gradually the spheres of routine work became divided between a number of secretaries with regular fixed and recognized positions; the secretary for correspondence, the secretary of petitions, the secretary of the privy purse, the secretary for legal affairs. An army of government officials, big and little, ranged below these secretaries. Two roads led to recognition with the emperor—first and best, ability to do the work and to do it well; but, to a lesser degree and yet more conspicuously, fawning and flattery to win his favor. On the other hand, to maintain his position as established by the constitution of Augustus, the emperor must retain the support of the voting populace. More and more, entertainments and corn doles became the familiar means to attain this end.

The reign of Claudius is perhaps the most significant in the development of the court life which grew up as the government centered more and more about one man. Claudius was supposed by many to be an imbecile. Certainly he had no qualifications for personally governing the Roman Empire. But he recognized the fact and he placed in all positions of trust men who had proved their ability. These were usually freedmen who, now that the competition was unrestricted, could ordinarily outstrip the scions of the old families. Their position depended on their success and the businesslike bureaucracy established under Claudius, all but shattered by the unfit advisers of Nero, restored and reinforced by Vespasian, was efficient and thorough and carried the empire through the four centuries that remained of her life.

If this efficiency had been the one result of the centralized government the trend of life and of letters would have been very different from what in reality it was. But when favors are the gift of an individual, when social position comes through the old political offices and those offices depend primarily on the nomination of the prince—the doors are wide open to influences of corruption, sometimes blatant and obvious, sometimes subtle and unseen, but always active. The court levees attain the utmost importance. If you can gain access to the morning reception of the prince, well and good. If not, then go call on the highest satellite that you can get to invite you, and gradually work your way up the precarious ladder to such social prominence as you can attain. The process is reciprocal. The emperor wants his court to be brilliant, his prestige maintained. So he offers entertainment to lure, not the courtier who is clamoring for admission, but the less sympathetic peer of real distinction who tends to cling to a stern and futile cult of opposition. The underling courtier, too, must maintain the brilliancy of his counterfeit salon, for he must at least appear to the world to be someone, even if it be at the price of the daily dole handed out to the still humbler souls that cling frantically to the fringes of society.

Between populace and emperor there is the same give and take. For the most part the prince gives and the proletariat takes. Games in the arena with all the strange animals of the world; gladiatorial contests where they can gloat over the streams of blood from a safe point of vantage in the serried seats of the amphitheater; horse races in the circus that could seat a hundred thousand; free distribution of corn; holidays, processions, fetes— an endless series of payments on an account never closed. And in return the populace will furnish enthusiastic applause and support the throne.

It is a curious outcome, this life of Rome in the first century—as unlike the world of Coriolanus or Camillus as the America of today is unlike that of Miles Standish and John Alden. Unlike too in more ways than we have seen. The artificial glamour of the court has dazzled the writers of ancient times and of modern till we almost forget that the Poppaeas and the Tigellinuses, and even at times the Neros, are but the play actors strutting behind the glaring footlights to the delectation or disgust of the substantial bourgeoisie in the orchestra and the penniless proletariat in the gallery. The Four Hundred at the top and the submerged tenth at the bottom loom big in the newspapers of today as they did in the literature of the early empire, but there was at Rome as there is in America the substantial remainder. Rome had more than a million inhabitants and centralization meant that the great majority of people were working to get a living without much interest in the court save as a subject for gossip. Rome, like every world city, had come to be a complex that no single view can fairly represent. The dead-beat, shiftless proletariat, the court society, the slave population, the great capitalists and the small businessmen, the old nobility and the day laborers—they all go to make up a Rome that has lost the simple unity of the city of Romulus. The Roman imperium that passed from king to people, that was absorbed for a time by the aristocracy, had fallen to the hands of the politician, where it finally lost its identity. For such a conception as that of the imperium can exist only when the people themselves have some realization that they constitute and are responsible for the power of the state and when the administrators of the government are consciously the representatives of the people. Such a realization was fast disappearing under the early empire. The principle of the imperium implies some degree of nationalism and with the decay of nationalism it too became an empty dream. Internal politics at Rome went hand in hand with imperial expansion to pave the way for cosmopolitanism.

IV

THE Rome of Nero's day was a cosmopolitan city. What, if any, was its philosophy of life, its religious tone, its habit of serious thought? It would of course be ridiculous to expect to find any unanimity of belief in so complex a society, or for that matter much of any serious thought at all. But each age, in perspective at least, shows a certain philosophic temper, superstitious it may be or scientific or skeptical or deeply religious, and from this general temper the literature of the day develops, either by way of reflection or protest.

It is safe to say that a people who would crowd the Dionysiac theater all day long to listen to plays of Aeschylus were essentially religious in their thought. The reason for Euripides' popularity was not that he led this same people into the lines of more modern beliefs and disbeliefs, but that he gave them what they, as a whole, wanted. And if the drama is not altogether a fair criterion, the same principle holds true elsewhere. Homer reveals the intellectual interest of his day just as well as does Sophocles. It was the conservative minority that put Socrates to death, vainly thinking that they were preventing the Athenian youth from absorbing dangerous doctrines. The Athenian youth, however, were better represented by Alcibiades and Socrates than by Anytus and the 280 hostile judges. The great philosopher was no doubt unpopular but not unrepresentative. There is no need to illustrate at length what is very nearly a truism. Better to trace the current of Graeco-Roman thought down to the Age of the Caesars to win, if possible, to some conception of the temper of the masses in the days of Nero.

Socrates was charged with inculcating disbelief in his city's gods. There could have been little enough belief in the Olympians at the end of the fifth century B.C. for anyone to destroy. They had become largely mythological characters whose adventures and amours made delightful material for Euripides and Aristophanes and served to maintain certain salutary tradition and ritual. But this tradition and ritual were bound up with the old Athens and the propagation of ideas that undermined them threatened at the same time to undermine the old civic organization. What caused panic in the hearts of the conservative minority was the outspoken expression of a skepticism that was daily becoming more universal.

Philosophy had long been offering substitutes for the religion of Olympus. The light of pure reason was not clear sunlight but it was for the time being all that was left to illumine the twilight of the gods. For generations the philosophers had been interested in the theories of physics and metaphysics that sought to make rational explanation of the universe and so to dispel the shadows of superstition. But even during the Peloponnesian War, Athens was fast losing her imperial position; her citizens were soon to find themselves without the supreme interest of civic activity to guide their every act; and very surely the time was approaching when each citizen must determine for himself his own conduct on the basis of something more than obedience to the needs and laws of his native city. The philosophy of behavior was coming to be much more important to him than any theory of metaphysics. Socrates led the way in this transfer of philosophy from clouds to earth.

When ethics became the chief interest of philosophy, abstract theories of being, of the origin and nature and end of the universe, became simply the dogma to give sanction to ethical precept. The schools that followed Socrates and Plato divided really along the lines of their practical principles of conduct, determined to be sure by fundamental theories, often loosely held, but far overshadowing those theories in the minds of all but the leaders. The change was not immediate. Greek curiosity still struggled with the riddle of the universe, giving rise to numerous schools, at variance on many points, often splitting hairs, frequently losing sight of reality in the manipulation of words. But the two most important schools in the fourth century were the Cynics and the Cyrenaics, sharply opposed to each other in their moral teaching. To the former, virtue was the one thing essential to happiness, to the latter, pleasure. Both theories were perhaps driven to extremes by the pressure of competition, the Cynic doctrine suffering most because of the excesses of Diogenes who emphasized in unpleasantly dramatic and extreme manner the negative side of Cynic teaching. If virtue was the proper end of man's efforts, then all creature comforts, all worldly ambitions, were worthless. Diogenes became a caricature of the somewhat ascetic school to which he gave allegiance, but unfortunately he became also a model for the Cynics of the future.

By the end of the fourth century, the ethical problems had become very nearly the only ones of moment in the philosophic world. Also they were receiving the attention of greater minds than those which the successors of Socrates had possessed. Zeno and Epicurus and Pyrrho applied themselves to the question of human behavior and, out of the somewhat loose confusion of doctrine, developed the foundations of the three great schools of later times, Stoicism, Epicureanism, and Skepticism. Zeno, whose doctrine was formulated in the voluminous writings of Chrysippus, adopted the Cynic ideal of a life of virtue in harmony with nature. To him the instinct of preservation was the most fundamental human trait and this was best satisfied by conformity with the plan of the universe, by adapting finite reason to the infinite reason. Life according to reason was the life of virtue and the only aim worth cherishing. Fundamentally he held with the Cynics, and Stoicism taught the supreme importance of virtue and the necessity of eliminating the worldly vices which stood in its way. But the emphasis was rather on the positive. While Stoicism never lost the Cynic tendency to combat vices and was often harsh and one-sided, sometimes to excess, it did maintain a dignity which was sorely lacking in the harsh, self-righteous, theatrical asceticism of the Cynic.

Epicureanism, basing its theory on scientific materialism, denied the Stoic belief in divine reason and found in the enjoyment of pleasure and in the absence of pain the only proper aim of mankind. Happiness was not the attainment of virtue, but the sum of pleasures. The successor of the Cyrenaic school, it was developed in the hands of the earnest and able Epicurus into a theory of life susceptible of widely differing interpretation, appealing to the scientific thinker and also to the thoughtless pleasure seeker who craved reputable sanction for his inconsequence.

Pure skepticism is the attainment (or the luxury) of the intellectual. It does not move the masses. And so it comes about that the Alexandrian world, largely bereft of religion, followed in the mass either the virtuous ideal of the Stoic or the scientific pleasure of the Epicurean.

This development does not, however, tell the whole story. After the passing of the Olympians, the intellectuals might fortify themselves with philosophic theories, but for the mass of the people the loss of the ancient gods threatened to leave a vacuum. To them philosophies could never serve either as incentive or narcotic. And since a vacuum is nearly as abhorrent in the moral as in the physical world, it is not surprising to find the more mystical religions of Thrace and the East slowly but irresistibly flowing into the empty spaces. All of these were sanctioned not by reason but by revelation, they were not intellectual but emotional. Their appeal lay in their mysteries and more than all else in the hope of a future life which these mysteries revealed and which in one way or another should compensate for the ugliness and sterility of the present.

The afterlife that the Graeco-Italic religions had held out could never have acted as a powerful moving force in life. Tartarus as a threat may have had some potency, but the Elysian Fields were scarcely a paradise. Both had vanished in the mists that shrouded the passing of the gods. Epicureanism allowed of no future existence. Stoicism either rejected it also (with Panaetius) or accepted it in a form so purely intellectual as to be worse than meaningless to the everyday man. But Dionysiac worship and the Orphic mysteries, the religions of Cybele and of Isis, Mithraism, Judaism, and, later on, Christianity, revealed religions all of them, and all of them appealing to faith rather than to reason, these held out to the individual the most alluring hope of future happiness to reward him for a life of devotion. By ritual and mystery they appealed to the emotions and their appeal awakened a response when the reasoned dogmas of the schools fell on deaf ears.

Repentance, purification, reward, in one form or another, these three elements appear in all of the religions that flooded the Mediterranean world. Their sanction lay in revelation and by their very essence they involved secrecy and a certain amount of exclusiveness. In other words they were antinational without being cosmopolitan. Even Christianity, when it came, taught the devotee that he was not of this world but belonged to a kingdom of God on earth, set apart and to a degree mysterious. Religion therefore tended to come at once into opposition with the essentially cosmopolitan systems of life, with philosophy. The latter, based on reason, taught a system of behavior for this world solely, rejecting revelation except insofar as Stoicism allied itself with Chaldaean astrology and so adopted a certain rationalized revelation. Nationalism narrowed the horizon still further. Religion made of this world a thing insignificant in the face of futurity and of the kingdoms of this world something less than the small dust of the balance. Perhaps it was in part this contrast that led the practical Panaetius to reject both immortality and astrology and so to bequeath to the Romans a Stoicism that accepted no future life and knew no system of astral revelation.

Pure philosophy could satisfy the purely intellectual seeker after truth. Other men needed something more. The utterly thoughtless man could call himself an Epicurean and could eat, drink, and be merry without compunction. The more earnest of the proletariat might accept the Stoic ethics but craved still some dogma more satisfying to their emotional selves. To them religion appealed. And even Stoics could feel the lure of Chaldaean numbers. They were not all as self-dependent as Horace or Paetus Thrasea or Juvenal, so that there need be no surprise at finding astrology at home in the court and the thoroughgoing Stoic attacking with equal ferocity the superstitions of the old paganism, the ecstasies of the new religions, and the nervous curiosity of the Chaldaeans. This is, however, to anticipate the introduction of philosophy into Rome.

Early Rome had been even more self-sufficient than fifth-century Athens. For Rome had a discipline which Athens never knew. There was no room for individual systems of behavior; the city did his thinking for the citizen and religion, like every other field of life, was state-controlled. And with keen intuition the conservative Romans like Cato fought hard against the introduction of Greek philosophy, the product of denationalized Athens, because they realized that it was essentially antagonistic to the communal spirit of nationalism which they upheld. But the fight was an unequal one. Rome too was already becoming less national or at least less communal and the leaders of the senate could not but realize that they were attempting the impossible. Men were bound to be thinking for themselves as individuals; the state could no longer command their whole conscious life.

In the second century the new thought found a sympathetic welcome in the circle of Scipio. With true Roman shrewdness the governing class at Rome, realizing that the two great types of philosophic thought were bound to spread, chose the one most closely allied to what was left of the old Roman religion. They lent the full force of their prestige to the school of the Stoa. Panaetius, the first important teacher of Stoicism at Rome, was well adapted to the role of amalgamator for he had modified Stoicism to the extent of adopting the Aristotelian mean, a theory congenial with the common sense of the Roman, a practical theory that could work in real life. Stoicism rapidly became the "orthodox" Roman morality. Panaetius had inculcated the positive doctrine of virtue and the negative teachings against avarice, ambition, luxury, and lust. These tenets were tangible and comprehensible and they corresponded to the best elements in Roman character. Stoicism soon became more a religion than a system of ethics, almost a faith. Epicureanism, scientific materialism, the doctrine of pleasure, came to be looked on as anti-Roman, as representing all the degeneracy, real or imagined, of the eastern nations. Stoicism came to be, at least in the literature as we have it, synonymous with morality, to represent Roman virtue rather than abstract virtue and thus to serve as a dogma of reform in opposition to all that the more conservative element felt to be encroaching on pure Roman tradition. It is hardly an exaggeration to say that Stoicism came to stand in the popular mind for righteousness and decency, for patriotism and honor, and for religion as against the selfishness and luxury and individualism of the nonreligious man—all of which were popularly looked upon as the product of Epicureanism but became in reality simply non-Stoicism.

The very violence of much of the Stoic literature of reform indicates the extent of the growth of luxury and selfish pleasure in Rome. We are apt to remember the emphasis that Augustus placed on the old-fashioned Roman virtues of courage, thrift, and loyalty and to take lightly the urbane protests of Horace against qualities of a different sort. But one cannot fail to sense a certain materialistic crassness, even in the Golden Age of Augustus, when one recalls that that exponent of old-fashioned simplicity gave, by his own account, eight gladiatorial contests in which 10,000 men contended; that he gave twenty-six wild-beast shows with 3,500 animals killed; that, beside these, he gave to the people more than thirty games not including the great secular games of 17 B.C.; that he built a lake with surrounding grandstands and gave there the spectacle of a naval battle in which some sixty ships and 3,000 men, not counting the crews, contended; that from 18 B.C. until his death thirty-two years later, he personally paid the taxes of some 100,000 persons and in addition made almost annual gifts of money or corn to the common people and the army. Successfully as he overshadowed the process by his public program of brilliant building and peace on earth, he was inevitably preparing the way for the social demoralization of the days of Nero by pauperizing the masses in the city of Rome and inaugurating the social changes which so sharply differentiated the classes of that later day. He flattered the senate and urged it to act independently but he also gave new and significant powers to the capitalistic class and, in spite of the germ of truth in his claim that he gave the government back to the senate and people of Rome, it was due to the system which he established that government became a business and that the individual came finally to have his prime interest in his own advancement and no longer felt himself even in theory a constituent part of a vital community government.

Augustus seems to have encouraged the self-made man. The conservative senate would hardly have allowed freedmen to emerge as they did after the reformation had they been able to prevent it. In many ways a republic makes the cruelest distinction between classes while an emperor can afford to encourage whom he will. It was altogether to the advantage of Augustus to gain efficiency in the administration of the empire. The most efficient men that could be obtained for the endless clerical positions of importance were more likely to be ambitious freedmen than not. And efficiency he recognized whether in a clerk like Licinus, a doctor like Antonius Musa, or a poet like Horace.

It is easy to see the trend of all these tendencies. The senate was bound to be brought into contradistinction with the emperor; the class of wealth was sure to grow daily in prestige and pomp; the ambitious, uncultured freedman was bringing into society an unwelcome but perhaps the only invigorating element; and the common people were learning to eat from the emperor's hand and to clamor for bread and the circus.

What role was philosophy likely to play in this situation? Obviously, in the great middle class that represented commercialism, philosophy had no room. Money was the goal and business interest determined the ethical code. But intellectual Stoicism was the most available bulwark of the representatives of the old regime, serving sullenly in the senate, and emotional Stoicism was the only comfort of the poverty-stricken proletariat when free doles failed to satisfy their stomachs and gladiatorial shows their souls.

V

THE temper of the Age of Nero was certainly materialistic. The literature of the time that has survived is largely the product of a protesting minority. Many of the Romans probably felt as Ovid had, glad that he had not been born at an earlier date. The age must have seemed to the financier, to the tradesman, to the speculator—in fact to all but the thinking minority—a golden age indeed. But such an age could not produce a sympathetic literature that should live to represent it. Whatever was written for the consumption of the masses must have been fugitive in nature. Probably there was no demand for literature by any but the few, and the few, either honestly or because it was good form, took the attitude of critics of modernism and uttered their protests either directly or by implication. No great creative literature like the Greek drama could have originated in the Age of Nero. There was no great communal interest left, no spontaneous support. There was no longer any cohesion in the potential audience. Each man was on the make for himself and none had time for ideas or incentive for developing them. The self-conscious literati in their own little circle wrote to amuse themselves but the environment in which they wrote was completely alien to the production of any great literature save that of Satiric criticism.

Self-conscious literati is not a wholly fair description of the group that produced the literature of Nero's day, but it is not very unfair. There has never been a more closely confined literary group if we may judge from the letters of Pliny. "Everybody writes" is the complaint of Persius and of Pliny and no doubt of each author between. All, however, that this means is that writing was the fashionable accomplishment, the fad of the smart set. This surely seems to have been the case, and it is precisely because of this great popularity of writing that rhetoric produced the effect which it did on the product. If there had not been the self-conscious rivalry between authors, the constant effort to outshine someone else at his own game, the extremes of rhetoric would never have been tolerated. As it is, this rhetorical element is an essential part of the Age of Nero, as important for an understanding of Seneca as the political or philosophical temper of the age and possibly more so. For in this age of the world, if ever, artificiality was genuine.

Rhetoric was originally to the Roman a very practical asset which he borrowed from Greece, the art of persuasive speaking. The treatises were practical textbooks for the orator, to be studied and applied by him in order to build up a technique that would enable him to persuade his fellow citizens in the forum and in the courts. They became the foundation of Roman advanced education because the ultimate purpose of the education was to produce orators. But with the establishment of Augustus' new regime the field of oratory became strictly limited. Political advancement no longer came as a result of success in swaying the popular assemblies or the courts. Some call there was for court oratory, for success there might bring social and even indirect pecuniary reward if not political, but the chief field of oratory left to the ambitious youth was that of the eulogy which is the least averse to rhetorical exaggeration. Nevertheless, education, with its familiar conservatism, continued along oratorical lines and the principles that were originally intended to produce orators were still inculcated in budding poets and even historians. For literature became the fashion very shortly after the Augustan Age. We are quite wrong to think that the early first century was devoid of literature. That its product has for the most part perished is undoubtedly fortunate, but writing was furiously cultivated and under unhappy auspices.

Persius died in A.D. 62 and, as he was but twenty-seven years old at the time of his death, his Satires must have been written in the late fifties. The first Satire is given almost wholly to a vivid description of a literary recitation. It is assuredly no copy of Lucilius or Horace, for even in Horace's day the literary bore could only with difficulty obtain an audience. The literary recitation was at its worst in its infancy, which it certainly is not in the Satire of Persius.

The picture presents the reader as dressed up in his new toga, his birthday ring, and the rest of his finery. He has gargled his throat and his eye is taught to roll ecstatically as his rippling measures produce the most alarming effects upon his hearers. The world of Rome is all agog for the latest poem and there is no dearth of producers: We all shut ourselves up and write, one in verse, one in prose, something grand that we may pour forth from surcharged lungs. Persius, while he admits the joy of real popularity, attacks bitterly what seems to be the prevalent view that the "bravo" of the literary circle is the highest attainment open to any writer.

We take it for granted that by the time of Martial and Juvenal the Roman world was full of little Vergils and little Ovids and little Pollios. But here, not later than A.D. 62, is a picture of the fully developed recitation in going order with throngs of reciters, a far cry from anything that Cicero could well have imagined. Persius speaks of the Phyllises and the Hipsypyles, of Attius' *Iliad*, drunk with hellebore, of the little elegies written by first citizens in fits of indigestion, in short of everything "produced on couches of citron." All the productions are smooth and all in the grand style. There is no real simplicity, no ability to do the simple thing. Archaisms and pretended admiration for the older poet, mere affectations to attract attention, he bitterly arraigns. Even orations are now showpieces filled with balanced antitheses.

All this seems proof, if proof be needed, that writing, such as it was, far from being discredited or banished by the court, was rampant in the first half of the first century. Persius cannot have drawn the picture from Horace; to think of his summoning it from his imagination is absurd. That the recitation nuisance should have sprung full-armed from the reign of Claudius is equally unthinkable. The Satirist's picture is more violent than that of Pliny in the next generation, and it surely has the Satirist's exaggeration, but it is sound evidence nevertheless of the existence of a custom.

This custom seems to have arisen out of the educational system under which the boys wrote and declaimed speeches to be listened to and criticized by the master, the rest of the boys listening also with either favor or disapproval. To show how it ought to be done, the master too made speeches before his classes, declamations intended to be models. There was "declamation" in the time of Cicero but it was simply the dress rehearsal of an orator in his own home without audience, for his own training. The Elder Seneca who died during the reign of Tiberius was old enough to have heard Cicero. He could therefore look back over the period in which declamation, in its later sense, became popular and his collection of *Controversiae* consists primarily of sententious commonplaces which he heard from the lips of great orators, not in real cases, but in declamations. These declamations Seneca states were modern. In his youth no orator gave public recitations. When the public began to be admitted there was an essential change which Seneca followed from its cradle.

In the introductory epistle to Book III, there is further sharp distinction between declaiming and speaking in court, between appealing to an audience and to the judge. The former he compares to "toiling in one's dreams." He still has in mind that at that period boys and young men, eager to learn, comprised the bulk at least of the audience, a type of audience, be it noted, not ill-suited to create a temptation to show off. Cestius (in Seneca) declaimed "in school" before his pupils.

It was Asinius Pollio who first, according to Seneca, read or recited what he had written to an invited audience, though "he never admitted the crowd to his declamations." Haterius admitted the mob even to his extemporaneous efforts and the fat was in the fire. The key to the change is to be found in a remark in the introduction to Book IX: "Montanus Votienus was so opposed to declaiming for the sake of showing off that he did not even declaim for practice." His reason was "that the man who prepares a declamation writes, not to persuade, but to please." So Labienus had already scorned recitations, as Seneca rather naïvely says, not only because the institution had not yet been invented but because he considered it a disgraceful and frivolous exhibition.

Seneca's collection bears witness to the very considerable number of orators who exhibited their wares before audiences at recitations, but the institution, once established, proved an equally welcome boon to the poets, such as Horace describes, who were so anxious to hear their own voices. If Pollio did not read selections of pure literature to his invited guests it was certainly not long before orations were only one of the types of literature that were first published by this means. It was made easier than it would otherwise have been to give vogue to this custom by the fact that the Romans had already been in the habit of sometimes circulating what they wrote before it really reached the publishing stage. Whether Tiberius read his Latin lyric or his Greek poems in public or Germanicus his Greek plays and epigrams and his *Aratea*, we do not know, but we have it on the authority of Suetonius that one emperor before Nero, Gaius, invited an audience to listen to his oratorical recitations.

Certainly by the time of Nero the recitation before an invited audience was the accepted method of publication. All literature was produced with the audience in mind, a restricted audience who would actually hear the reading and who must be influenced through the ear and not through the eye. This audience therefore becomes of prime importance to an understanding of the character of the literature.

The listeners at the recitations were the people whose development we have considered in earlier pages, increasingly in a hurry over nothing, increasingly superficial, increasingly jaded in the nerves and ever more eager for speed, noise, novelty, excitement of any kind. In fact not greatly different from our own postwar generation. Society in the days of Augustus still consisted in large part of those who, by inheritance and opportunity, had some real background of culture and of those who, by real worth, had earned their place alongside of the scions of the older stock. But the following century saw a steadily increasing proportion of intruders within the sacred portals of society. Even if we discount largely the attacks of philosophers, satirists, and wits, it is obvious that money was the best passport into the desired realm and aggressive obsequiousness the best weapon of assault. The *nouveau riche* and the clamorous upstart were in all likelihood the most patient and appreciative listeners at the average recitation. It is undoubtedly true that there were numerous readings which, like those of the Younger Pliny, were given for the sake of getting real criticism, but on the whole these seem to have been rare. Even Pliny was well aware of the more common kind at which the interest of the audience was calculated. It is worth while to stop long enough to realize what was the educational background of the average audience to which, if he was to gain any fame, a poet must address himself and whose tastes he must satisfy.

This audience was not the broad group which we think of today as the reading public. Without the popular theater and the printing press and without general public education or a widespread intelligent middle class, it was confined, so far as concerns any literature in which we are interested, to the upper classes, the society of the day. The members of this society had had for the most part a fairly uniform education. They had been taught as children the fundamentals of reading and writing in Greek and Latin, some little mathematics, and some grammar. It was, however, the more advanced instruction of the school of the rhetor that had the greatest influence. After the age of about fourteen a boy was trained primarily in rhetoric with enough philosophy and literature to provide him with some powers of allusion and illustration. This latter study might be carried further abroad but too much of it was not considered either safe or altogether in good form. There is a shade of bitterness in the comment of Tacitus that the good sense of Agricola's mother restrained the ardent youth from getting more philosophy than was good for a senator. The higher education was intended to develop oratorical power and oratorical power was the power to persuade. The historian and the poet underwent the same training as the professional orator and the audience which all three addressed had been through the same mill.

The character of this training is made clear to us not only from innumerable casual references but specifically from the casebook of the Elder Seneca and from the critical discussions of Tacitus, Petronius, and Quintilian. Fictitious cases were furnished the boy and he prepared speeches to present to the master and his fellow pupils, arguing on one side or the other of the case or on both. The master too would present model speeches for the edification of the pupils. The quality of the argument was no longer that of Cato, whose principle was: *rem tene, verba sequentur*. The facts were laid down and must be accepted; adherence to truth or search for truth was never the aim, but rather the entertainment and persuasion of the audience. To conservatives like Tacitus this was a marked degeneracy from the old days. In his *Dialogus*, the somewhat old-fashioned Messalla twits the young man Aper on his scholastic declamations and his admiration for the new-fangled orators in preference to the older standards. Aper springs to the defense of the moderns. "Who today," he asks, "would sit patiently through the five books against Verres? Who would bear with the speeches for Tullius or Aulus Caecina? The judge in our day anticipates the speaker and unless, by the flow of argument, or by colorful phrases, or by brilliant and learned descriptions, he is allured and prejudiced, he is against you. The general audience too and the casual, drifting listeners have learned to demand pleasure and beauty in a speech." This is a long cry from Cato's standard. And Aper elaborates further: the young students expect to get from the speeches that they hear something distinguished to take home in their memory for their own use. They pass on the bits that they gather "whether it be the flash of an epigram embodying some conceit in pointed and terse phraseology or the glamour of some passage of choice poetical beauty."

To Messalla these trappings are all meretricious but his judgment was not the popular one of the day. In spite of despairing protests on the part of the conservatives, the convictions of Aper formed the generally accepted creed. It is the very protests that make this clear. Messalla would have it that the trouble lies with the laziness of the boys, the carelessness of the parents, the ignorance of the teachers, and the decay of old-fashioned virtue. Quintilian wrote his handbook "to recall to sterner standards the art of speaking, now corrupted and shattered by every vice."

Tacitus and Petronius, in their individual ways, attribute most of the trouble to the futility and unreality of the rhetorical education.

It is worth quoting at length the comment of Tacitus put into the mouth of Messalla in the *Dialogus* (Sec. 35). It is hostile criticism, to be sure, but the hypothetical cases of the Elder Seneca furnish evidence that it has a basis of truth and the satire of Petronius lends it confirmation.

"But nowadays our boys are escorted to the schools of the so-called 'professors of rhetoric,'—persons who came on the scene just before the time of Cicero but failed to find favour with our forefathers, as is obvious from the fact that the censors Crassus and Domitius ordered them to shut down what Cicero calls their 'school of shamelessness.' They are escorted, as I was saying, to these schools, of which it would be hard to say what is most prejudicial to their intellectual growth, the place itself, or their fellow-scholars, or the studies they pursue. The place has nothing about it that commands respect,—no one enters it who is not as ignorant as the rest; there is no profit in the society of the scholars, since they are all either boys or young men who are equally devoid of any feeling of responsibility whether they take the floor or provide an audience; and the exercises in which they engage largely defeat their own objects. You are of course aware that there are two kinds of subject-matter handled by these professors, the deliberative and the disputatious. Now while, as regards the former, it is entrusted to mere boys, as being obviously of less importance and not making such demands on the judgment, the more mature scholars are asked to deal with the latter,—but, good heavens! what poor quality is shown in their themes, and how unnaturally they are made up! Then in addition to the subject-matter that is so remote from real life, there is the bombastic style in which it is presented. And so it comes that themes like these: 'the reward of the king-killer,' or 'the outraged maid's alternatives,' or 'a remedy for the plague,' or 'the incestuous mother,' and all the other topics that are treated every day in the school, but seldom or never in actual practise, are set forth in magniloquent phraseology."

Petronius (Sec. 1) is more concise: "I believe," says Encolpius in the Satyricon, "that our boys are made utter dolts in the schools for they neither hear nor see anything of ordinary life but pirates standing on the shore in chains, tyrants writing edicts, ordering sons to decapitate their fathers, oracles uttered in times of pestilence calling for the immolation of three or more virgins, honeyed sweet-bits and words sprinkled with sesame and poppy seed."

There is no need to labor the point. It is clear that the education led in large part to superficial adornment and that an audience so educated looked first for decoration rather than substance. Nor were these conditions confined either to the producers of speeches or to their audiences. The crowd that listened at the law courts would contain the same men that were gathered together to listen to a reading of poetry; the writer of the epic or the drama had behind him the same education as the orator and felt the same urge to lure his hearers by means that appealed to them.

CHAPTER III
THE PROLOGUE

THE dramas of Sophocles would surely have been even less generally popular in the Rome of Nero than on modern Broadway. But the self-conscious group of Roman literati were wholly unconcerned with popular taste. They attempted all types of literature into all of which they introduced the artificial taste of the day. This introduction of an alien feeling into the drama is chiefly what made of it a new type. That it was a new type seemed obvious in the *Oedipus*, but if we are to understand clearly what the writers of sixteenth-century England knew as "our Seneca" we must analyze the elements of the tragedy to see what, in concrete detail, Seneca did and what was the result which he left to posterity.

To begin, then, at the beginning of the play if not at the beginning of the problem. Leaving out of consideration the fragmentary *Phoenissae* and the presumably spurious *Octavia*, there are seven Senecan plays beside the *Oedipus*. The prologue of the *Troades*, like the one we have studied with some care, is spoken by the chief character. It is fairly long—sixty-six lines—and laments the fall of Troy and the terrible lot of the aged Queen. But it begins with something of a philosophic generalization:

> Whoso puts faith in might or rules supreme
> In royal halls, nor fears the fickle gods,
> Yielding to pleasure with a credulous heart,
> Let him but look on me—ay and on Troy:
> Never hath chance proven more ruthlessly
> How insecure the pinnacles of pride.

In these two prologues, the *Oedipus* and the *Troades*, there is one element in common, the presentation of a state of desolation, an atmosphere of gloom and terror. The two expositions even proceed from the same point of departure, the futility of royal power. An apparent distinction in technique should, however, be

THE PROLOGUE

noted: a second speaker is present in the *Oedipus*, or at least appears after eighty lines of Oedipus' monologue, to break in and give it the superficial form of dialogue. Hecuba, on the other hand, concludes her complaint by addressing the chorus, but only to rouse them to lamentations and not to initiate a conversation.

The *Medea* too is opened by the heroine herself in tones of deepest tragedy, and she likewise prepares the ground by means of generalization:

> Ye gods of wedlock and thou guardian queen
> Lucina, watcher o'er the marriage couch,
> And thou that taughtest mankind to master ships
> To dominate the sea, thou ruler fierce
> Of all the vasty deep, thou Titan too
> Dividing with thine orb the coursing days,
> Thou Hecate of triple form whose beams
> Glance at all secret rites, ye gods by whom
> Jason once swore to me and whom methinks
> 'Tis seemlier far Medea should invoke:
> Chaos of night eternal, realms the gods
> See not, all impious shades and thou the lord
> Of blackest hell and thou its mistress too—
> I call ye all with my ill-omened cry.

Throughout the fifty-five lines of this prologue, Medea addresses neither another character nor the chorus. She begins in the form of a prayer to the gods of wedlock and continues in pure monologue addressed to herself. When the chorus does speak out at line 56, it is not in response to Medea's speech. This prologue is completely isolated from the rest of the play and is pure monologue. At the same time, it is, like those of the *Oedipus* and the *Troades*, spoken by the leading character of the play and it creates an atmosphere of horror.

The heroine in the *Phaedra*, following the song of Hippolytus which makes the opening of the play unique, laments loudly to her native Crete the ills that have befallen her. In technique this is quite parallel to the prayer of Medea, and it too is followed by a monologue addressed to the speaker's own soul. The interruption of the nurse, however, relieves the situation by producing a long dialogue which continues up to the first choral ode.

In the *Hercules on Oeta*, the hero addresses a prayer to Jupiter in which he complains at length of his exclusion from heaven. In the course of this complaint he creates an atmosphere of tragic terror. At the very end he addresses five lines to Lichas, who is evidently a silent listener, thereby creating a faint illusion of realism and giving to the prayer a tenuous relation with the action.

These five prologues show minor variations in technique, but the most striking thing about them is their similarity. Each one consists in essence of a long monologue spoken by the leading character in the play, presenting something of the background of the plot and, except for the *Oedipus*, giving the name of the speaker. Primarily, however, each one creates an atmosphere of terror.

The remaining three prologues are different. In the *Hercules Furens*, Juno speaks the prologue:

> I, sister of the thunderer (for this name
> Alone is left me) have abandoned Jove,
> Who hates me ever, and the spacious ways
> Of lofty ether: banished, I yield my place
> To courtesans, for harlots hold high heaven.

Here three things are at once evident. The speaker is superhuman, appearing from heaven to give a divine motivation for the play. She is not a character in the play nor does she reappear later, but she has the sole function of furnishing this motivation from outside the action, giving the prologue an even more thoroughgoing detachment from the rest of the play. She identifies herself immediately. In the *Agamemnon*, the ghost of Thyestes rises from the lower world to instigate tragic deeds and speaks the prologue. His lines are black with horror, but it is noteworthy that he too is a character not otherwise appearing in the action, that he gives to the play a motivation which is external and supernatural, and that he identifies himself at once. The same is true of the ghost of Tantalus in the *Thyestes*. A touch of melodramatic variety is added by the presence of a Fury that drives Tantalus on to pursue his hideous plan and thus gives to the prologue the specious appearance of a dialogue.

There are, then, two sorts of prologue in the plays of Seneca, neither of them closely knit to the body of the play, but those of one sort comprising in the main a monologue by a character concerned in the later action, while the other sort presents an external supernatural motivation. Even a hasty glance makes it clear that the prototype of neither group is to be sought in Sophocles. It is true that in the *Ajax* of the Greek poet the prologue is spoken in part by Athena who foretells the madness of Ajax, but the technique is not that of Seneca: it consists of a well-constructed dialogue between two people who meet perfectly naturally; there is no long harangue; the short speeches and the identification of the scene and of the speakers are characteristically Sophoclean. It is also true that in the *Trachinian Women* we find a closer approach to Seneca. Deianeira makes a fairly long speech with little motivation, giving her pedigree and mourning over her uphappy state. Two of the characters, however, the nurse and Hyllus, take part in the prologue relieving the monologue, and the most that can be said is that we have here the least typical of the Sophoclean prologues. It is the closest approach made by the earlier poet to the prologues of Euripides, as will be clear presently; it is not, however, a model for the tone poems of Seneca.

This matter of the prologue is one of prime importance in any study of the technique of the drama, justifying a glance backward to the prologues of Aeschylus and even to what went before them. The origin of the Greek drama was in a choral dance in which song and movement comprised the whole ceremony and which presented no dramatic divisions such as a prologue. Thespis, according to a fairly probable tradition, was responsible for the addition of an actor who spoke his lines in the interludes between choral songs. This did not produce a prologue but it was the first breaking up of the choral matter into divisions. Neither Thespis nor any of his contemporaries, so far as we can judge, developed the dramatic element beyond this point. The *Suppliants* was the earliest of the extant plays of Aeschylus. In it he made no great strides beyond the art of Thespis. The drama opens with a choral passage of 175 lines and the choral element predominates throughout. Aeschylus did, so tradition tells us, invent the device of a second actor, but in the *Suppliants* he made only sparing use of it. In the *Persians* he strikes out more boldly. In both plays, however, the chorus opens the action, if action it may be called, and in both instances the first chorus gives a general idea of the situation. Such exposition was probably not necessary when the range of the choral subject matter was strictly limited, but, with the extension of this range, it must have been as necessary as in the subsequent plays. The fact remains that here in a play the choral song comes first. There is nothing that can properly be called a prologue.

With the *Seven Against Thebes* Aeschylus introduced the innovation which led to the formal prologue. The play opens with a proclamation by Eteocles. To give verisimilitude to the situation, some citizens must be present, but they certainly are not the women who make up the regular chorus, for, in the course of the proclamation, Eteocles bids his hearers man the bulwarks of the city. As he finishes his speech a messenger enters to report the actions of the enemy and, after reporting, departs. Eteocles makes a prayer to the gods and presumably departs also, though his exit and subsequent entrance are not carefully motivated. Only after he has gone does the regular chorus of women enter and sing a long hymn of horror at the approach of war, a hymn generously interspersed with prayers.

This introduction of a speaker in advance of the chorus is a real innovation, one which emphasizes the dramatic side of the performance as against the choral, and one which evidently commended itself, for there is no return to the choral opening in any of our extant plays with the exception of the problematical *Rhesus* of Euripides.

In the next of the plays of Aeschylus that have come down to us, the *Prometheus*, we encounter a prologue much more like that of the *Oedipus* of Sophocles. Kratos and Hephaestos, with the function of fastening Prometheus to the cliff, open the play with a dialogue which gives the scene, the situation, and the names of the characters as they appear. This is in part informational, but it is also an integral part of the action as was the proclamation of Eteocles and his order which inaugurated the conflict. In both instances, however, the material of an introductory sort has been with considerable care introduced dramatically and previous to the entrance of the chorus. In the *Prometheus* there is a further element. When Hephaestos with his henchmen departs and leaves Prometheus suspended on the cliff, the hero of the play pours forth his protest against the injustice of Zeus, expressed in a long monologue addressed to the air and sea about him. In a static play like the *Prometheus*, there are many long speeches and they must of necessity be considered part of the action. The present speech is not detached from the action. It is, however, decidedly an innovation in tragedy, a real soliloquy.

There remain the three plays of the *Oresteia*. The *Agamemnon* opens with the speech of the watchman, a soliloquy without even a silent audience. This watchman has no further part in the action. In technique, therefore, he is like the auxiliary prologue characters of the *Prometheus;* in the nature of his speech he resembles more Prometheus himself. What he has to say gives the setting for the play, though not actually the motivation: it is really the first step in the action, so introduced as to make clear the essential situation. He sufficiently identifies himself and disappears from the play when his function is fulfilled. The first choral ode follows directly. Of the opening of the *Choephoroi* much seems to have been lost, but the indications are that we have again a simple speech, this time by the leading character of the play, Orestes, who identifies himself though without giving his name in the text as we have it. His speech is in part a prayer to Zeus, in part a soliloquy, giving the setting of the play and starting the action. At the very end he addresses Pylades by name, showing that this character has been present in silence throughout the prologue. The opening choral ode follows the speech.

In these two plays the prologue is technically not unlike that of the *Seven* in that it is a single speech preceding the entrance of the chorus. In no case is there a deliberate statement of the pedigree of the speaker, but in all the situation is made clear. The *Eumenides* is a *tour de force* with elaborate movements of characters off from the scene and onto it. The coming and going of the Delphic prophetess, the appearance of Apollo and the departure of Orestes, and finally the entrance of the ghost of Clytemnestra all combine to produce a result hard to analyze but fortunately without imitators. The chorus has no long ode. This whole play is rendered unique by the change of scene during the action and by the sensational chorus of Furies. It is easy to understand why it did not commend itself to imitation. Yet even here it is not difficult to see a certain similarity to the technique of the first two plays of the trilogy. The Delphic prophetess opens the action with an elaborate prayer in which she identifies herself, followed by a brief proclamation. Her visit to the shrine is followed by an account of her discovery there of Orestes, an account delivered to no apparent audience. After the change of scene, Orestes speaks what is in effect a second prologue, offering his prayer before the temple of Athena. He does not have to identify himself, for that was done (not very clearly) in the earlier scene. He does, however, identify the place. The chorus follows with an ode.

In Aeschylus, then, we find two plays which open with choral odes and therefore have no actual prologues. All the rest have some sort of monologue, sometimes spoken by the chief character of the play, again by a character not appearing elsewhere in the action. This monologue may be speech, prayer, or soliloquy. Care may or may not be expended on its dramatic realism and likewise it may or may not be supplemented by dialogue.

It is clear that Aeschylus was an experimenter. He originated the prologue as a distinct division of the tragedy preceding the first choral ode, but he did not settle upon any stock form of prologue, if we are to judge from the plays that have survived. If we may draw any inference from Aristophanes' treatment of the prologues of Aeschylus we should conclude that the *Choephoroi* shows as typical a form as any. It is this drama from which the generalization is drawn in the *Frogs* that the prologues of Aeschylus were repetitious and lacked clarity. The Comic Poet may have meant no more than that the prologue exhibited a certain amount of tautology. Unfortunately it is exceedingly fragmentary in its present condition. It is apparently not unlike some of the prologues of Euripides and among the plays of Aeschylus may most nearly have served as a model for Sophocles.

This later poet, as we have already seen in the *Oedipus*, was concerned with the realism of his prologue. His technique was fairly consistent. The first speaker regularly gives the setting dramatically—not in a storytelling form—and addresses by name a second speaker who in turn gives naturally the name of the first. In the *Oedipus at Colonos* there are three prologue characters, as in the *Tyrannus*, but of these only two engage in the conversation at any given time. First Oedipus and Antigone engage in dialogue, then, Oedipus and the stranger, then again, Oedipus and Antigone. The nearest approach to a long speech is a prayer which Oedipus makes to the Erinyes. The *Antigone* has but two speakers in the prologue, Antigone herself and Ismene, and there are no extended speeches. Athena and Odysseus open the prologue of the *Ajax* with a dialogue that is wholly natural (except for the fact that Athena is a goddess) and this is followed by a conversation between Athena and Ajax. There are no long speeches. Athena is interesting as a character not otherwise appearing in the play and yet to a large extent furnishing the motivation which is therefore from a supernatural source outside the action. Otherwise there is nothing unusual about this prologue. In the *Elektra*, an auxiliary character, if we may call it so, is introduced into the prologue, in the form of the paedagogos, to avoid a monologue by giving Orestes someone to talk to. He is not, however, merely a prologue character like Athena but returns later to take part in the action. A novel turn is introduced also at the close of the prologue by having Elektra enter, singing a lament in which the chorus joins. The *Trachinian Women* has a nurse corresponding to the paedagogos and, with her as an audience, Deianeira makes a long opening speech not motivated with Sophocles' usual skill. This play too has three speaking characters in the prologue but only two engaging at a time in the conversation. In the *Philoktetes*, there are but two speakers and while the speeches are a little long, the conversation is natural.

In general then, the prologues of Sophocles present the leading character of the play in natural conversation, realistically presented. They furnish the necessary facts dramatically and are an integral part of the play. As such they are as much within the dramatic illusion as any other part of the whole and must be given the same natural motivation. The Athena of the *Ajax* is the single exception: though dramatically handled, she suggests the later *dea ex machina*.

Of Euripides we have seventeen plays (not counting the *Cyclops* and the *Rhesus*) and the opening lines of seven others are cited by Aristophanes in the *Frogs*. One thing is noteworthy at once about the prologues as a whole. The employment of a long and formal speech with which to open the play has become the regular practice. All trace of the old choral opening has disappeared, as has also the attempt carefully to motivate an introductory dialogue that shall be truly dramatic. Details vary but always the first speaker is forced to identify himself to the audience and the usual effect produced is that of a prefatory introduction often detached from the play proper. This is putting it strongly, and in most cases a natural dialogue follows the opening speech. But it is hard to find dramatic justification for the opening lines, for example, of the *Iphigeneia among the Taurians*:

> Pelops the son of Tantalus once went
> With his swift steeds to Pisa, so to win
> The daughter of Oenomaus to wife.
> Of her was Atreus born and Atreus' sons
> Were Menelaus, Agamemnon called;
> His daughter I, grandchild of Tyndareus,
> Iphigeneia named.

This is to ignore the dramatic illusion with a vengeance for the sake of getting before the audience the necessary facts in a businesslike way. Iphigeneia proceeds to tell the rest of her story not to any carefully produced character in the play but merely to the audience. The only attempt at motivation, or at least at explanation, of Iphigeneia's presence is her prayer and offering to avert the evil omen of her dream. In the *Phoenissae*, Iokaste comes forward similarly, making a prayer to Helios. In both plays the heroine retires when her immediate function is performed and two other characters complete the prologue with a dialogue which is dramatically conceived and which really begins the action.

In seven of the plays[1] the opening is of the same sort, but the original speaker does not withdraw and is joined by another character, the two engaging in a natural conversation which continues through the prologue and until the entrance of the chorus. In the *Andromache* the second character is purely a prologue character, that is, does not appear again during the play. She is a maid, the confidante of Andromache. The opening speaker is usually the chief character of the piece.

In the *Suppliants*, Aithra prays to Demeter, and her expository prayer comprises the entire prologue; there is no dialogue following it before the entrance of the chorus.

A second distinct type of Euripidean prologue is that in which a deity or ghost makes the expository speech. The speech may stand by itself as the entire prologue, as it does in the *Bacchae*, the *Hecuba*, and the *Ion*, or it may be followed by a dialogue between two divine speakers, as in the *Alcestis* and the *Trojan Women*, or finally, as in the *Hippolytus*, the god may depart and a conversation between two characters may complete the prologue. In each of the plays of the first group, the prologue god begins with an abrupt ἥκω, I come. In all of these plays in which the first speaker is a god (or, as in the *Hecuba*, a ghost), this is his only appearance. Exception might be made of the *Bacchae* but it would hardly be justified, since the prologue Dionysus is the god himself in his own person, while the Dionysus of the play proper is in disguise, taking the role of a mortal, and at the end, only his voice is heard.

From another point of view, important for the study of

1. *Elektra, Helen, Herakleidae, Herakles, Iphigeneia at Aulis, Medea, Orestes.*

Seneca, the prologues of Euripides may be divided according to the introductory device used by the first speaker. The commonest is that of direct statement like the one already quoted from the *Iphigeneia among the Taurians*. This is the manner also of divinities when they open a play. The *Elektra* represents an exclamatory type of introduction:

> O ancient land of Argos and ye streams
> Of Inachus, whence with his thousand ships,
> Rousing fierce Ares 'gainst the walls of Troy,
> Sailed Agamemnon.

Finally, there are prologues, still similar in general character, beginning with a sort of philosophizing tone of generalization. So Iolaos opens the *Herakleidae*:

> Long since I am persuaded of this truth:
> The honest man doth benefit his kind;
> But he whose soul is given up to gain
> Is useless to his city, ever hard
> To deal with, yet to himself the best of men.
> Such knowledge have I from experience.

Similar is the opening of the *Orestes*. The *Medea* begins with a tone of complaint in the speech of the old nurse, not inconsistent with the philosophizing manner.

The fragmentary prologues that have come down to us confirm the analysis made of the surviving plays. The *Phrixus* began abruptly:

> Cadmus, Agenor's son, abandoning
> His house in Sidon, came to the land of Thebes.

The same seems to have been true of the *Hipsypyle*, the *Melanippe*, the *Archelaus*, the *Meleager*, and probably the *Antigone*. Two seem to have had the opening, I come. The *Oineus* and the *Telephus* began with a somewhat exclamatory greeting to the scene of the drama, and the *Stheneboia* opened with the philosophizing comment: No man in all the world is wholly blest.

One thing is common then to all the prologues of Euripides: they open with long speeches, not dramatically motivated and addressed largely if not wholly to the audience, giving the necessary information for an understanding of the play, the Senecan model, to a large extent, so far as form is concerned.

They, the Euripidean prologues, are to this extent the models for the Senecan in form but not to any extent in content or tone. They are very largely conveyers of information. Take, for example, the prologue to the *Phoenissae:*

> O Helios that o'er the way of heaven
> Star-studded makest in thy gilded car
> Thy daily journey while thy wind-swift steeds
> Speed on thy light, with what unhappy ray
> Thou camest unto Thebes the day when once,
> Leaving Phoenicia's sea girt land behind,
> Kadmos of old sailed first unto this land,
> Husband of Harmonia, Kypris' child,
> Begetting Polydorus who they say
> Was father of that Labdakus whose son
> Was Laius.

And so on through the early history of the ill-fated family, bringing it up to the moment of the play. Even such a gloomy drama as the *Troades,* or perhaps even better the *Hecuba,* does not stress the terrifying atmosphere of black horror that we have seen to be a characteristic of Seneca. In the Euripidean prologue the facts are presented and the motivation, often by a character external to the play, a god or a ghost, but, even if something of a threatening tone is given by the first speech, it is not the exaggerated one of the Roman dramatist.

If we recall the purpose of Sophocles in his prologues, the exposition of the plot with the presentation of one or more of the leading characters, all properly motivated and wrought into the fabric of the play as a whole, it is not difficult to guess at the reasons for the change which is evident in Euripides. The younger dramatist, it is generally conceded, was an intellectual, delighted with the quibbles of the sophists and concerned with cleverness. He dealt less with great psychological presentations and with important human relations than with the lesser crises of life, the minor contacts; not with the great moving forces of Fate and heredity, but with the transitory relations of daily life. To him, therefore, the prologue was a convenient means of putting his audience quickly into a position of familiarity with the main situation; it was a playbill or program of a sort.

Confirmation of this position can be had from a glance at the prologues of Plautus and Terence. It has never been wholly (or at least generally) realized to what an extent the New Comedy in Athens and its child, the comedy of Rome, are the descendants of the Greek tragedy. If they take their Comic atmosphere from the Old Comedy, it is really about all the inheritance that they have from that ancestor. Their form and most of their technical characteristics come from the other side of the family.

In the comedies of Menander and Plautus the plots were no longer the old and familiar myths, not even the less familiar myths of Euripides. They were invented stories, unfamiliar to the audience. Hence it was necessary to give more explicit explanation. The prologue took a new departure and did not maintain even a tenuous connection, dramatically speaking, with the play proper. It was now frankly an address to the audience, giving necessary and often unnecessary information to the spectators. It was not absolutely essential. Plautus showed himself entirely capable of developing the exposition without a prologue. But it was a convenient device and gave the playwright, once it had been divorced from the plot, a welcome opportunity to talk with his audience.

In such plays as the *Miles Gloriosus* and the *Mostellaria*, Plautus did not use a prologue, or at least none has come down to us, and the exposition is easily handled by means of a conversation. In the one the hero talks with a parasite, the lineal descendant of the confidante of tragedy, in the other two slaves develop the situation. The *Casina* has a prologue followed by an expository dialogue. There is the same device in the *Poenulus*, the *Asinaria*, and others. In the same way, whether there is a prologue or not, the play proper may open with an extended monologue. The *Mercator* has no prologue, the *Truculentus* has one, but in each case Act I begins with a speech by a leading

THE PROLOGUE

character. In other words, the prologue has become an element detached from the play proper and no longer affects its technique. As a result of this fact, it is frankly addressed as a general rule to the spectators. It may or may not give extensive information about the background of the plot. Usually it does. The prologue of the *Menaechmi* is fairly typical:

> A greeting first and foremost unto you,
> Spectators, I pronounce—to you and me;
> Plautus I bring to you—by word of mouth,
> Not by the hand—I beg you, hear him well.
> And now, attentive, hear the argument
> Which I'll present you in few words and clear.

After a few lines, giving the location of the play and the origin of its chief characters, he continues:

> There was a merchant old of Syracuse
> To whom were born two sons, and they were twins.

The complication antecedent to the play is expounded but the play could have been understood without the prologue, which is chiefly characterized by its ineptitude. In other words, this member of the drama has become in Plautus a means of interesting and appealing to the audience. He uses it to beg them to be attentive, he is jovially familiar with them, he talks about his play and its source.

Terence took the last step in the divorce proceedings between play and prologue. He used the prologue for literary criticism and for self-defense against his own detractors. By this time different prologues could be used for different performances of the same play; indeed, the same prologue could be used for different plays, so far had its nature changed from the Sophoclean concept of a first act preceding the entrance of the chorus, and to such an extent had it been detached from the play proper.

Now Seneca will scarcely be suspected of deriving from the Comic poets. He is rather a second branch of development, so far as the prologues are concerned, from the same point of departure: Euripides. The necessity for dramatic realism in this member of the drama has ended with Euripides, and Seneca scarcely feels a remnant of it. He follows his favorite predecessor in his long prologue speeches and he inherits also the various types of prologue: the directly explanatory type with the announcement of the speaker "I, so and so, have come" (*Hercules, Agamemnon*), the exclamatory type including invocations and rhetorical questions (*Medea, Phaedra*, after the unique choral passage suggested by the later song in Euripides' play, *Thyestes, Hercules on Oeta*), and the philosophizing (*Troades, Oedipus*). In general, he has followed the lead of Euripides in detaching the prologue from the play, carrying the development to a greater length, not merely by having more than a third of his prologues spoken by characters outside the play (the *Hercules, Thyestes,* and *Agamemnon*), but by concerning himself in the prologue less with the factual background than with setting a tragic tone.

It is this tone quality which chiefly distinguishes the prologues of Seneca. These are no longer mere expositions of antecedent fact, certainly not integral parts of a dramatic action. They are rhetorical introductions, intended to bring the audience into the proper mood for appreciating the recital of horrors. This is probably a distinctively Roman development, and the result of their method of higher education. Because of the importance of oratory in the days of the republic, all the advanced training of the better-class Romans was in rhetoric and after the days of independent politics this training continued, becoming more stereotyped and artificial in proportion as it was less vitally connected with life. The rhetorical system, dating back to the days before Cicero, divided a speech into definite parts, *exordium, narratio, divisio,* etc., and assigned to each part its function. The exordium was an introduction designed to put the judges in the proper frame of mind to look with favor upon the case of the speaker, or, in the words of the treatises, to make the judges attentive, amenable, and well disposed. To do this, both their interest and their sympathy must be aroused. Various methods for accomplishing this were taught by the rhetoricians, and each type of case had its own type of exordium, but in each there were

THE PROLOGUE

present the two functions of fastening the interest of the hearer upon the immediate case and of setting the proper tone for the case, so that the hearer would be in a sympathetic mood. Originally intended for orations, this doctrine seems to have spread perfectly naturally to the other types of literature. It is encountered, for instance, in history and in the didactic essay. With growth of the practice of public recitation it received a new impetus, and, in a normally emotional form of literature like the drama, it is not strange that it developed a more emotional tone.

It has often been assumed that there is little differentiation between the prologues of different plays, that Seneca wished merely to make his audience gloomy and vaguely apprehensive. Gloom there is in abundance in all the prologues—that was the fundamental quality of tragedy to Seneca. But there is also at least the attempt on the author's part to give an appropriate tone to each of the several plays. For example, the Juno of the *Hercules* prologue is not merely the dejected outcast wife; she is something of a virago and whips herself to a fury which is sharply distinguished from mere gloom or mere terror:

> Up wrath and on, crush the presumptuous churl
> That still aspires, tear him with thine own hands,
> Nor leave thy will to others; let be wild beasts
> And all the Titan host. Dost seek a match
> For Hercules? There is but one—himself.
> With his own self let him wage war—call thou
> From lowest hell the stark Eumenides
> With flaming locks and in their savage claws
> Wielding the viper scourge. Go now proud fool
> And, scorning earth, assail the firmament:
> Dost think thou hast escaped the Stygian realm,
> The abode of Shades? Here will I make for thee
> A very hell.

All of the learned astronomy that is crowded into this prologue cannot destroy the ferocity of it. So far as tone is concerned it is the proper and successful preparation for a play in which madness plays the leading role.

Again, in the *Hercules on Oeta,* there is something less than the usual heavy note of melodramatic gloom. There is more of defiance in the claim of the son to recognition by his father, now that he has performed his great tasks.

> Now father of the gods, thou at whose hand
> Both realms of Phoebus feel the thunderbolt,
> Rule thou secure: I have wrought peace for thee
> Wherever Nereus bounds the solid earth:
> No need of thunder—impious kings are fallen
> And cruel tyrants. I have shattered all
> That called thy lightning forth. And yet to me
> Is heaven still denied?

The tone is certainly not, throughout the rest of the prologue speech, a light one, but it conveys a sense of terror produced by brute power and anger, in addition to the atmosphere of gloom and horror.

The *Troades* is a play neither of revenge nor of defiance. From its Greek source it inherited something of the tone of pacifist propaganda, but, in its transformation into a Roman tragedy, it developed less an atmosphere suggestive purely of the horror of war than one of despair and human misery. Seneca chose Hecuba, the too long-lived, to present this tone in the prologue, as he chose the wronged wife Juno in the *Hercules Furens* and the defiant hero himself in the *Hercules on Oeta*.

The *Medea* is in much the same category as the *Hercules Furens*. The heroine is a slighted wife and an imperious one. She has not the regal divinity of Juno, but she is the untamed barbarian with magic power and she has the consuming rage of a woman scorned. Except for the *Phaedra*, the remaining plays are true tragedies of horror. The prologue speakers are the ill-starred Oedipus, the ghost of Thyestes, and the ghost of Tantalus. The tone of horror is developed extensively in each of the monologues with the additional color of revenge in the last two.

The *Phaedra* requires a further word of comment. It is of course influenced strongly by its model, the *Hippolytus* of Euripides, and yet it is an obvious attempt at originality. The Greek play opened with a prologue in which Aphrodite foretold in a general way the disasters to come, followed by the romantic entrance of Hippolytus with his huntsmen, all of them singing as they return home. Seneca discarded the divine motivation, congenial as it was to him, and opened directly with a song which indicates that Hippolytus is off for an extensive hunt; he is departing instead of coming home, in spite of the fact that he will be needed after 350 lines while the day is still young! When he is gone, Phaedra begins a monologue which to some extent takes the place of the prologue with its tone of despairing gloom. This is not, however, detached from the play proper, in the usual Senecan fashion, by the chorus. Having departed once from his normal practice, Seneca goes further and follows Euripides' example by having a dialogue (the nurse and Phaedra) follow the prologue speech. Obviously this tragedy is something of an exception and the author did not furnish the key to its rhetorical tone by the usual prologue method. It is a play of intrigue with fatal consequences and, considered as a whole, less of a rhetorical tone picture than the others.

The Senecan prologue seems then to come primarily from the Euripidean. Like its Greek model, it is detached from the rest of the play and consists of a monologue either by one of the leading characters of the play or by a supernatural speaker not otherwise appearing in the action. Unlike its ancestor, it did not regularly include dialogue nor was it primarily concerned with the exposition of essential facts. These it did supply when necessary, as well as motivation for the tragedy, but its truly Roman contribution lies rather in its function of setting the tone for the play, a tone of revengeful fury, defiance, despair, or sheer unadulterated horror.

CHAPTER IV
DRAMATIC TECHNIQUE

WHEN we pass from the prologue to the plays proper it becomes even clearer that the striking differences that appeared between the Greek *Oedipus* and the Roman are typical. Before taking up various elements of the tragedy one by one it will be convenient to consider a number of the more mechanical phases of dramatic technique which influenced English drama and which, deriving their origin from the Greek, nevertheless appear sometimes in Seneca in a form greatly modified if not wholly changed.

One fundamental characteristic of ancient tragedy was not altered in the transition from Greece to Rome. The dialogue continued to be in verse and the verse used continued to be the iambic trimeter. Neither drama in prose nor prose passages inserted into verse drama were ever attempted so far as we know by the classical playwrights. The iambic trimeter, once determined upon as the suitable meter, was retained without exception. It has the advantage of being dignified and satisfactorily rhythmical while at the same time approaching more closely to prose than any of the possible substitutes.

The plays of Seneca were, then, like their Greek models, verse dramas, with the dialogue in iambic trimeter. Occasionally a more emotional meter was introduced for short passages and even, in a few cases, lyric meters. Between the episodes, a chorus regularly sang an ode in some lyric meter or meters. This general form was not the original vehicle of tragedy which, evolving from a choral exhibition, took on its final character gradually, but in Seneca the type is fixed.

Another characteristic of the Senecan play derived without change from the Greek was the conventional limitation of the number of characters. Except for the chorus, which, it will appear later, was disappearing as a character in the play, there are never more than three speaking characters on the scene at once. Traditionally it is supposed to have been Arion who first separated the chorus leader from the chorus and introduced dialogue into what had been a choral exhibition. Thespis added an actor and made drama possible. Aeschylus is credited with adding a second actor while Sophocles is supposed to have contributed the idea of a third actor and to have thus given to Greek drama as much range as it ever attained. The limitation was undoubtedly due in large part to the simplicity of the action which not only originated in a choral exhibition but was always to a large extent conditioned by the presence of the chorus. Furthermore, the size of the open-air theater required simplicity of action and sharp differentiation of characters and any multiplicity of parts would surely have led to confusion, with chorus and actors filling the orchestra. It is not necessary to ascribe the rule of three actors to Athenian parsimony: it, like all the so-called rules of the drama, was the practical outcome of natural conditions. Such was not the case when tragedy reached the hands of Seneca. For him there was no reason for limiting the number of parts. He simply accepted tradition and passed on the convention that there should never be more than three actors on the stage at once.

Another convention that received its final sanction from Seneca is that every play must consist of five acts and of five acts only. The Greek episodes were not by rule fixed in number but in practice it is more usual in the plays of Sophocles and Euripides to find three episodes than any other number. These, with the prologos and the exodos, correspond to the five acts of Roman tragedy which Horace stipulates as correct.

By practice, too, the Greek playwrights established the unities of time and place. The constant presence of the chorus made it not only natural but almost necessary to confine the action to one place and to the time of one day. In Seneca, the scene is never clearly defined and it is therefore hardly possible to say more than that the unity of place is on the whole respected. The instance of confusion of scene in the *Troades* is not in reality a change of scene, even an unintentional one, but merely a slip due to the fact that the setting was undefined and, from Seneca's point of view, unimportant. The unity of time is faithfully observed.

Finally, the Greek tradition of mythological subjects and characters was accepted by Seneca. Historical subjects did not prove acceptable to the Athenian playwrights and the surviving *Octavia* indicates that, given his type of play, Seneca was wise in following the mythological convention.

In these respects, then, the Roman plays simply continued the practice or tradition of the Greek. But in the mechanical handling of the action, in what may be called dramatic technique in a narrow sense, the difference between the two is marked. For example, even in the prologue Sophocles was always careful to create and maintain an illusion of reality; from the first word spoken in any drama, no character was allowed to step outside the play and talk directly to the audience. Euripides was quite unconcerned over this dramatic illusion in the prologue but, outside that element of the play, no serious charge can be brought against him on this ground. Such is not the case with Seneca. His prologues were even further detached from the plays than those of his favorite model and he does not stop there. In the plays proper he has small regard for dramatic illusion.

The handling of the mechanics will be most easily seen by following through a single play. The *Troades* is typical. It opens with the usual gloom, in this case partially but not wholly localized.

> Who trusts in power of royalty, in might
> Rules a proud court nor fears the fickle gods,
> But with prosperity lulls his credulous soul:
> Let him but look on me; on me and then
> On thee, O Troy. Never has fortune proven
> More ruthlessly how insecure the heights
> Where proud men stand; lo, shattered and o'erthrown,
> Lies now the columned strength of Asia's pride:
> The masterpiece of gods.

The general location is made clear: the play will be near or at Troy and the lines that follow confirm this, adding detail to the

DRAMATIC TECHNIQUE 85

picture of the fallen city, still burning; at line 36 the speaker identifies herself as Hecuba. She goes even further and indicates that the Greeks are about to divide the human spoil. At line 62 a minor difficulty occurs. There has been no indication of anyone present to whom Hecuba's complaints are addressed. With a knowledge of Euripides' undramatic prologues, the reader is not disturbed by this. He is, however, surprised when Hecuba says abruptly:

> Ceases our lamentation? Ye captive throng,
> Come, bare your breasts and sound the mourning plaint,
> The righteous due of Troy. Long since 'tis meet
> The slopes of Ida, big with fate, the home
> Of that most ill-starred judge, should sound with woe.

Thereupon the chorus begins the dirge for captured Troy. Quite clearly this is not at all an impossible situation. Granted a Roman theater, supplied with a curtain which saved the playwright the necessity of finding a plausible entrance for his opening characters, it would probably be captious to ask for more precision. Presumably the scene might be thought of as opening with the captive Trojan women grouped on the stage. Hecuba sufficiently identifies herself and them. There is, however, a different feeling from that produced by a Greek play in which the entrance of the chorus is regularly motivated and in which that entrance occurs *after* the prologue. We have an inclination to look for stage directions or to turn to a program to make sure just what the antecedent situation is. Seneca was not interested in explaining the presence of the chorus at the opening or of creating a plausible entrance for them.

The trouble becomes more complicated at the end of the choral passage called for by Hecuba and provided by the captives. Hecuba herself has not withdrawn but has taken part in the lament, guiding the chorus throughout with directions as to what they shall mourn. But, at line 164, a new character appears and abruptly, without introduction by himself or anyone else, bursts into exclamations which are met by the chorus with a question as to their meaning, a question which elicits a speech from the newcomer addressed entirely to the chorus. Hecuba has vanished utterly from the scene, entirely without comment. The manuscripts tell us that the newcomer is Talthybius, herald of the Greeks. He may be, but he is not performing the functions of a herald but rather of a messenger. The technique is that of a messenger's speech not too well done. His first remark is correctly exclamatory but it is *not* excited or terrified:

> Oh long, how long, the endless stay in port,
> Whether the Greeks seek war or sail for home.

The chorus asks the expected simple question:

> What is the reason that the Greeks delay?
> Tell us, I pray, what god doth bar their path?

Suddenly the messenger galvanizes into horror. He makes a few terrified exclamations, then begins in proper epic style the story of the appearance of Achilles' ghost.

> Titan was touching with his rising rays
> The topmost peaks and day had conquered night,
> When, with a sudden groan, etc.

The story is told effectively but this abrupt and foreshortened opening suggests the technique of one who is not thinking of the stage effect but simply sketching a conventional framework for a bit of melodramatic recitation. The suspicion is confirmed by the close of this speech. With crude suddenness, on the withdrawal of the ghost, supreme calm returned to the ocean and in the distance was heard "the hymeneal chorus of the Tritons," which, while affording ample contrast with the threatening address of Achilles' ghost, is ludicrously irrelevant. Furthermore, the incident ends on this hymeneal note; not a further word from the messenger, not a syllable of comment from the chorus who have asked for the story and should be interested in it, and not an indication of how the messenger is disposed of. Disposed of he must be, for in the next line a new character is speaking, once more unannounced, and most certainly not conscious of the presence of the messenger. He is not talking to himself:

> When thou wouldst spread in joy returning sails,
> Thou thoughtst not of Achilles by whose hand
> Alone Troy fell.

It develops that the reader is eavesdropping on a violent argument between Pyrrhus (Achilles' son) and Agamemnon, the young man demanding the sacrifice of Polyxena to his father's spirit. They seem to have no knowledge of the ghost's demands or if they have they ignore them. The argument consists of one long passage for each, then several shorter ones, finally a line and even half a line apiece as the heat of passion rises. Then suddenly (l. 349), Agamemnon (who has been sufficiently identified but never named) closes the argument with the statement that he will summon Calchas and abide by his decision. In the very same breath, he addresses Calchas and asks his decision! In businesslike fashion and in only eleven lines, Calchas demands the death of Polyxena and, for good measure, adds the sacrifice of Astyanax. Without motivation, Agamemnon, Pyrrhus, Calchas disappear, and the chorus sings the best of the Senecan odes: "Is it true or an idle tale," excellent as a nondramatic lyric but quite detached from the play. With the close of the lyric recital, the chorus is addressed by an unheralded woman who expresses her misery in well-turned epigrams and proves to be Andromache with young Astyanax. An interlocutor materializes from nowhere—the manuscripts call him "senex"—and, by his questions, gives her the opportunity to recount, with the technique of the messenger's speech, a dream which she has had. In the dream, Hector bade her hide Astyanax. This she finally does in the tomb of Hector but no sooner has she finished than she sees Ulysses, the first character in the play to be dramatically introduced.

> Earth open wide and thou my consort burst
> The depths beneath and into Stygian night
> Bury what here I left. Ulysses comes
> With dubious step and countenance. He plans
> Within that wily heart some clever ruse.

The contest of wits between Andromache and Ulysses is on the whole good but disproportionately long—nearly 300 lines, or one quarter of the play. No exits are prepared for at its close.

After another choral passage Helen enters and announces herself. In the midst of her reverie she stops short and addresses Andromache who has evidently either remained during the choral ode or drifted in again. Presently it develops that Hecuba too has appeared unannounced: she is speaking to Helen when she sees Pyrrhus coming. Nothing develops from this for he does not speak and the act ends with the usual unmentioned disappearance of the characters while the chorus sings an ode in Horatian meter. This is their last appearance, but, contrary to his usual custom, Seneca provides for their departure from the stage at the close of the play. The messenger orders them off to the Greek ships. As their last ode comes to an end, this messenger enters breathless with the usual exclamatory preface. On being questioned, he tells in deliberate fashion the story of the twofold catastrophe, the deaths of Polyxena and Astyanax.

Several facts should be noted. There is no evidence of the exact scene of the action except the presence of the tomb of Hector. Presumably, this is outside the city but near the wall. This fact makes such scenes as the argument of Pyrrhus and Agamemnon somewhat unnatural and the sudden arrival of Calchas absurd. The setting meant little to Seneca as is indicated by the messenger's account in the last act. He describes a spectator to the tragedy as climbing the tomb of Hector to obtain a better view, and this while he is talking to people who are and have been throughout at the tomb of Hector and yet know nothing of the tragic deaths.

The failure to motivate entrances and exits or properly to introduce characters is quite sufficient evidence that the play was never intended for acting. It was for recitation solely.

It is clear that forms like the prologue, the chorus, the messenger's speech have become hardened into fairly fixed and conventional types and that the chorus is merely a formal division between acts.

Finally, there is a considerable amount of monologue. The

characters do not address the audience directly but they talk freely to themselves.

These same points were all evident in the *Oedipus* and they are equally clear in the other plays. The entrance of the chorus is almost never motivated and in no play but the *Troades* is a reason given for its departure. In two instances, however, the chorus seems to be thought of as coming in at the end of an act. In the *Hercules Furens*, Theseus says that he sees a crowd coming with wreaths on to celebrate Hercules, and there follows a regular choral ode, one of the four, in honor of Hercules. Similarly, in the *Agamemnon*, Clytemnestra sees coming what she assumes to be a crowd of Trojan captives with Cassandra and she is proved right by the ode which follows immediately. This does not mean that the chorus is thought of as regularly leaving the stage at the close of an ode. (Very occasionally the chorus will be found playing the part of a character.) It simply indicates the diminished importance of the chorus in the mind of the playwright and his failure to be dramatically consistent, because the play is not an acting piece. In these two instances, it is probable that the chorus in its preceding appearances was thought of as differently constituted. The choruses are never well identified except in the *Troades*. In the *Medea*, the only indication is the singing of a wedding song for Jason and Creusa which makes the chorus appear to be friendly to Jason and this is confirmed by their strong condemnation of Medea. In the *Phaedra* the chorus seems to be made up of sympathetic women but the fact is not made obvious and in the *Thyestes* all indication is lacking. There is not much more to go on in the *Oedipus* though the (second) ode to Bacchus seems to open with a call to bacchantes: "Bind your flowing locks and seize the thyrsus in your soft hands." Aside from this there is nothing inconsistent with the male chorus that we should expect. In the *Hercules on Oeta*, it is clearly intended to have two different choruses. The first identifies itself as a group of Oechalian women, the second Deianeira addresses as her maidens, women of Aetolia. In the *Agamemnon* there is one Trojan and one Argive chorus.

It is not alone the chorus that is left unexplained in its entrances and exits. The well-motivated arrival or departure of any character is exceptional. The great majority appear utterly unheralded and leave as mysteriously. The device of a creaking door or something equally mechanical is about all that is used in the small minority of motivated entrances. And, furthermore, a new character is hardly ever identified promptly or clearly. It is hard to believe that, at the recitation of the plays, the name of the speaker (at least in the case of a new character) was not read out by the performer.

Although the monologue will be more thoroughly treated in a later chapter, its dramatic handling should be noted here. At line 85 of the *Phaedra*, the heroine, without any explanation of where she is or how she comes to be there and with no one apparently present for her to address, invokes her island home of Crete, complaining of Theseus' infidelity. Her charges against her husband soon give way to self-pity for her own distraught state of mind and, at line 112, she addresses herself: *quo tendis anime?* A moment later the nurse breaks in and gives some dramatic realism to the situation. There are many monologues of this type usually with an exclamatory opening but almost always without dramatic preparation. One of these is of particular interest for the present discussion. Clytemnestra (*Agam.*, l. 108) makes her initial entrance addressing her own soul in an effort to arouse her own fury. After some fifteen lines of this, the nurse addresses her:

> Queen of the Greeks, of Leda's noble stock,
> What dost thou plan in silence?

The dramatic illusion is shattered completely.

There seems to be a further extension of the monologue in one or two instances in which the speaker appears actually to address the audience. For example, in the fourth act of the *Medea* the nurse recounts the doings of Medea in direct narrative. It is barely possible to imagine that the chorus is her audience but no indication of this is given. In the fourth act of the *Agamemnon*, Strophius enters at line 918:

DRAMATIC TECHNIQUE

> I, Strophius far-famed, with trophies won
> At Elis, now return. My purpose is
> To bring congratulation to that friend
> By whose all powerful hand great Troy has fallen
> After ten years of warfare. But who now
> Is this that comes with flowing tears and look
> Of frightened sorrow?

Obviously his opening words have not been addressed to Elektra and no other logical audience is provided.

In the *Thyestes* there is at least one actual aside. The third act opens with the entrance of Thyestes accompanied by his son Tantalus. He pronounces a monologue which Tantalus is evidently not supposed to hear if we may judge by his question at the close. Thyestes continues, addressing his soul, until a second question by his son leads him into direct conversation. After a rather long dialogue, Atreus enters with what cannot but be regarded as an aside:

> The net is spread, the quarry caught therein:
> I see the man himself and, with his sire,
> The son of loathed race. At last my hate
> Has opportunity; Thyestes falls
> Into my grasp.

This continues for some fifteen lines. Then he reminds himself that he must deceive his brother and proceeds:

> 'Tis joy to greet a brother. Come to my arms.
> All hate that was is past. From this day on,
> Let piety and brother's love be ours.

Ulysses, in the *Troades* (l. 605), is addressing Andromache when he too breaks off into an aside:

> I shall with joy report unto the Greeks
> High fate accomplished, mighty Hector's stock
> Destroyed—Ulysses, where thy wonted wit?
> The Greeks will take thy word, but thou, whose word
> Art thou accepting? What a parent says?
> Nay, could a parent lie in such a plight
> Nor fear the omen of her husband's tomb?

> Yet they fear omens who have naught to fear
> That's worse than omens. But she bound her faith
> By oath. She did and if she break her oath
> What worse hath she to fear? Come soul of mine
> Summon thy wit, thy tricks, thy cunning wiles,
> All that becomes Ulysses. Truth will out.
> Scan thou that mother's face; she weeps, she groans;
> And yet she paces restlessly and seems
> To listen for some sound with anxious ear.
> More than her grief, her fear. Now show thy wit.—
> Some women I should comfort in their grief
> But thee, poor Queen, I must congratulate.
> Thy son is lost for whom a cruel death
> Was waiting even now.

In a less striking way Jason comments on Medea (1. 445) in her presence without her hearing him.

It cannot be said that the aside was a frequent practice of Seneca. But there is evident in his plays a strong tendency to forget all dramatic illusion and to address remarks directly to the audience. The precedent of the aside has been established and there is no longer apparent any compelling obligation on the part of the playwright to exclude the audience from the action.

As to the convention of stage horrors, it seems clear that Seneca did not follow Horace's dictum at all so far as his artistic principle went, for Iokaste kills herself "on the stage" and it is very hard to see how Megara and her children can be saved from publicity in their deaths. And yet, with no artistic inhibition as explanation, it is at first hard to understand why Seneca, with his love for exaggeration and the melodramatic, does not go further in the matter of bloody exhibition. But it is no mystery when we recall the fact that these were not acting plays. These horrors must, under any circumstances, be read, not acted, and the easiest way by far to gain his melodramatic effect was to have them reported from "off stage." One of the horrors on stage is strong corroboration for the conclusion that these were not acting plays. Hippolytus has been hurled to death and dragged by his horses until his body has been torn to fragments. These fragments have been in large part collected and are being

DRAMATIC TECHNIQUE

placed in approximate order by Theseus. One piece he finds too shapeless to identify and finally, after vain surmise, he puts it in an otherwise vacant place in the pattern. This passage is bad enough when read: acted, it would be either impossibly horrible or (much more likely) impossibly ridiculous. The *effect* of horror in a play *wholly recited* is greater as a general rule if an interested messenger can elaborate on his account of it with melodramatic comment than if an attempt is made to present it as actually happening on the stage. In fact, the presentation of horrors on stage in a recited play raises very real difficulty while their description by a reporter offers a congenial opportunity for rhetorical display. In each of the cases cited of horrors enacted on stage the action is far from clear and of course has to be inferred from the spoken word. Seneca, therefore, set an example of rhetorical horror but not of "stage horrors."

CHAPTER V
LONG SPEECHES

FROM the point of view of dramatic construction, there is significance in the relative importance allotted by a playwright to chorus, dialogue, and long harangue. In general the chorus has about the same prominence in Seneca as in Euripides or Sophocles. But the nonchoral parts are very different. The Roman poet as a rule devotes more than one half of his whole play to long speeches, never more than a third to what may be called dialogue. Now Sophocles had used the long speech sparingly; Euripides, with his oratorical tendency, had developed it to a certain extent, but even he never gave it such prominence as did Seneca. His true dialogue runs regularly to something over six hundred lines, an amount never approached by Seneca, who has about four hundred lines in his longest play.

The matter of long speeches is more important than it appears at first glance. Obviously, they are of two types: first, the long harangues that really form a part of the action on stage, and second, the narratives that are either a messenger's speech or its equivalent. In either case, these latter speeches recount some event off stage and therefore, because of the requisite unity of scene (in the Greek theater at least), are an essential part of any play making pretense to reasonable range of action. It will be simpler to take the latter type first.

It has always been something of an accepted commonplace to speak of the plays of Aeschylus as a combination of choral lyric and epic poetry. There is a certain amount of epic language in Aeschylus to bear out this observation; otherwise the epic element is not as obvious as might be expected. (Incidentally, of course, it is not certain that we should call the forms epic.) In the earliest play of Aeschylus, the *Suppliants*, there is little narrative that would suggest epic poetry. Such of the play as is not choral is largely taken up with dialogue. In the *Persians*, we have indeed the long account of the battle by the messenger, one part of which begins with a phrase that will be very familiar in form before we are through with messengers' speeches: There is an island hard by Salamis. Here is narrative of a good epic style introduced by a description of the setting of the story. The speeches of the messenger in the *Seven Against Thebes* are pictures of the heroes matched by the pictures drawn by Eteocles. The account of the ceremony of the oath comes nearer to the narrative report of an incident off stage. In the *Prometheus*, there is nothing that can really be classed with this present type of speech, although Io's story and the long harangues of Prometheus serve to lend romantic color by bringing in what must have been exciting material that lay outside the scope of the immediate action. Finally, the three plays of the *Oresteia* produce no real narrative accounts of events off stage. It seems clear that to Aeschylus the tragedy was still more of a choral performance than a drama, with enough dialogue to interpret the lyrics and with longer speeches introduced largely for their spectacular or romantic effect and then only sparingly.

With Sophocles we have already seen that the dramatic element came into its own. Plot furnishes the central interest. Complications have a new value, for the play is no longer a static picture but an advancing action. The range of the action is largely extended although the exactions of the physical production make it impossible for the scene to change. (In the *Ajax*, it does actually change as it had in the *Eumenides* of Aeschylus. These two examples stand alone in Greek tragedy.) Events bearing on the main issue must be brought in by some device and the most ready device is that of a reporter who narrates the off-stage event.

It is Sophocles, therefore, who must be looked upon as the inventor of the traditional messenger's speech. To him it would seem to have had a special function, namely, to report the catastrophe. Sophocles did not bring on to the stage any acts of violence (with the exception of the suicide of Ajax in a play which is also most unusual in that it has a change of scene), but used them rather as symbolic of the more real suffering of the spirit. He did recount them in speeches which show more of rhetoric and less of dramatic suitability to the character of the speaker than the rest of his lines. Four of his plays have such speeches. Of the rest, the *Ajax* presents the catastrophe before the eyes of the spectators; the *Philoktetes* has no real catastrophe and furthermore comes nearer to a character study, like the *Prometheus*, than do any of the others; in the *Elektra*, the dramatic method of announcing the death of Clytemnestra to Aigisthos eliminates any chance of a messenger's speech. Of the four speeches announcing the catastrophe, three begin with an adverb of time as does the incidental speech of Hyllus in the *Trachinian Women*, announcing the effects of the Nessus robe on Herakles. And so Tekmessa, reporting the mad acts of Ajax, begins: At dead of night when burned no more the lamps. The old Paedagogos also, in the *Elektra*, coming to tell the fictitious story of Orestes' death, begins his tale: For when he came to that famed land of Greece. The narrative use of γάρ is noteworthy here as in two of the narrations of catastrophes. The same technique is found in the only true messenger speeches in Sophocles that do not tell of a violent fate—the report of the guard in *Antigone:* For when we came obedient to thy threats; and the account by a messenger of the speech of Calchas in the *Ajax:* For Calchas rising from his seat alone.

Other speeches in Sophocles have slight but not remarkable resemblances to what we think of as the typical messenger's speech. Evidently there was already a tendency to give to this member of the drama a fixed form, but it had not gone far in Sophocles and the messenger's speech was confined to a fairly narrow function.

It is necessary, at this juncture, to make a still sharper distinction between different sorts of speeches and the differences will now be more readily apparent. The true messenger's speech reports an action which is actually a part of the plot and in that sense is actually the equivalent, so far as the advancement of the plot is concerned, of a scene enacted "on the stage." This contribution to the action or development of plot may be made by one of the characters in the play or by a messenger used for this purpose only. So, in the *Trachinian Women*, Hyllus reports the donning of the Nessus robe by Herakles and the nurse tells of the end of Deianeira, whereas, in the *Antigone*, a messenger who has no other function in the play reports the deaths of Haemon and Antigone.

Now, along with these speeches which advance the immediate action of the plot, we have also extended accounts of facts which have a bearing on the story, to be sure, but which are extraneous to the immediate plot, usually antecedent facts not brought out in the prologue; in other words, more pertinent to the exposition than to the action proper. Such is the speech of Oedipus in the *Oedipus Tyrannus* at line 771. Iokaste has asked Oedipus why he is anxious to hear the slave who was with Laius when he met his death. In answer, Oedipus recounts at considerable length (63 lines) his (supposed) parentage, his departure from Corinth, his experiences at Delphi and, afterwards, on the way to Thebes. In the *Ajax*, Tekmessa (ll. 282–330), in response to a question of the chorus, tells of the madness of Ajax which is the immediate antecedent of the plot. She begins in a manner more typical of a messenger: At dead of night when burned no more the lamps. A third speech of this sort is especially interesting. In the *Oedipus at Colonos* (l. 1284), Polyneices, in response to Antigone's request, tells the story of the Army of the Seven, gathered to attack Thebes. It is an account of antecedent fact but it develops (in its true light) into a plea to Oedipus for help. It is followed by two colorless lines by the chorus, after which Oedipus answers in a speech nearly as long as that of Polyneices. The first speech, therefore, in its setting, becomes rather part of an argument than a narrative and as such falls into a class that is more familiar in Euripides and which lies outside the class of messenger speeches even in their wider interpretation.

To proceed, then, with the messenger speech in Euripides. It would be tedious and unprofitable to go through all the plays in detail. Two have no messenger speeches at all, the *Alkestis* and the *Troades* which in other respects also show unique peculiarities among the Euripidean plays. In the case of the *Troades* it is possible to find an explanation in the fact that the play is more a pageant of the woes of war than a tragedy in the strict sense. Of the remaining plays (including even the *Cyclops* and the *Rhesus*) just over half have the catastrophe recounted by a messenger, the rest have messenger's speeches to introduce other incidents directly in the stream of the plot. Fourteen of these messengers' speeches begin with ἐπεί, when, so many of them that this becomes a recognized conventional opening. "When came your twofold offspring with their sire." "When we arrived at Phoebus' famed abode." "When he, Creusa's husband, with the child / had left the shrine." "When to the heights along the shore we came." All of these give the setting of the story which the messenger is about to tell and this setting usually includes the place where the incident occurs. There are half as many more that give the time or place or both, but with other openings. "It happened from the country I was come / within the gates." "I was proceeding with the royal herds / onto the uplands when the sun burst forth / warming the earth."

In almost every instance the messenger comes in at a high pitch of excitement and a few lines of dialogue give realism to the entrance before he settles down to his narrative. Usually the messenger reports some event of a more or less violent nature though, occasionally, as in the first narrative in the *Bacchae*, it is simply something that could not be presented on the stage because of the difficulty of changing scene. Euripides avoids with considerable care the direct presentation of scenes of physical violence or horror. His messenger speeches are rhetorical but vigorous and vivacious. He uses, with rare exceptions, a messenger rather than some character in the play. Talthybius in the *Troades* is perhaps a little more than an ordinary messenger and Odysseus performs the function in the *Cyclops*.

Euripides may be said to have taken the messenger speech from Sophocles and to have used it to a much greater extent than did his older contemporary. In part this extension was due to his desire to broaden and complicate the action, in part to his delight in thrilling narrative. On the whole, he made these speeches dramatic in that he furnished a suitable audience, properly developed the opening and the close, and gave to his messengers sufficient individuality to make their parts realistic. At the same time he somewhat conventionalized the type of speech, making it a familiar element of the drama. That this is true is evidenced not only by the facts as we shall find them in Seneca, but by the development in the New Comedy, as illustrated by Plautus. Grotesque as he is, the "running slave" is the direct descendant of Euripides' messenger.

With a more objective prologue, Euripides had less need of the other type of informative speech noted in Sophocles. In the *Iphigeneia among the Taurians* (1. 939) Orestes recounts his past experiences to his sister as his other sister does to him in the *Elektra* (1. 300). Both speakers begin λέγοιμ' ἄν, I will tell you, and both speeches are narrative but not like the messenger speeches proper. They correspond to the expository instances noted in Sophocles and their true literary ancestor is to be found in such recitals as those of Prometheus, elicited by the chorus, in Aeschylus.

The narrative type of speech does not, however, represent all the extended recital in the Greek drama. One very popular type of speech in Euripides has been suggested already by an example from Sophocles. It is commonly called the argument scene because, in Euripides, it most often forms part of a debate. One speaker makes a long address followed by one of approximately the same length by another character, the two separated by a commonplace remark of the chorus. The mannerism of Euripides was at least a common practice of Sophocles, although the older poet did not develop the rhetorical balance and almost conventional form of the younger. But Oedipus and Tiresias, Antigone and Kreon, Ajax and Tekmessa, Agamemnon and Teucer all argue in this general form, although perhaps the more noteworthy fact is that Sophocles did *not* develop the device into a mannerism. In Euripides, it is too familiar to dwell on at length.

Every play shows at least one instance and most of them more than one, some as many as four. It is perhaps worth while noting one elaboration of the device, illustrated in the *Andromache*: Peleus and Menelaus have two sets of speeches of this type, the two sets divided by two lines of chorus. There is an even more elaborate pattern when Andromache and Menelaus argue in the same play.

This is the sort of thing that we should hardly expect to find in Aeschylus: argument is not the stuff of dramatic poems so much as of realistic dramas. Yet it is not impossible to see the origin of the typical form in Aeschylus. Prometheus and Oceanus argue in the *Prometheus Bound* and, while the chorus does not interject any commonplace, the debaters have five lines each between the long speeches. Furthermore, Aeschylus was perfectly familiar with the device of breaking up the monotony of long narratives or harangues by interjecting lines by the chorus who are quite often the only other actors present to hear the speaker. Examples are the speeches by the King in the *Suppliants*, by Clytemnestra in the *Agamemnon*, by Orestes in the *Choephoroi*, by Prometheus. The herald's speech in the *Agamemnon* is broken by dialogue, and Atossa interrupts the messenger's narrative in the *Persians*, with comments or questions. A somewhat more intricate pattern is formed in the *Seven* by the pairs of speeches by Eteocles and the messenger, each pair divided from the next by five lines of chorus. The bulk of the speeches in Aeschylus, however, is addressed to the chorus and falls into another category, but the germ of this type, the paired argumentative speeches, is already present, a germ which developed in Euripides into something almost stereotyped, as familiar as the thrust and parry of his rapid argument which was of course equally the rhetorical development of something already present in the drama.

But to return to the long speeches. Quite apart from messengers' speeches and the set argumentative discourses, there are many speeches of considerable length that fall into neither category. In the simpler form of the early drama, these normally had the character of addresses to the chorus, although at times this audience seems to be well-nigh forgotten. The King and Danaus talk directly and at length to the maidens of the chorus. Atossa addresses the Persian elders and Eteocles does the same to the women of Thebes. Prometheus almost forgets the ocean nymphs in his long outbursts, as both Clytemnestra and Agamemnon forget the chorus when they are holding forth with no one but this group of Argives to listen to them. But it is the chorus, nevertheless, to whom these long speeches are formally addressed. Orestes and Elektra keep the chorus well in mind in the *Choephoroi*, Orestes not so clearly in the *Eumenides*.

At the same time, Aeschylus by no means limits himself to the chorus as the recipient of long addresses. Eteocles makes his opening proclamation to what might be called an auxiliary chorus though it does not speak; Prometheus is always present and listens to Io's long narrative (which, however, is more like a messenger's speech and has already been discussed); in the *Eumenides*, Orestes appeals to Athena who answers—both are long speeches—and Apollo and Athena address each other. In the *Agamemnon*, there is an interesting interchange between Agamemnon and Clytemnestra which has something of a pattern, like the debate scenes: two speeches followed by thirteen lines of stichomythia, then two shorter speeches. In general these would seem to be either long addresses to the chorus or somewhat extended conversational speeches between actors, although the latter may reach the proportions and attain the character of long independent speeches.

In passing, some comment should be made on the lengthy remarks of the ghost of Darius in the *Persians*. The form has already been noted. In substance this is largely suggestive of a misplaced prologue. Its purpose is like that of the divinities of Euripides that speak at the opening of the play and furnish the motivation of the action.

When we turn to Sophocles it is necessary to remind ourselves that the dramatic interest is for him supreme, that he did not stop with the presentation of a choral entertainment, made comprehensible by a limited amount of recitative, but that real drama, the development of plot through character, replaces in his work the great dramatic pageants of his predecessor. This does not mean that he was wholly realistic but it certainly means at least that he was more observant of the dramatic probabilities.

There are, however, plenty of situations in which a person may with perfect naturalness harangue a group of persons such as are represented by a Greek chorus. Sophocles did not discard the address to the chorus. At the end of the parodos in the *Oedipus Tyrannus*, the King answers directly the appeal which has sounded in the choral song and speaks at considerable length, explaining to the elders of Thebes what the situation is and what he plans to do about it. Equally natural is the speech of the same king, now a blind exile, to the men of Colonos in the same relative situation in the later play. In the *Antigone*, Kreon follows the parodos with his vigorous proclamation which is the source of all the plot, and the heroine of the *Elektra* opens the action in a similar way. In each case, the speech does much more than advance the action, for all four are what might well be called character speeches, presenting one of the leading personages in such a way as to make him at once clearly known to the audience. But their speeches are realistically motivated and the chorus is not wholly a lay figure, simply furnishing a passive audience. In the *Elektra*, they come closer to being confidantes, and the motivation is less clear-cut. The same situation arises in the *Trachinian Women* when Deianeira twice addresses the chorus at length. It is such speeches as these that verge on monologue. After Oedipus has blinded himself and emerges from the palace, he begins to address the chorus but soon almost forgets them in his reminiscences, especially when he bursts forth into exclamations. So, too, the chorus is largely forgotten by Ajax in his horror at what he has done while mad. Most of his first long speech and much of his second are really monologue, while his third actually disregards the chorus as he calls upon the gods one after another. Antigone, addressing her tomb as she is led away to be buried alive, has little thought of the chorus or of any audience, and the same is true of Herakles in his exclamatory speech during his death agony and of Philoktetes as he suffers through two monologues. For monologues they really are. At the same time, they are entirely natural, occurring as they do at moments of the highest emotion.

These speeches all have real importance in furthering the action and in presenting the character but they have a natural tendency to become undramatic. This is less true of those speeches which are simply enlarged members of the dialogue, like those of Theseus and Oedipus, or of Elektra and Chrysothemis. There may be nothing at all distinctive in such speeches beyond the fact that they are longer than just a few lines, but it is from such that the debate scenes developed and along another line the ardent appeals of one sort or another that become familiar in Sophocles, such as that of Polyneices to Oedipus or of Neoptolemus to Philoktetes. They may also lead to long narrations, at which point they approach the messenger-speech type. One instance in Sophocles stands apart, the speech of Tiresias in the *Antigone*, telling of his divination and pronouncing his prophecies. In this he is somewhat remotely akin to the ghost of Darius: he is a supernatural element introduced to influence the action.

It has an unhappily mechanical sound, this cataloguing of types, but there is some value in the analysis, even if it is more satisfying to forget the tags. For the tendency in Euripides, and much more so in Seneca, would seem to have been toward the hardening of forms into conventional types. So it is as well to think of the speeches in characteristic groups: the informative speeches, narrating either antecedent events or contributory parts of the drama, the latter the messenger speech proper, the former either expository or decorative; the proclamation group, also informative but not narrative; the extended conversational speeches, tending along one line toward appeals and along another but not very different line toward debates; and finally, perhaps the oldest of all, the address to the chorus, developing into the addresses to confidantes other than the chorus and into the true monologue.

Sophocles brought the drama to its highest point so far as cohesion and unity of plot are concerned. He required little in the way of the spectacular to hold the attention of his audience as he unfolded his tensely dramatic plots. Euripides found the drama already brought down from the heights of Olympus but not yet reduced to the trivialities of daily life. To this last step we may be sure he never quite proceeded, in spite of the criticisms of Aristophanes. But he did move toward it. His plays are not in the grand manner to anything like the same extent as those of Aeschylus or even Sophocles. The characters of mythology become in large degree ordinary human beings; there is more realism in his dialogue; his interest is less in the strict development of the plot than in the presentation of human characters and moving scenes. It is not surprising, therefore, to find that he also delights in showing off to some extent in the sophistic manner popular in his day. We have already noted the readiness with which he discarded the restriction of making his prologue dramatically plausible. We shall find a similar tendency in other speeches of the longer types. For the conventional messenger speech and the debate scenes served to hold the interest of the audience as did the romantic geographical excursuses of Aeschylus and, while to a certain degree undramatic, they cannot but have been popular. These two types of extended speech have probably been discussed at sufficient length, but something more must be said about the address to the chorus or to a confidante which, in Euripides, finally became a real monologue.

This last development can be seen in various speeches of Medea. At line 364 she begins speaking to the chorus about her plans which are as yet only vaguely outlined in her own mind. She even addresses the chorus as friends. Yet, before she has concluded the speech, she has practically forgotten her audience and cries out:

> So be it then, Medea, spare thou naught
> Of all the wiles thou hast.

This self-address is indicative of the nature of the speech—a monologue very thinly disguised. In line 764 she has a similar speech, though without the address to herself, but when, at 1021, she speaks at length to her silent children, she addresses her own soul and practically all pretense of an audience is abandoned.

Hippolytus (l. 616) has a genuine monologue on the character of woman which is, however, in response to a statement by the nurse, who is present throughout and is technically the recipient of his remarks. Achilles, in the *Iphigeneia at Aulis*, has a monologue in which he addresses himself by name. The *Helen* has four monologues and one speech by Helen to the chorus. The reflections of Iphis, in the *Suppliants* (1080), assumes the chorus for an audience, and, in the *Herakles* (451), Megara addresses her first word, εἶεν, to the chorus, although her monologue, cast in the form of a prayer to Herakles, ignores them. Amphitryon has been present throughout, listening, and addresses her when she concludes, so that it is perhaps incorrect to call this a true monologue. Iphigeneia (*Iph. in Taur.* 344) also begins a long speech with εἶεν, addressed to the chorus, but in this case she presently addresses herself, ὦ καρδία ταλαῖνα, and certainly forgets the chorus. In the *Orestes* (366), Menelaus enters with exclamations, ignoring the chorus, and, during the course of his speech, addressing himself by name. This does not by any means exhaust the illustrations that might be given of monologues in Euripides. They are not wholly undramatic but they have a tendency to become so. They no longer occur merely at the moment of highest emotional tension, although they are always highly emotional in themselves. The exclamatory opening is common and the general tone is often reflective. There is a strong tendency toward self-address.

These monologues are one of the most characteristic of the innovations of Euripides. He uses also the extended speech of an expository nature giving information, usually by request, such as that of Adrastus to Theseus, telling of the heroes at Thebes, and that of Elektra to Orestes, and he presents numerous instances of longer speeches in dialogue. The device of a second motivation from without (Iris in the *Herakles* and Tiresias in the *Phoenissae*) is familiar from Sophocles; but Euripides has an extension of this in a new and favorite use for the long speech, the device of the *deus ex machina* to order the conclusion of the play. This is employed in nine of the extant plays.

It is high time to return from this digression on origins and to see what Seneca did with the long speeches which, as we have seen, formed a considerable part of his plays. It will be instructive to run through one play as a whole, taking for example the *Hercules*. The prologue is a speech by Juno, already noted, 124 verses in length, calling down Fury and tragedy on Hercules and his house. At the close of the parodos, the chorus announces the approach of Megara and her children along with Amphitryon. The latter, however, does not seem to realize the presence of anyone else, not even the chorus, but launches into an unmotivated monologue (with the empty courtesy of an address to Jupiter), recounting the labors of Hercules and urging him to return. When he has had his say for 74 lines, Megara takes her turn, without any attention to Amphitryon or the chorus, but with a little more recognition of Jupiter. Some editors make this all one long speech by Megara and nothing is lost (or gained) by this arrangement, a fact in itself significant of the undramatic quality of the whole. The two speakers suddenly become aware of each other and a short dialogue follows. Then enters Lycus who fails to see the others until he in turn has pronounced a monologue, whereupon, after one aside by Lycus and one by Megara, quite undramatic and following the comic technique rather than the tragic, there follows an argument scene between the two but without choral lines separating the speeches. Then a long aside by Megara followed by rapid dialogue for 100 lines. Chorus and end of second act. Hercules enters addressing the gods, telling about himself, and wondering about the situation. He has a few words with Amphitryon who appears from nowhere and then, as Hercules evidently departs to exact vengeance of Lycus, Theseus, who must have been with him, gives an account of their adventures in the familiar form of the messenger speech, punctuated by short questions on the part of

Amphitryon. Chorus, ending Act III. The fourth act is unusual. It begins with Hercules preparing sacrifice after the slaying of Lycus, accompanied by prayers, in the midst of which the madness, foretold by Juno, comes upon him. This is presented by his monologue with interjected warnings by Amphitryon. As Hercules goes within, Amphitryon from the doorway reports what happens there, the killing of the children and Megara. The voices of those within can be heard too. Act V opens with a long monologue by the restored Hercules, bemoaning what he has done, and concludes with dialogue between him and Amphitryon and Theseus.

First of all, the fourth act may be set aside except insofar as to note the mad scene as a monologue. The whole is, in reality, a melodramatic decoration, supplying the thrill that was furnished in the *Oedipus* by the hocus-pocus of Tiresias and in *Medea* by her incantations. The romantic need in Aeschylus' day might be satisfied by imaginative travelogues, but the taste of the Age of Nero was more jaded. In this particular instance, the treatment is unique, but the element of romantic melodrama is a subject by itself. The monologue in which Hercules raves in his growing madness is noteworthy.

We have, then, in the *Hercules*, the messenger speech, the extended dialogue speech, the argument scene, and the monologue. All of them are familiar from Euripides and some of them are, to a considerable extent, exaggerated and even conventionalized in his Roman rival. For example, the messenger speech, in this case spoken by a character, begins with a description of the entrance to the lower world, opening in a leisurely narrative manner quite foreign to the somewhat excited setting in which it occurs:

> The land of Sparta rears a rugged height
> Where Taenarus with thick grown woods juts out
> Into the sea.

This description passes on to a picture of the lower world and its denizens, stretching to 110 lines before the adventure of Hercules, the subject of the narrative, is introduced at all. Ixion, the Danaids, Sisyphus, all the paraphernalia of Hades are passed in review and Seneca's whole vocabulary of Stygian adjectives marshaled to enhance the effect. The epic atmosphere is emphasized by similes and by Vergilian reminiscences, but the overemphasis and lack of restraint are wholly un-Vergilian.

Similarly overstrained is the monologue of Hercules when restored to sanity. The first twenty-two lines are almost entirely composed of frantic questions addressed to no one. These continue, interspersed with wild exclamations, during the rest of the speech (twenty-five lines more) which, to be sure, he concludes by addressing Theseus and Amphitryon. In the course of the speech, Hercules harangues his own courage, bidding it to mount, although he does not actually address himself.

Equally overdone, speaking from a dramatic point of view, are the two long monologues of Amphitryon and Megara in the second act. Over a hundred lines are devoted to the labors of Hercules and the appeal to him to return. In brief, a considerably larger portion of the nonchoral part of the play is given to speeches than to dialogue and these speeches are of an overstrained character, showing at times an exaggeration of the exclamatory monologue, at times too much of the influence of the epic.

These will be found to be general characteristics of the plays of Seneca. He has two ways of beginning a messenger's speech, one giving the time setting, the other, that used in the *Hercules*, the place. If the time is described the normal opening is like the Euripidean, using a temporal conjunction: *ut profugus urbem liquit*. This occurs in the *Phaedra*, the *Hercules on Oeta* (*ut omnis Oeten maesta corripuit manus*), the *Agamemnon* (*ut Pergamum omne Dorica cecidit face*), the *Medea* (*namque ut attonito gradu / evasit*), and the *Oedipus* (*Praedicta postquam feta et infandum genus / deprendit*). But there is a variation of this type occurring twice in the *Troades*. Each instance is the story of a ghost scene, either dream or vision, so that the time is important. In one, Andromache recounts the dream she had: *partes fere nox alma transierat duas*; the other is Talthybius' story of the appearance of Achilles: *summa iam Titan iuga / stringebat ortu*.

LONG SPEECHES

The "place settings," which are more numerous, begin with a general statement of location: *est una magna turris e Troia super; est in remoto regiae sedis loco; est in recessu Tartari obscuro locus; est procul ab urbe lucus ilicibus niger; in arce summa Pelopiae pars est domus.* This is sometimes varied in phraseology but not in characteristic quality: *Spartana tellus nobile iugum; Euboica tellus vertice inmenso tumens / pulsatur omni latere.* This "place" type is reminiscent of Aeschylus' line: "There is an island hard by Salamis," just as the "time" instances are suggestive of Euripides' more usual practice.

That these are familiar epic usages it is hardly necessary to suggest. *Urbs antiqua fuit* springs immediately to mind and there are many similar phrases (e.g., *lucus in urbe fuit media; terra procul vastis colitur Mavortia campis; turris erat vasto suspectu*) in Vergil and also in Lucan who was a contemporary of Seneca's (e.g., *fonte cadit modico,* etc.; *colle tumet modico,* etc.; *lucus erat longo,* etc.). And the time setting is just as common, more so in Lucan. *Caesar ut* is almost a conventional paragraph opening with the Neronian poet and his greater predecessor did the same thing frequently: e.g., *ut pelagus tenuere rates; ut belli signum Laurenti Turnus ab arce / extulit; Turnus ut infracto,* etc.; *Turnus ut Aenean,* etc. The opening of Aeneas' great account of the fall of Troy is familiar to everyone: *Troianas ut opes et lamentabile regnum / Eruerint Danai.* The extended descriptions, too, and the learned allusions are, even if overdone, at least more suitable to epic than to the drama. The elaborate setting is not the only sign of exaggeration in these messenger speeches of Seneca. Perhaps the most marked is the ferocious nature of the horror descriptions.

The proper use for which the messenger was invented was to report the catastrophe which, for various reasons, was not presented before the audience and which afforded the Greek playwright his best chance to dwell on horrors. This method is adopted by Seneca in five plays and these are the only instances in which he uses an actual messenger. I have included the report of the banquet scene in *Thyestes*, for, while this is not actually the catastrophe in an exact sense, it is in reality the tragic climax and would seem to have been so considered by Seneca. In the remaining eight "messenger" speeches, with a single exception, one of the regular characters of the play speaks and reports a matter really antecedent to and sometimes not wholly necessary to the plot of the piece. This is not an extraordinarily large number of messenger speeches. Those that deal with matters not constituting the dramatic climax of the play have for their subjects Hercules' visit to Hades, the dream of Andromache, the visit of Achilles' ghost, the account of Medea's magic, the raising of Laius' ghost, the fall of Troy, the poison of Nessus, and the infidelity of Hercules. While these have in the main an atmosphere of horror, they are not accounts of the tragic catastrophe and therefore are sufficiently distinct from the "normal" messenger speeches. They correspond to such speeches as that of Oedipus to Iokaste in Sophocles, telling of his killing the old man at the triple crossroads. Only the account of the necromancy of Tiresias approaches the use of messengers, made by Euripides, to extend the scope of his action, such as, for example, the tale in the *Bacchae* of what the Theban women are doing on the hills, or in the *Iphigeneia* of the capture of Orestes and Pylades. So Sophocles told of the first ceremonial burial of Polyneices. The necromancy scene, in Seneca's *Oedipus*, would not have been necessary if Tiresias had been the genuine Greek seer instead of a Roman haruspex in disguise. It offered a chance, not to extend the scope of the action, but to present the weird and gruesome.

One curious use of the messenger I have omitted. It is in the *Medea*. At line 879 a messenger comes in with the familiar concise announcement of trouble:

> All, all has perished and, our kingdom lost,
> The princess and her sire are both consumed.

He makes three short answers to questions, giving the necessary information about the effect of the fatal robe. But as we settle down to hear the extended account that would normally follow, the nurse turns to Medea urging her to flee and, in their discussion, the messenger is forgotten: so far as the text indicates, he is still standing there with his story untold. Had this scene been developed, it would have been the report by a messenger of a crucial event pretty much, though not wholly, in line with the reports of tragic climaxes. As it is, it is unique: the bald announcement of a fact essential to the progress of the play. It is tempting to suspect, in this instance, a case of incompleteness of text or failure on the part of Seneca to finish the play for publication, but it is more probably simply another case of crude workmanship.

Turning to the other types of long speeches, it might seem curious at first that the debate scene is not more popular with Seneca. In an age of litigation, like the first century B.C., it very likely bulked large in tragedy, but it must be remembered that, busy as the courts were in the time of Claudius, there was a tendency even then toward one-sided cases, influenced by the reigning power, and that this tendency had gone far in Nero's day. There was not the general participation in litigation that had made every Athenian an orator. Quintilian, not so long after, could write his essay on the causes of decline in oratory and Petronius put the case more pungently in the *Satyricon*. His picture in the opening paragraphs of the fragments as we have them presents the orator as far removed from the type of lawyer who argued facts and stuck to the laws of logic. Petronius used extravagant rhetoric but his claims are, in part at least, borne out by the evidence. Rhetoric was no longer the art of logical argument but the pseudo-art of melodramatic fiction.

There are debate scenes in Seneca but they are not such conspicuous purple patches nor so clearly recognizable as those of Euripides. Pyrrhus and Agamemnon have a pitched battle of words in the *Troades*. It is a curious scene in some ways. Talthybius has just made his announcement to the Trojan chorus of the imminent departure of the Greek ships, inspired by the ghost of Achilles. With no indicated change of scene, Pyrrhus and Agamemnon appear in serious argument. At the end of the debate Agamemnon says that he will consult Calchas whom he addresses in the next line. No response by either of the contestants is made to the seer's pronouncement which abruptly ends the scene. Even for Seneca, this is careless construction. It gives to the debate scene an element of isolation; the whole thing is a rhetorical insertion. Pyrrhus opens with a speech of forty-seven lines which is answered by Agamemnon in forty-two. A one-line question by the younger man is answered in eight lines by the commander-in-chief to which Pyrrhus retorts in nine-and-a-half lines. The interchange is gradually reduced to stichomythia and even to lines divided between the two, then slightly expanded, till Agamemnon breaks off the discussion abruptly with his reference to Calchas.

In the same play there are argument scenes between Ulysses and Andromache and between Andromache and Helen but they do not follow this formal plan. The fragments of the *Phoenissae* are composed in large part of argument but, as we have not the whole (or the completed) play, it is impossible to say more than this, that there are here long argumentative speeches that might well have been parts of scenes of debate. In the *Medea*, the heroine argues with Kreon. The long speeches are forty-nine and twenty-nine lines respectively, framed by shorter speeches. Very similar is the set debate between the nurse and Hippolytus in the *Phaedra*, and a few other less well-marked instances of the type occur. But these are in no way comparable in form with the debate scenes in Euripides. The matched argument was not an appealing rhetorical adornment for Seneca.

But, if the Cordovan playwright did not find acceptable material in the court practice of first-century Rome, the case stands very differently with the monologue, not, I presume, because the people of Seneca's day were given to talking aloud to themselves or philosophizing to some helpless confidante. Here, I think, is evident the rhetorical practice as evinced not only in the schools, with their formal *suasoriae*, but by the social readings that made much of the widespread respect for the superficialities of philosophy. Proverbial wisdom passed for philosophy. It had been somewhat popularized by the Satire and had spread thence to other branches of literature in which it played the role of adornment. As such it will be found in generous measure in the tragedies of Seneca. At present it is not so much the commonplaces of ethical dogma that are under discussion as the philosophizing speeches which furnish the milieu for many proverbial and sententious epigrams. Euripides had gone far in developing the undramatic monologue and in Seneca he had an apt pupil. Atreus' speech, at line 885 of the *Thyestes*, is a good example. He is alone except for the chorus and exulting in his vengeance on Thyestes who is even at the moment consuming the unholy banquet prepared for him. He does not address the chorus and there is no indication that they are so much as present.

> Companion of the stars I move, above
> All mortals raised, touching the vault of heaven
> With my proud head.

As he proceeds with his exultation, he orders the doors of the palace opened, evidently calling to the slaves within. His remarks up to that point can be addressed to no one but himself (or the audience). Clytemnestra, in the *Agamemnon* (108, also 192), twice addresses herself: *quid segnis, anime, tuta consilia expetes*, and *accingere, anime, bella non levia apparas*. In the same play (228), Aegisthus similarly lashes himself: *quid terga vertis, anime;* five lines later he addresses himself by name. Aegisthus has both Clytemnestra and the nurse "on the stage," though he does not notice them for the space of at least eight lines. Clytemnestra too had someone on stage to whom she might have spoken, but the nurse actually interrupts the monologue before she is noticed and then, after a conversation of some thirty-seven lines, she is again wholly ignored throughout a forty-one line monologue. Perhaps one of the clearest instances of all is the speech of the nurse in the first act of the *Hercules on Oeta*. Iole, after a long anapestic complaint, has departed within. From nowhere appears the nurse in exclamatory mood:

> What fatal madness goads a woman's heart
> When one house harbors concubine and wife;

> Less fearful Scylla and Charybdis dire,
> Lashing the straits to fury, no wild beast
> But has a kindlier nature.

In this vein she continues until interrupted by the sound of the creaking door, indicating the entrance of Deianeira. She does, in the course of her monologue, give some expository information with regard to the relations between the mistress and wife of Hercules; otherwise the speech seems to exist simply for its own sake. In the *Medea*, there is one address to the soul of the speaker and, in the *Phaedra*, four. Lycus, in the *Hercules Furens*, does not address his soul or himself but he is talking to himself, and Megara and Amphitryon, who are on stage but whom he does not see for some time, do not hear what he says. This is one of the worst instances of the undramatic monologue. In the majority of cases in which there is really a monologue in Seneca there is at least a conventional listener. Amphitryon prays to Jupiter (*H.F.* 205); Megara addresses Hercules who is still absent in the lower world (*H.F.* 279); Hercules appeals to Phoebus (592); the nurse is present to serve as unnoticed hearer of Phaedra's monologue (*Ph.* 85) and later of Theseus' (*Ph.* 835); another nurse renders the same service to Clytemnestra (*Ag.* 108), a satellite performs it for Atreus (*Th.* 176), and even the silent Astyanax for Andromache (*Tr.* 461).

The tendency is strong to preserve at least the convention of realism and, with the tradition of a chorus always present, it is difficult to say positively that any speech, aside from the prologues, is addressed to no one at all. The chorus, however, in Seneca is only on the rarest occasions treated as a reality within the play. In the *Phaedra*, the chorus leader addresses two lines to the nurse, asking about the Queen, and the answer is addressed either to the chorus or to the leader, acting as a character, but there is no response at the end: the chorus is forgotten. Exactly parallel is *Troades*, 164 ff. There are two other instances in which the chorus serves as recipient of a messenger's speech, with no other character on stage, and converses with the messenger as well. There are three instances of kommatic lamentations in which a character (Hecuba, Cassandra, Iole) alternates with the chorus in expressing the situation. Finally, there are nine instances in which the chorus announces the entrance of a character, six of them in the form of a question, seven beginning with *sed* (*sed quis, sed quid, sed ecce*), and two referring to the creaking of the door. Two to five lines suffice for this most mechanical type of entrance device. Beyond this, the chorus might be removed from the plays without being missed so far as the procedure of the action is concerned. Even when used by the playwright, it is regularly dropped unceremoniously and was quite obviously never felt as an omnipresent reality. This is very clear in the third act of *Medea*. The nurse exclaims on her fear and horror at the impending tragedy and then recounts (to the listening audience, presumably) the mumbo jumbo that Medea has been performing. This speech is not a monologue but a report of off-stage action, made to the audience instead of to a character in the play, quite as undramatic as the Senecan prologue.

Obviously Seneca developed the messenger speech and the monologue from Euripides, in each case creating a more inelastic type with something of a fixed form. The expository monologue he borrowed and the monologue of a somewhat reflective nature, opening regularly with an exclamation and often including an address to the speaker's wretched heart. The debate speeches were not so popular with Seneca and the *deus ex machina* he did not use at all. It is especially noteworthy that, whereas Euripides always had another character present for the messenger to address, Seneca failed to provide this proper audience in five of his thirteen messenger speeches, a failure entirely in keeping with the general tendency on the part of the Roman writer to produce material for recitation rather than production.

CHAPTER VI

THE SHORTER SPEECHES. DIALOGUE

INASMUCH as long speeches of one sort and another make up the bulk of all the plays, it is probable that Seneca was not greatly interested in the technique of the dialogue composed of shorter speeches. A play that was written to be read would quite naturally be more effective with less of the rapid conversational give and take and more of the rhetorical speechmaking element. But Seneca could hardly eliminate the former. In the acted drama there was a premium placed on naturalness and speechmaking is not wholly natural in everyday life. That there is, however, a certain amount of conversation in Seneca's plays, and what use is made of it, will be seen from a summary of one play, for example, the *Medea*.

The first act consists of a monologue in which Medea calls upon a large assortment of deities, including those of the lower world and "chaos of eternal night," to help her take vengeance on Jason. She hints that this vengeance may come through her children and winds up: The home I won by crime, by crime I'll leave. The chorus sings a marriage hymn which, the hearer is expected to guess, is in honor of the wedding of Jason. At any rate Medea guesses correctly and proceeds to flog herself into a fury. This brings the nurse into the action and at line 150 the first dialogue passage begins. Nothing is accomplished for the progress of the play in the twenty-nine lines that follow. Their purpose is to give a chance for brilliant epigram. The nurse is little more than a foil. A few lines will illustrate.

> *Medea.* Light is that grief that can take careful thought
> And hide itself: great ills are not concealed.
> I'll act in the open. *Nurse.* Check your mad impulse,
> My daughter; silence scarce can save you now.
> *Medea.* Fortune fears brave men, cowards are its prey.
> *Nurse.* Try Fortune then when courage finds some scope.

DIALOGUE

> *Medea.* There is no time when courage has no scope.
> *Nurse.* No hope points out the way in your distress.
> *Medea.* Who has no hope, he never need despair.

And so it goes, coming down to half-line and quarter-line repartee, until Medea winds up:

> Fortune may take my wealth but not my spirit.

Then abruptly she calls attention to the sound of the palace door opening and Kreon enters.

In the scene that follows between the King and Medea (the nurse, no longer needed, has disappeared), the plot *is* advanced in the course of conversation, for Medea wins her request for a day's delay before she is banished. Kreon opens with an order to Medea to depart. There is some epigrammatic sparring:

> *Medea.* What crime or fault shall my flight expiate?
> *Kreon.* 'Tis for an innocent woman to ask the cause.
> *Medea.* If thou'rt judge, try the case, if tyrant, order.
> *Kreon.* Just or unjust, thou'lt heed the King's command.
> *Medea.* No regal power unjust can last for ay.

Then Medea is given a chance to present her argument in forty-nine lines and Kreon answers in twenty. In the short dialogue that follows, she produces the request for delay. Kreon grants it and rushes off to the wedding.

The choral ode which ends this second act is a long exposition of the daring efforts of mankind, winding up with the famous lines: That day shall come when earth no more shall have / a farthest Thule.

The nurse as confidante is on hand again when the chorus finishes. She tries to address Medea who pays no attention. The result is two monologues, one by the nurse, one by Medea, before the latter consents to recognize the other's presence, which she does only with another bombastic phrase: My only peace, to see all wrecked with me. To save them from the necessity of further conversation, the author makes Jason enter at this point but prevents his noticing the other characters until he has pronounced a monologue of fifteen lines. Then, without even preparatory conversation, Medea bursts into her defense before Jason. At the close there follows the longest section of dialogue in the play, seventy lines. In part it has dramatic value too, for, at the end, Medea has determined on the nature of her revenge. Jason tries to prove that he has been lenient in having Medea exiled instead of killed. This gives ample opportunity for epigrammatic fireworks. Abruptly, in the midst of her violent railing, Medea asks for permission to take her children with her. When Jason says he cannot bear to lose them, she sees her opportunity, pretends to be softened, and begs Jason to keep a memory of her kindlier side. The change is too swift to be convincing to anyone but a Senecan character like Jason, who departs with smug advice. Medea, left with the nurse, bids the latter get a robe and chain that were gifts to Aeetes from the Sun and which she now proposes to enchant and send to the bride.

The chorus ends Act III with an ode on the fury of a woman scorned. The nurse opens Act IV with the equivalent of a messenger's speech with no apparent audience. She describes the brew with which Medea plans to work her sorcery and, as she finishes, by some stage magic, we are supposed to hear at least, if we do not see, Medea at work, singing her foul enchantment. At the close there are six striking lines. In effect she says: It is done, call my children to carry and present the gift. Go children, win your stepmother with this gift and come back for my last embrace. All attempt at stage technique is abandoned. Here was the time for effective dialogue and dialogue there is none. In fact, there is little more than a stage direction or a note by the reciter. The chorus sings a brief comment, dividing the fourth act from the last, which begins with the entrance of a messenger. The chorus receives him with the usual questions which he answers excitedly. He does not, however, settle down into a speech. Instead, the nurse interrupts to bid Medea flee at once and messenger and chorus are forgotten, never to be recalled. Medea glories in her act but goads herself to further frenzy for over eighty lines. Toward the end she kills one of her children just before Jason enters and proceeds with the body and with the living child to the top of the house. From that vantage point she talks with Jason who begs her to desist. She kills the other boy and tosses the bodies to Jason as she flies off in her dragon-drawn chariot. There are fifty lines of conversation but there is too much melodramatic action to allow of any really effective dialogue.

It is pretty clear from this survey that the dialogue is not the means for character presentation that it had been in the Greek drama, nor the normal channel through which the plot is developed. Primarily, it furnishes an opportunity for the display of verbal brilliancy. This conclusion is confirmed by the other plays. A good instance is the argument between Pyrrhus and Agamemnon in the *Troades*. The Greek tradition had given a precedent for that type of repartee in which one speaker picks up a word or phrase from another and gives to it a new turn. This appealed to Seneca because of its spectacular possibilities and as usual his tendency was to exaggerate. Achilles' right to the sacrifice of Polyxena is the bone of contention: Pyrrhus is boasting of his father's prestige.

> *Pyrrhus.* Then mighty Hector, scorning thy threatening arms,
>   Quailed at Achilles' song; midst general fears
>   There was deep peace around the Thessalian ships.
> *Agamemnon.* Ay, and around those same Thessalian ships
>   There was deep peace even for Hector's sire.
> *Pyrrhus.* Royalty's right is giving life to kings.
> *Agamemnon.* Why did thy right hand then rob life of kings?
> *Pyrrhus.* True mercy oft gives death instead of life.
> *Agamemnon.* Is't mercy then that seeks a virgin's death?
> *Pyrrhus. Now* think'st 'tis outrage, virgin sacrifice?
> *Agamemnon.* A king must place his country o'er his child.
> *Pyrrhus.* No law spares captives or forbids revenge.
> *Agamemnon.* What no law would forbid, that shame forbids.
> *Pyrrhus.* Whate'er he will, a victor has the right.
> *Agamemnon.* Who has the right to much, should will the least.

After a little more of this, Agamemnon says abruptly:

> Well might I check your words and your bold self
> With punishment, but even captive maids
> My sword can spare; let god's interpreter,
> Calchas, be called; if fate ordains, I yield.

In part, it is the abruptness which makes the technique seem purely mechanical but it is equally noteworthy that, in this meeting, the contrast between the impetuous youth and the experienced commander, which Seneca suggests (l. 250) and which would have had real dramatic value, is not developed. Each speaker is equally skilled in epigram and equally lacking in consistent personality. And yet this argument approaches as nearly as any in Seneca to a character presentation.

No play fails to have at least one conversation consisting almost entirely of an exchange of sententious epigram. The *Phaedra* has the shortest and least striking and it may even be argued that Phaedra pronounces all of the epigrams while her interlocutors largely ask questions or urge her to disclose her thoughts. It is, however, a matter of degree: the conversations of Phaedra with Hippolytus and Theseus are not as glittering as other creations of Seneca but they are not the dialogue of realism; there is an unnatural rhetorical sparkle to them. The other plays present ample parallels to the stichomythia from the *Troades*.

It is not intended to suggest that the ordinary dialogue of drama does not exist in Seneca. There is a striking passage in the *Oedipus* which consists of such dialogue and at the same time furnishes a good illustration of its quality when it does occur. Beginning at line 764, Oedipus, the play three quarters finished, begins to suspect that he may be the murderer of Laius, as the supernatural powers have declared. He makes inquiry of Iokaste and learns the time of the murder, the age and circumstances of Laius, and the incidents of the catastrophe. The old man from Corinth then enters and, in sixty lines of rapid conversation, Oedipus learns of the death of Polybus, of the fact that he is not the child of Merope, that he was a foundling, and that he is the child of Laius and Iokaste. Here then is the use of dialogue to further the plot but it bears little resemblance to the use in the Greek tragedy. There is no effort at realism, no characterization of the different speakers, no dramatic suspense. The author seems simply to hurry over something that must be done and on

DIALOGUE

the doing of it he wastes as little time as possible. All the great dramatic suspense of Sophocles is gone. In order to save time for melodramatic recital and other congenial material, Seneca crowds the bulk of the plot development into three hundred lines.

Again, Seneca does make use of the dialogue to frame or to introduce a messenger speech. This is a device familiar from Greek tragedy but again it is, as a rule, done perfunctorily in Seneca. The familiar use in the Greek playwrights, to introduce new characters, practically does not exist in Seneca who feels no responsibility for introducing his characters at all.

It seems safe to say then that Seneca used the more rapid dialogue, not from any desire to be realistic or to advance the plot in a natural way, but rather in three functions only, the first, to advance the plot artificially and as quickly as possible in order to save time for things which he considered more important; second, as a perfunctory setting or framework for longer speeches; and third, for the display of rhetorical fireworks. When he was using dialogue to serve the first two functions, he evinced no enthusiasm in its development. Only the third type did he develop as though it were really a congenial task. And it requires but a glance at the argument between Tiresias and Oedipus, in Sophocles, in comparison with the Agamemnon–Pyrrhus argument, in the *Troades* of Seneca, to see how the purpose has changed and how rhetoric has triumphed. The Roman conversation consists almost wholly of highly seasoned rhetorical repartee, the sort of thing that would definitely please the members of the reading circle that listened, to whom details were all-important. This effort at sparkling detail is wholly consistent with the rhetorical descriptions that have been noted already.

The making of epigrammatic phrases, especially if they were the crystallization of some general truth and therefore came under the title of *sententiae,* was one of the great objects of most of the writers of what we call silver Latin. It was a recognized element of the regular education and part of the glory of even so great a writer as Tacitus lies in the ability to do this thing extremely well. In the plays of Seneca, many a line is perfectly turned and for that reason many a line reappears in new garb in the Elizabethan dramatists. But they are not dramatically convincing; they indicate clearly a type of drama quite different, in purpose as well as in quality, from the Greek.

Inasmuch as this polishing of sentiment and phrase was a distinct characteristic of Senecan tragedy and one wholly congenial to his English admirers of the sixteenth century, it is worth while to illustrate it to some extent. The primarily philosophic epigrams will be noted later. To a considerable degree, however, there is moral content in a large proportion of the epigrammatic creations of Seneca. *Qui non vetat peccare, cum possit iubet*[1] (*Tr.* 291); *Amor timere neminem verus potest* (*Med.* 416); *Curae leves loquuntur, ingentes stupent* (*Ph.* 607); *Credula est spes improba* (*Th.* 295). These are taken at random to illustrate the general tone. One sentiment is constantly recurring and seems to have suggested itself to Seneca from his own bitter experience, that the instigator, who profits by crime, is guilty rather than the helpless tool. *Cui prodest scelus / is fecit* (*Med.* 500); *Ad auctorem redit / sceleris coacti culpa* (*Tr.* 870); *Haud est nocens quicumque non sponte est nocens* (*H.O.* 886). Other epigrams as well show real insight and are perhaps the best expressions of their particular content: *Quaeritur belli exitus / non causa* (*H.F.* 408); *Qui statuit aliquid parte inaudita altera, / aequum licet statuerit, haud aequus fuit* (*Med.* 199). There are reminiscences of Horace, such as: *Sequitur superbos ultor a tergo deus* (*H.F.* 385), or of Vergil: *quae fuit durum pati / meminisse dulce est* (*H.F.* 657), but the wording is Senecan: the first century placed a premium on the restatement of an old idea that is not easy for us to appreciate. There are sententious epigrams too that have a strangely familiar ring to Christian ears: *Nam sera numquam est ad bonos mores via; / quem paenitet peccasse paene est innocens* (*Ag.* 242); *Respiciet deus / bene cogitata* (*Th.* 489). It strikes us, too, as somewhat ironical that these sentiments, which we associate with non-

---

1. The success of an epigram consists so much in the wording that translation seems futile.

pagan ways of thought, are put into the mouths of Clytemnestra, Medea, and the young child Tantalus, son of Thyestes.

This sententious habit in the literature of the early empire was only one of the ways in which a deliberate attempt was made to adorn the style in order to give it interest of detail. The larger conception of composition had almost disappeared, not alone from tragedy but equally from the other classical form of extended poetic expression, the epic. Lucan furnishes an excellent parallel to Seneca. His *Pharsalia* fails miserably in unity of conception but won unstinted praise for its sententious brilliance. Seneca was responding to the demand of his small, cultivated audience whose jaded nerves required brilliancy of epigram and could not appreciate the dialogue which, to our taste, is the chief substance of a drama.

CHAPTER VII
THE CHORUS

AN English reader of the *Spanish Tragedy*, unfamiliar with the classical drama, might be puzzled by the words of the Fury, addressed to the ghost of Andrea: Here sit we down . . . and serve for chorus in this tragedy. Any chorus at all would seem to him unnecessary, while to the classical scholar, unfamiliar with the beginnings of English drama, this remnant of a chorus in the *Spanish Tragedy* would certainly seem curiously inadequate. As a matter of fact, the process by which the chorus dwindled from the central member of tragedy to this pitiful vestige and finally disappeared is the most distinctive single development in the classical drama, co-extensive with its history and easily followed throughout its course.

There is still disagreement between authorities as to the exact origin of Greek tragedy, but there cannot but be general acquiescence in the theory that, whatever its ceremonial source, the drama was, in its first stages, choral. It was the introduction of dialogue, made possible by the separation of the chorus leader from the chorus and the addition of a speaking actor, that changed a choral to a dramatic exhibition. And when the dramatic element grew stronger and became predominant, it was still in large measure the chorus that gave to it strict continuity. For, after its entrance in a Greek tragedy, the chorus was continuously present and continuously an integral part of the action. How its importance diminished and, in the plays of Seneca, almost disappeared can be readily observed and the change not only accounts for the type of chorus which appears in English drama, but, incidentally, to a large extent for the lack of smooth continuity in the Senecan plays, a lack fraught with important consequences for the English stage. Previous chapters have touched incidentally on the Senecan chorus, with regard both to its form and content, but sufficient importance attaches to it, as an

THE CHORUS

integral member of the normal classical drama, to justify a separate discussion.

Familiar as the facts are, it is worth while to recall the position of the chorus in the earliest Greek play that has survived, the *Suppliants* of Aeschylus. The piece begins with the entrance of the chorus chanting in anapests. Like the prologue characters of a later day, they identify themselves as the daughters of Danaus and indicate the scene on the shore of Argos. After 29 lines of anapests, they settle down to a regular choral ode with strophic arrangement. This ode is long, 134 lines, and elaborate. In addition to eight strophes and antistrophes, it contains three stanzas that are each introduced after a strophe and repeated after the corresponding antistrophe. At the end of the ode, Danaus, identifying himself, addresses the chorus directly and prepares them, in the course of a short dialogue, to meet the strangers whose approach he notes. The King of Argos enters and he too directly addresses the chorus. There is a mutual explanation of identity and a long dialogue follows, the chorus, at line 359, bursting into lyric meter. Their speeches have strophic arrangement. At line 532, the King retires (Danaus has already gone off to the city) and the chorus sings a formal ode of 76 lines, closely related in content to the plot. Danaus then returns with a favorable report, addressed to the chorus, on the attitude of the Argives. In the scene that follows, the chorus sings an 80-line prayer of thanksgiving to Zeus with strophic arrangement and converses with Danaus, partly in trimeter and partly in lyric meter with strophic correspondences. Danaus, who has seen the Egyptian pursuers approaching, makes his exit at line 775 to go for help. A regular stasimon follows at the close of which, with the arrival of a herald from the ships, a new act begins with lyric dialogue between the chorus and the newcomer. The choral parts of this are strophic and continue to be so even after the herald has subsided into trimeters. The King reenters and protests to the herald, while the chorus temporarily withdraws from the conversation. They sing in anapests during the interval between the departure of the King and the entry of

Danaus and finally, after his long harangue, they wind up the play with a strophic ode.

It is clear that the chorus is, in this play, not only a character but the leading character. This does not, as is sometimes assumed, exclude the *Suppliants* as evidence. Rather, it indicates the origin of tragedy in a chorus that was, if not the entire show, at least the center of interest. As a character in the action, the chorus engages in ordinary conversation, in lyric dialogue, and in nonstrophic songs, and, in addition to being a character, it furnishes the formal strophic odes during the intervals when the orchestra is otherwise empty. It should be noted in passing that other characters indulge in lyric meters only in conversation at high tension with the chorus.

All of these characteristics of the *Suppliants* are emphasized by the nature of the chorus but, with perhaps less vivid clarity, they persist throughout all the plays of Aeschylus. The chorus never ceases to be one of the important characters, although, in the *Prometheus*, the playwright has gone a long way toward a radical reform of its function. In the first place the prologue has, in the interval, become a recognized dramatic member as that part of the play preceding the entrance of the chorus. The Nereid maidens do not open the action but are themselves announced by Prometheus who is terrified by their approach. They do, however, immediately address Prometheus and assume at once a role in the drama by stating their loyal purpose in coming to support the hero in his misfortune. Through half of the first episode and all of the second, they alone share the dialogue with Prometheus, and, even during the long Io episode, the author takes pains to keep them in the action as interested participants. In the final act, Hermes comes as an outsider while the chorus, now fully identified with Prometheus, refuses to be separated from him and go down with him in the final cataclysm. The change that has come in the function of the chorus is simply this: they have ceased to be the central character and have become a supporting character. So far as the mechanics of the drama is concerned, there is no vital change.

THE CHORUS

In Sophocles, the development of the predominant interest in plot and character inevitably diminished the importance of the chorus and it is in his plays that the formal choral odes, the songs between episodes, take on a more definite character. In fact, the episodes themselves become more sharply defined, thus emphasizing the function of the choral odes to mark off the stages of the plot development. Nevertheless, the chorus is still a character, though one of decidedly minor importance, and regularly takes part in the action. It participates in the ordinary dialogue with one or more of the other characters. At the same time, in its role of sympathetic supporter of hero or heroine, it has become a distinctly less independent character, inclined to be timorous and more and more reflecting the emotions which, at each stage of the action, the playwright is seeking to produce in the spectator.

The *Oedipus* furnishes clear illustration of the Sophoclean practice. It is noticeable, in the first place, that effort is no longer made carefully to motivate the entrance of the chorus. The prologos ends with the orchestra empty: the suppliants have been dismissed by Oedipus and the King and Kreon have retired within to prepare for the discovery of the murderer of Laius. Oedipus merely gives order that someone call together the citizens to hear his decree. This is to a certain extent motivation, but no one announces the approach of the chorus nor is time allowed for the gathering of the people. The anapests which, in Aeschylus, regularly accompanied the entering march of the chorus have disappeared and have been replaced by a beautiful strophic ode. In the episode that follows, the chorus is the recipient of the King's address, answers certain questions necessary to the exposition, announces the approach of Tiresias, and finally, in four lines of trimeter, thoroughly noncommittal in character, makes suitable mechanical division between the long speeches of Oedipus and the blind priest. It is the same throughout the play: the elders respond in the same timorous way to Kreon, Iokaste, Oedipus, and the messengers, and finally conclude the play with seven lines of trochaic commonplaces.

The treatment of the chorus in the *Antigone* is almost identical with that in the *Oedipus*, and in fact there is no great divergence from this type in any of the seven plays. In the *Ajax*, unique in other ways as well, the chorus has an anapestic marching song, reminiscent of Aeschylus, before its first formal ode, but throughout Sophocles the chorus as a character has little force and retains hardly more than a useful mechanical function. At the same time Sophocles' formal choral odes reached the highest point of artistic perfection.

Aristotle was responsible for the belief that there was a gulf between Sophocles and Euripides in the matter of the chorus. He referred to the formal odes and criticized Euripides for allowing odes irrelevant to the subject matter of the play. On the whole this is a position hard to defend. The practice of Euripides is not very different in this respect from that of his older contemporary. Both of them separated the formal odes from the dialogue more sharply than did Aeschylus and if Euripides went slightly farther afield for the subjects of his odes, it was not to any great extent. His chorus is still almost always the sympathetic supporter of the hero or heroine; it takes a certain colorless part in the action, performing mechanical functions of a useful sort, as did that of Sophocles; and it sings formal odes intended to carry out the emotional tone of the action. It is in this last respect that there is something of a change. It is not, I think, that Euripides consciously detached his chorus from the action, but that he was a poet of the newer school and that his treatment of the odes, in a more allusive and far less conventional form, led to the charge of irrelevance. The first song of the washerwomen in the *Hippolytus* may serve to illustrate this manner. The chorus of simple women have heard that the Queen, Phaedra, is ill. They have heard it in the gossip of the crowd at the riverside, washing their clothes, and they wonder what is the matter. This is the prosaic content of the ode. But the setting is given in the first strophe and antistrophe in language that would have been unintelligible to the washerwomen, but which presents nevertheless a poetic picture of real beauty. The second strophe and antistrophe consist of conjectures as to the source of Phaedra's illness. Is it madness from Pan or Hekate or the Korybantes or Diktynna? Or perhaps it is love. Is her husband unfaithful or is she in love with some wayfarer from Crete? An epistrophe concludes the ode with reflections on the hard lot that nature has given woman and the relief that Artemis brings to one in labor. This ode is strictly relevant to the action and serves as an introduction to the first episode in which the nurse and Phaedra appear. But the indirect expression, the poetic diction, and the wealth of allusion, often obscure, might readily have made it seem, to one with conservative tastes, to be inappropriate. It would appear to be this quality, in part at least, that provoked Aristophanes to satiric comment, comment that was not, to be sure, without justification; for this illustration from the *Hippolytus* is not extreme.

The fact remains, however, that, on the whole, the odes of Euripides are relevant to the action of the play, and that, so far as the other functions of the chorus are concerned, he was not materially different from Sophocles.

The history of the chorus, then, in Greek tragedy seems to be this. The proportion of choral to dialogue, so high in the *Suppliants* of Aeschylus and gradually decreasing through his other plays, was fairly constant for Sophocles and Euripides. But the chorus as an essential character of the drama was losing ground through the later period. In Sophocles, the leader of the chorus very regularly took part in the dialogue: the members of the chorus were vitally interested in the situation and concerned in the outcome. In every one of the seven plays the chorus is kept definitely within the action throughout. At the same time, the opportunities for the actual choral odes are provided by natural pauses in the action when the stage is otherwise clear. The songs with which the chorus fills these natural pauses have varying degrees of relevance to the action of the play itself but relevant they always are. The chorus is no longer the most important element in any given play but it holds its own with the other leading elements.

Euripides' plays show only a slight difference from Sophocles' in this respect. But the difference is more marked in the later plays. By the close of his career the change in the chorus, which is said to have been completed by Agathon, had already gone far. The chorus leader no longer plays a large role in the dialogue. Short speeches he has, to be sure, largely unimportant comments serving to punctuate more important utterances, but, as a character in the play, he has decidedly lost caste. Equally, the chorus as a whole was steadily reduced in importance from Aeschylus' day to Agathon's. With more complicated plots, it became more difficult to make convincing a chorus always present and yet never revealing secrets with which often they had no sympathy. More and more they receded into the background so far as the plot was concerned and came to have as their chief function the filling of the gaps between acts. This being the case, it is not strange to find the subject matter of their odes less and less closely related to the subject matter of the plays. Except in a few instances, this process did not go to an extreme, but in general the odes become more elaborately mythological or else more rhetorically moralizing in content and less pertinent to the matter in hand.

Such a change in the function of the chorus must have had a strong influence in favor of the process which accompanied it, namely, the breaking down of the strict unity of plot. So long as the ever-present chorus was a leading character in the play, the story had perforce to be developed along simple lines and from one point of view. As the chorus decreased in prominence its unifying influence decreased. This is not immediately germane to a discussion of the chorus itself but must be noted in passing, to be more fully discussed later.

With Seneca, the tendencies noted in Sophocles and Euripides go farther. The *Hercules Furens* will serve as a good illustration of the Roman use of the chorus. Juno, as prologue speaker, departs with the remark that day is dawning and this remark serves the chorus as an opening motif for the first ode. The connection is tenuous and the ode has almost no relation to the play.

THE CHORUS

> The paling stars and few
> Fast leave the sky;
> Night yields and day is born
> Ere long to die.
> Great Titan's reign begins;
> From Oeta's height,
> Trodden of Bacchanals,
> The moon takes flight,
> And toil and care return
> After the night.

This is, in abbreviated form, the opening of an ode which presents first a charming picture of the simple life of the country, the tranquil peace of the lowly. Then follows, in harsher tones, a presentation of the artificial life of the city along almost Juvenalian lines. Greed and fear are abroad in the towns. The pathetic morning caller at the door of the rich, the miser bending over his hoardings, the seeker after public applause, the raucous political lawyer, these are swiftly presented as typical of the city. The moral pointed is the need to snatch the best from swiftly moving time as it goes, and to be content with the humble lot which spells security. There is much that is Horatian in tone and in phraseology, the popular Stoicism of the satirist; and there is something too of the more personal, subjective moralizing.

At the close of this ode, the chorus calls attention in three lines to the approach of Amphitryon and Megara. This is their only participation in the action of the play.

The second choral interlude is more pertinent to the plot than the first, but it is awkwardly interjected to make an act division. Amphitryon has just been speaking and winds up with the exclamation that the earth is shaking and groaning and that he hears the steps of returning Hercules. Whereupon the chorus sings, in sixty-eight Asclepiadeans, the hardness of fortune which has sent Hercules to the lower world, with a picture of Orpheus for comparison. The opening lines lead one to expect another moralizing ode:

> O Fortune jealous ever of the brave,
> Uneven in thy gifts.

It is a subject dear to the heart of Seneca but in this case he contents himself with the pertinent illustration of his thesis, adorned with no little mythological lore.

The third ode is in construction almost the reverse of the second. The beginning deals with Eurystheus' dispatch of Hercules to the lower world and at the end there is an awkward return to the situation caused by the success of Hercules. But the body of the ode is a fine picture of the innumerable shades, winding up with a truly Stoic paradox: *prima quae vitam dedit hora, carpit*. This is immediately preceded by a very personal, subjective bit of moralizing: "None comes too late to that retreat whence, once arrived, he never may return. Why hasten on our unforgiving fate? All of the throngs that wander through the earth shall one day go below and make the voyage across the lifeless waters of Cocytus. For thee, o death, are all things growing, all that the rising and the setting sun beholds, all we prepare for thee, o death. Spare us for we shall come. And though thyself art slow we hasten ever on. Our natal hour that gave us life fixed that life's end."

The fourth and last ode is directly connected with the plot. It consists of exclamatory horror at the slaughter of his children by Hercules. It contains a beautiful address to Sleep who is urged to heal the spirit of the hero.

The *Hercules Furens*, as regards the chorus, is not untypical of the plays as a whole. About one half of the odes bear directly on the subject matter of the plot and the other half deal with the commonplace subjects of Stoic philosophy or satire. Moderation and the danger of extremes, especially of greatness, are perhaps the favorite themes, but Fate and the daring of mankind, the sureness and desirability of death, are also constantly recurring topics.

In no play does the chorus assume an important part in advancing the plot. In one, the *Medea*, aside from four remarks to the nurse, each of less than a line in length, its only function is to sing the choral odes. In the *Oedipus*, it announces four characters, one in answer to a question, and makes one comment, a total of

THE CHORUS

sixteen lines; in the *Phaedra*, it announces three characters, asks one question, and makes two comments, all in a total of twenty-four lines. These are all perfectly mechanical functions, used for convenience by the playwright. In the *Thyestes*, the function is almost as mechanical but it is handled with at least some attempt at art. In one scene a messenger appears with no one to address. The chorus steps into the breach and asks: "What news do you bring?" Nine times during his long speech they make the proper comment or ask the proper question to bring out his narrative and keep it going. Quite undramatically, their end accomplished, they are silent when he has finished. They speak a total of twelve lines. If the text of the *Hercules on Oeta* ordinarily adopted is correct, they do the same thing in that play, speaking five lines but remaining silent at the end. One manuscript tradition gives the lines to the nurse. Once in the *Agamemnon* and twice in the *Hercules on Oeta* they briefly introduce new characters. In three plays they have a further function, reminiscent of the Greek Kommos. One of the characters (Hecuba in the *Troades*, Iole in the *Hercules on Oeta*, and Cassandra in the *Agamemnon*) sings a long lament, calling on the chorus to join, which they proceed to do. The passage in the *Hercules on Oeta* seems to be by an auxiliary chorus and is perhaps not in its final form. This play is a difficult problem in many ways and has this peculiarity of a second chorus in common with the *Agamemnon*. For the groups that sing with Cassandra and Iole are the foreign maidens accompanying them in an alien land and are sympathetic with neither the hero nor the heroine. Two further exceptional uses of the chorus occur also in the *Hercules on Oeta*. They interject into Hercules' long speech beginning at line 1131 three short passages of anapests, thirty-two lines in all, and they wind up the play with fourteen lines of anapests. Of iambic trimeter, the choruses speak less than a hundred lines in all the plays together.

Seneca has also gone further than Euripides in detaching his chorus from the play by not clearly identifying them. The choral songs might almost always be suitably assigned to any group of singers and we are not even, in most cases, informed as to who the singers are. He has also made them dramatically less acceptable because he takes no care to create a natural pause in which to have them sing their odes. This change should be particularly noted because it is distinctly characteristic of Seneca and the rhetorical drama. It would probably not have come about in tragedy written for the stage and actually acted. It is sufficiently important to justify illustration at some length.

At the end of the second act (l. 516) of the *Hercules Furens*, Amphitryon says:

> Ye mighty gods, thou sire of all the gods
> Before whose thunderbolts all mortals quake,
> Stay with thy power the impious hand of this
> Most impious king. Yet why unto the gods
> Should I appeal in vain? Thou, thou, my son,
> Come, wheresoe'er thou art. Why suddenly
> Shakes the whole house? Why trembles so the ground?
> I hear—it is the step of Hercules.

At line 592 Hercules appears with exclamations, greeting the light of day. Amphitryon is evidently still present. There had been nothing to suggest his departure and at the end of Hercules' speech he addresses his son. Between these two passages, and with the entrance of Hercules imminent, in fact already audible, the chorus sings an ode of sixty-eight lines on Hercules in the lower world. This is quite foreign to the Greek tradition of using a formal choral ode only when the orchestra was empty of all characters except the chorus—in other words, when there was a natural break in the action. At line 829, Theseus, at the end of a long narrative, sees coming a crowd of people singing the praises of Hercules. It is hard to avoid the inference that the chorus is thought of as not present and as reëntering at this point. None of the characters leave while the choral ode that follows is being sung although Hercules does enter at its close. During the chorus that begins at line 1054 Hercules is again present, though unconscious, and Amphitryon and Theseus must be present also.

In the *Hecuba* the chorus begins an ode at line 1009 with the heroine present, or at least without any indication of her departure, and when they finish, at line 1055, she is there to receive the messenger. Medea is evidently present while the chorus sings the first ode in the *Medea*. At the end of the following act, Medea tells Kreon that the one day's grace which he has granted her is more than enough for she too is in haste. Kreon departs for the wedding of Jason and his new bride. After a long choral ode on the daring of mankind, the nurse asks Medea where she is hurrying from the palace. The most natural interpretation would be that the action is here again continuous, ignoring the chorus, and that the nurse enters only at this point. It is of course possible to think of Medea as going within and coming out again. The fact is that Seneca is not concerned with stage management but with recital, and it is impossible to decide which interpretation is correct. In the *Phaedra*, Theseus is undoubtedly present during a choral ode (958-989).

These instances merely indicate what is clear by now, that the Senecan choruses serve as useful breaks in the dramatic recital but that they do not necessarily, as did the Greek, fill natural intervals in the action. It is a further step in the decline of the chorus as an essential part of the play and therefore another factor contributing to its ultimate elimination. If the slight mechanical function of the chorus were handled as it readily might be by some more dramatic device and the three laments were omitted, the chorus in Seneca would have become what it had long been in the process of becoming, an undramatic interlude between episodes. Already it *makes* the breaks between acts instead of *filling* breaks created by the natural dramatic progress of the play.

Metrically there is a great gulf between the Greek tragedies and Seneca, a gulf quite comprehensible when the essential fact is borne in mind that the former were written for acting while Seneca wrote for recitation. The choral passages have therefore a conventional value only. The Greek odes were to be sung and accompanied by the choral dance. The meters are therefore choral with strophic correspondence. Seneca uses the meters of the Latin lyric, in one case at least stanzaic, but usually not. Of thirty-three odes, eleven are wholly in anapests, seven in lesser Sapphics, four in lesser Asclepiads, two in Glyconics, one in Sapphic stanzas, and the rest in mixed meters. Several of these mixtures are simple combinations of the preceding meters (for example, in one case, the lesser Sapphic combined with the lesser Asclepiad, in another, the lesser Asclepiad combined with the Glyconic and the dactyllic hexameter, in still another the Glyconic combined with the Euripidean). This leaves four so-called polymetric choruses and the last ode in the *Medea*, written in short lines of three trochees each with anacrusis, punctuated by catalectic lines at irregular intervals to give the semblance of stanzaic arrangement. This ode may have been intended to represent the frenzy of Medea. Whatever its purpose, the result is not pleasing. Even less attractive are the polymetric choruses —two each in the *Oedipus* and the *Agamemnon*. These use all the more common lines (including the dactyllic hexameter which is strikingly out of place in a choral ode) without any apparent system of arrangement.

Much the same criticism may be made of the subject matter of the odes as of their meters: they are a somewhat indiscriminate medley of ideas and conceits already made familiar by Roman poets. This is not the same as saying that the odes are wholly irrelevant to the subject matter of the plays. Rather they are consistent with the tone and character of the plays that have been found to be essentially different from the Greek and their author has culled here and there the themes of Satire and lyric as they seemed suitable to the tone he was trying to produce. Fate is perhaps the most popular of these themes. The second ode in the *Hercules Furens* is addressed directly to Fortune:

> Fortuna, jealous ever of the brave,
> Uneven is thy hand:
> Eurystheus' lot to rule in easy sloth:
> Alcmene's son foredoomed
> With might divine
> To battle ever with earth's monster brood.

More Horatian is the ode to Fortune in the *Agamemnon* (ll. 57 ff.):

> O Fortune hostile ever to the lot of kings,
> On steep and dangerous heights
> Hast placed the exalted great:
> No peace is theirs;
> The␣scepter wins it not;
> No certain day:
> Care follows hard on care,
> And evermore new tempests rend their souls.

The last ode of the *Phaedra* expounds perhaps most explicitly the familiar Horatian theme that, as the highest peaks and the loftiest trees are those that are most exposed to the blasts of the tempest, so the most exalted humans are in the greatest danger from the attacks of Fortune.

Akin to this subject is that which is largely dwelt on in the *Medea*, the daring of mankind that has challenged the wrath of heaven. Horace's "heart of oak and triple bronze" is the inspiration of such odes. *Audax nimium* is the opening of one (ll. 301 ff.) and, although Seneca never took over enough of a line to make it sure that he was copying a definite poem, the reminiscences of Horace are unmistakable. The text of the last ode in the *Troades* seems to come from Lucretius but the thought may have been a commonplace long before Seneca's day, that misery loves company, or more precisely that no one complains of his lot if everyone else is miserable, that none is wretched except by comparison, a sentiment which Horace too expressed. Death and its imminence are a frequent choral subject, and also moderation, the "golden mean," and the *virtus* which is hard to define, so mixed is Seneca's conception, in his plays at any rate, a virtus that is half Stoic virtue and half Roman valor.

If, however, these choruses of Seneca recall the themes of Horace and contain also reminiscences of Catullus and Lucretius and Ovid, they have one quality that these poets escape in the main. Senecan odes are far too often learned. The information which the author gives by means of them would have forced most of his readers to an encyclopedia. It may be the learned list of Greek cities in the *Troades* (ll. 814 ff.), some thirty of them, or the signs of the zodiac in *Thyestes* (843 ff.), or simply an accumulation of mythological learning, as in the *Phaedra* (274 ff.) and in the *Medea* (579 ff.), but almost always there is something that is, to say the least, not familiar knowledge.

To summarize, the odes in the Senecan plays have not a natural and necessary function but are used almost exclusively to mark divisions between acts. They are not either choral or truly lyric in quality but use lyric meters and would probably have been designated as such if a Roman critic had tried to classify them. They develop the themes of current popular wisdom, dressing it up with a considerable amount of learning. They are rather an accessory to the play than an integral part of it.

CHAPTER VIII
SUPERHUMAN ELEMENT

ORDINARILY we think of Aeschylus as the most religious of the Greek dramatists and quite correctly. There is in all of his plays an air of unquestioning belief in the superhuman forces which guide human experience. The *Suppliants* is not far removed from the stage of dramatic development at which the chorus was practically the whole show. The fifty maidens open the play with a prayer to Zeus and the keynote of dependence on the supreme Olympian is maintained throughout. And yet there is no divine intervention either direct or indirect in the course of the action to guide or change it. Whether the *Prometheus* was an expression of heterodoxy or, as part of a trilogy, a defense of orthodoxy makes little difference from the present point of view: the underlying feeling is religious, and in this case, most of the characters are divine. But even Zeus cannot or does not guide the action by any arbitrary or external means. Through Hermes, even the supreme god acts as almost a character in the action. Into the *Persians* enters the first evidence of superhuman interference (unless we count the thunderbolt at the end of the *Prometheus*) injected into a human plot. Atossa, by simple prayer and libation, without any hocus-pocus whatever, calls up the ghost of Darius. His is not, however, a very potent ghost. It asks for information and tells of the great disaster, but it does not cause or instigate any action. In the *Seven*, the family curse is assumed as the active motivation throughout, but there is no intervention; in the *Agamemnon*, Cassandra foretells the murder but does not instigate it; and in the *Choephoroi*, while the chorus says that Clytemnestra's dream caused her to send them to the tomb and while Orestes declares that he is acting under the orders of Apollo's oracle, still, as far as the play itself is concerned, there is no divine intervention. The *Eumenides* is unique. The preliminary scene at Delphi presents the whole motivation: Apollo in person promises aid to Orestes if he will proceed to Athens and the ghost of Clytemnestra appears and addresses the sleeping Furies, goading them on to pursue Orestes. In the play proper, Athena appears as a participant, the deciding judge in the trial, distantly anticipating the *deus ex machina* of a later day. Obviously, the preponderance of religious atmosphere, with the chorus what it is and many of the characters constantly praying at length to the gods, is the normal atmosphere of tragedy to Aeschylus. At the same time he did not employ the gods either as symbols or as showpieces to motivate or guide plots otherwise human.

In Sophocles there is less of Zeus and more of Apollo, less of prayer and more of oracles and prophecies. It would seem as though Sophocles believed chiefly in Fate that could not be changed and less enthusiastically in the gods, powerful but themselves subject to Fate. Prayer to the gods was therefore not only politic but effective in minor matters but the chief effort of man should be to ascertain, by whatever sign possible, the program of destiny. Hence, the motivating force of oracles. Only in the *Philoktetes* does a *deus ex machina* appear to solve the problem. Otherwise, except for the *Ajax*, there is no direct divine interference. Orestes, in the prologue of *Elektra*, explains his whole action as due to the oracle at Delphi and this is the whole motivation, for Clytemnestra's dream is merely a warning of trouble for her. Herakles speaks vaguely of an oracle from Dodona. In the *Oedipus Tyrannus* the oracle from Delphi and the speech of Tiresias the seer cause the action which brings on the tragedy. Another oracle from Delphi serves as motivation in the *Oedipus at Colonos*, the *Philoktetes* has behind it a prophecy by Helenus, and in the *Antigone*, which is very human in its motivation, the inspired speech of Tiresias turns the course of action. The *Ajax* opens with the goddess Athena (probably invisible to the audience as she is to the actors) showing to Odysseus the madness of Ajax and its results. It is an unusually melodramatic scene for Sophocles and is merely a device to present the situation, adding nothing to the motivation. More effect is produced on the course

SUPERHUMAN ELEMENT

of the play by the report of Calchas' prophecy that the madness of Ajax would be for one day only.

Down to the time of Euripides, therefore, so far as our extant material indicates, there was precedent for the use of dreams, oracles, and ghosts as determinants of action; the use of a god or goddess either to motivate the action or to resolve the complications, while not unknown, was far from being a familiar device.

Euripides uses a divinity five times and the ghost of Polydorus once to motivate the play in the prologue. This is regularly a detached prologue quite independent of the action of the drama. In two more instances there is divine motivation introduced into the middle of the play, Lyssa and Iris serving the purpose in the *Herakles* and Athena in the *Rhesus*. There are nine instances of the *deus ex machina*, not including the sun chariot of Medea. Once (in the *Elektra*) there is an oracle in the background causing the action; in the *Phoenissae*, Tiresias tells Kreon he must slay Menoikeus; and in the *Iphigeneia at Aulis* the demand of Calchas determines the plot. In addition to these cases of divine interference, there is the magic robe prepared by Medea, the Eumenides seen by Orestes but not by the herdsmen, the curse of Poseidon used against Hippolytus, and the magic of Dionysus in the *Bacchae*.

It would be foolish to question the traditional picture of Euripides as a critic of religion, himself a sophist and at least not orthodox from the religious standpoint. The gods are still useful to him as machinery and as such he employs them with more than a suspicion of symbolism. This suspicion rises to a certainty in the *Hippolytus* when Aphrodite speaks the prologue and Artemis serves as the *dea ex machina*.

To Seneca of course there was no shred of reality left in the gods of Olympus; they were as much then as today literary material to be used as period decoration. Even so, the spirit of the period was not successfully achieved, for too much of the Age of Nero intruded itself. Juno is the only divinity that appears in any play and when she speaks the prologue of the *Hercules Furens*, she shows little enough of the dignity of the Queen of

Heaven. She is a very angry woman but has for dramatic purposes the power of a goddess which she is about to use to turn Hercules into a raving madman. She lashes herself into a fury for 124 lines, but except for the fact that she is a goddess and can therefore accomplish her threats, her speech is no different from the other prologue speeches that develop the tone of horror that Seneca felt suitable to tragedy. The gods were not very useful to Seneca who has but this one prologue divinity and no *deus ex machina*.

This is not to say that he made little use of the supernatural. For the ghost of Laius conjured up by Tiresias' magic, he seems to have gone back to Aeschylus and the ghost of Darius, but he has abandoned the simplicity of his model. The ghost of Achilles he presents only at second hand through the account of Talthybius. It seems to have arrived with considerable violence. Still further removed from the audience is the ghost of Hector who appears to Andromache in a dream. All of these ghosts have influence on the plot. There are two more ghosts, that of Thyestes in the *Agamemnon* and the Fury-driven shade of Tantalus in the *Thyestes*. These are prologue speakers both of them and explain the motivation of the plot. But, like all the other prologue speakers in Seneca, they are largely producers of tone and they were, I suspect, wholly to their creator's taste, for they added the sensation of melodramatic gruesomeness that Juno at her worst could not produce.

This desire for the melodramatic seems to be the key to an understanding of all of Seneca's use of the supernatural. Instead of following the simple model of Aeschylus, when a ghost is to be summoned from the lower world, Seneca had recourse in one case, the *Oedipus*, to the scene in which Kreon reports the exorcising rites of Tiresias and Manto, and in another, the *Troades*, to the messenger's speech of Talthybius, recounting the appearance of Achilles' ghost. This latter is shorter and less melodramatic than the *Oedipus* scene but it is done with enthusiasm and furthermore is left almost entirely detached from the rest of the act in which it occurs. Talthybius appears with an exclamatory entrance and is questioned in two lines by the chorus as to the reason for the delay of the Greek ships in leaving Troy. He then proceeds, after an appropriate shudder, to describe the setting of his story.

> Titan, just rising, touched the highest peaks
> And Night had conquered Day when, of a sudden,
> With dreadful groans, Earth parted to unfold
> Its lowest depths, the forests shook their tops,
> The lofty woodland and the sacred grove
> Thundered with mighty crash, the Idean rocks
> Rolled from her shattered peak. Not Earth alone
> Trembled; the Ocean knew Achilles too
> And smoothed its surface. Then the valley split
> In twain, exposed immeasurable caves
> When gaping Erebus, through sundered Earth,
> Produced a passage to the upper air,
> Leveling Achilles' tomb, till forth there flashed
> The mighty shade of that Thessalian chief.

When the ghost has given its message of horror, that Polyxena must be sacrificed before the Greeks can return in peace, it sinks again into the earth which closes over it and the recital ends with a thoroughly melodramatic contrast.

> All tranquil lay the waters of the sea
> Motionless and the winds forgot their wrath;
> The placid ocean ripples murmured soft
> And from the deep came sound of sweetest song:
> The hymeneal chorus of the Tritons.

The recital ended, Talthybius disappears as mysteriously as he arrived, with no comment from the chorus and no word of departure. He forgets even to rear again the tomb of Achilles on which Polyxena is to be sacrificed. The whole scene is a purple patch for recitation purposes.

There is one dream used by Seneca to motivate action and this vision involves the ghost of Hector. Andromache dreams that the spirit of her husband comes to her to warn her of the danger to Astyanax. The form of presentation is once more the messenger-speech type. After some exclamatory remarks, Andromache is led by the old man's questioning to recount her experience.

> Fair Night had traversed full two thirds its course
> The seven stars had turned their glowing wain;
> And rest, unknown to my afflicted state,
> Had come at length; a brief and troubled sleep
> Breathed on my weary cheeks, when suddenly
> Before my eyes stood Hector, not as once
> When leader of the battle 'gainst the Greeks
> He sought with Idean fire the Argive ships,
> Or with great slaughter drove the Danai
> And from a feigned Achilles won true spoil;
> Not such his countenance that once had flamed
> With joyous wrath; wearied he came, downcast,
> Heavy with mourning and his hair unkempt.
> Yet was it joy to see him. Shaking his head
> He spake: "Have done with sleep, my faithful wife,
> And save our son. Have done with weeping too.
> Dost weep that Troy has fallen? Would to god
> All, all had fallen. Up with haste and save
> The last weak scion of our house." A chill
> Of fear roused me from sleep. This way and that
> I turned my eyes in dread, forgot my child
> And sought but Hector. Through my empty arms
> His spirit fled.

I have yielded to the temptation to translate the whole speech because, by its exceptional restraint and vividness, without overpowering elaboration, it serves to make more obvious the usual exaggerated rhetoric of these speeches. Its brevity is compensated by the long soliloquy which follows, but both narrative and soliloquy are extraordinarily good.

The ghost was destined to have a remarkable career in English drama and should therefore be given more detailed study here. All five of Seneca's ghosts are the shades of men who have been or think they have been wronged. Laius had been murdered by his own son, even though that son had no intent to commit patricide; Achilles demands recompense for his services in the capture of Troy and believes that Polyxena should be his prize even though he is dead; Hector has lost everything, but is exceptional in that he is seeking the safety of his son and not any revenge or the punishment of any victim; Thyestes and Tantalus can hardly be said to have been wronged, but they have suffered such punishments themselves as to desire equal sufferings for others, and they have become Fury incarnate to spur on the tragic acts which comprise the plays to which they furnish prologues.

Obviously there are different conceptions here of the functions of a ghost. He may represent the demand for revenge that was a pious duty in the Greek tradition and so may be the counterpart of the Eumenides which had once haunted the guilty slayer. He may be no more than a cherished memory that warns of danger to dear ones. He may represent a sense of injustice demanding recognition. Or, finally, he may be the personification of furious wickedness, the inherited curse, the madness that drives to crime. It is the two prologue ghosts, Thyestes and Tantalus, that perhaps had the greatest progeny in English drama, but with the added element of revenge borrowed from the ghost of Laius. Gorlois, in the *Misfortunes of Arthur*, is such a revenge ghost in the prologue and to a lesser extent Andrea, in the *Spanish Tragedy*, the latter requiring considerable prompting from Revenge who plays the part of the Fury in *Thyestes*. The exorcism of Laius' ghost somewhat overshadows the speech of the specter itself but Laius is a ghost demanding revenge and the legitimate ancestor of Banquo. Achilles, too, is really in the same class, although the technique used in his case is different and the end that he seeks is not strictly revenge so much as satisfaction. When the result, however, is melodramatic death, the distinction is rather a fine one.

Hector is in a category by himself. The use of a ghost appearing in a dream to warn of danger introduces a different type of motivation and suggests that Seneca may have had a somewhat more advanced psychological conception in the use of ghosts than is generally conceded to him. If the spirits of the dead can come back with good purpose as well as evil, they are not the mere equivalent of Furies, not simply the spirit of Revenge. They may represent the persisting influence of personality which at long last becomes the motivation of many a play of inheritance and even of the conscience drama. Surely Banquo's ghost is midway between the Senecan Laius and the guilty conscience of Lady Macbeth. It will not do to push this point too far. Seneca, the prime minister, must have been well acquainted with the pangs of conscience and had discussed with Nero the voices that haunted him after his mother's murder, but Seneca the playwright was usually objective and concrete, and the ghosts which he bequeathed to posterity were fairly tangible.

Like the incantation scene from Tiresias, only perhaps more gruesome, is the mixing of the brew with which Medea poisons the robe she sends to Creusa.[1] Or rather it would be so if it were not overloaded with the learning which appealed too much to Seneca.

> Now, now is time for action far beyond
> The common ken. Hither unto my brew
> Let come that serpent huge that flows in heaven
> Like a great torrent, whose circumferent folds
> The two bears know, the lesser and the great,
> The one the lodestar of Pelasgia,
> Sidonia sails by the other; hither come
> With flowing poison Ophiuchus dread,
> His grip relaxed, and, answering my call,
> Let Python hasten, he who dared attack
> The twin divinities, Hydra return
> And all that serpent brood Hercules slew
> Reviving still by its own slaughter; come
> Thou dragon too that in the Colchian land
> First knew my incantation.

After the serpents, which are somewhat reminiscent of the digression on African snakes in Lucan, there is a paragraph on herbs. All this is in narrative by the nurse. At the close of her description, Medea herself enters singing the incantation into which is crowded a deal of mythological lore.

---

1. It seems appropriate to include this scene in the evidence for the use of the supernatural, for the poisonous brew has certainly powers beyond the natural.

One of the most striking contrasts between the supernatural in Seneca and in the Greek dramatists has already been noted in the *Oedipus*. Tiresias, who in the Greek play had always the dignity and the force and the inspired knowledge of the accredited representative of Apollo, has become in the Roman drama a mere haruspex with neither force nor inspiration of his own. He interprets the entrails and, for the raising of Laius' ghost, resorts to cheap necromancy.

Cassandra in the *Agamemnon* should perhaps be included among the prophets, for she has visions. So far, however, as their effect on the action is concerned, they are empty ravings. On the other hand, Calchas in the *Troades* gives a decision briefly and inartistically to furnish motivation and Kreon's report of the oracle in the *Oedipus* is short and effective. Both instances represent a businesslike use of the supernatural to facilitate the action but neither of them is of any real dramatic interest.

Beyond these adaptations of familiar types of the supernatural, Seneca borrows the curse of Theseus, gift of Poseidon, against Hippolytus, with the sea monster that the god of the Ocean sends to fulfill the curse. He uses the sun chariot to effect Medea's departure at the close of the play. Deianeira sends the robe of Nessus to Hercules in the *Hercules on Oeta* but with true Senecan forebodings of horror before she has any reason to be disturbed, and finally Hercules speaks from heaven at the end of the same play.

Such is the use made of the supernatural in Seneca. No play is without some manifestation of extrahuman power, but in none does the manifestation have religious significance or impressiveness. It is always melodramatic, theatrical, showy, a rather extraneous adornment except when it is used crudely to manage the plot quickly and easily. The ghost motivation is established as a prologue form, with or without the accompanying Fury, and the incantation scenes are thoroughly developed too. Oracles, dreams, curses, and magic are recognized as legitimate dramatic devices. The supernatural is on the whole exalted for its effect while religious atmosphere has been banished wholly.

This statement is sweeping, perhaps too much so, and demands a consideration of the religious tone and point of view of the tragedies apart from the mere devices for introducing the supernatural into the plot. The conventionalizing of those devices is in itself an indication of the decrease of religious conviction. If the great types of religious motivation have been degraded into exhibitions of the rhetorical art, it is hardly to be expected that the fiber of the plays should remain religious. In reality, they have not retained even as much of the religious atmosphere as did the average play of Euripides.

The gods of Olympus and of the lower world exist of course: the drama has not discarded its ancient framework wholly. So long as the myths furnished the plots, the gods could not be eliminated. But they are almost as much literary conventions to Seneca as to a writer of today. Titan may be used to mean the sunlight or Mars to personify war; Venus may represent the passion of love, Ceres the produce of the earth, without implying or even suggesting belief in any of them as actual divinities. Nor does a traditional hymn to Bacchus sung by the chorus in the *Oedipus* or one to Apollo and sundry others in the *Agamemnon* give a religious tone to either play. With the possible exception of the *Troades*, the choruses are no longer closely enough wrought into the fabric of the plays to dominate the tone, even if their own religious tone were in itself convincing. The choral hymn in the *Agamemnon* is as good an illustration as any and the *Agamemnon* may serve as typical throughout of the poet's religious attitude.

The motivating prologue is reserved to the ghost of Thyestes alone: he announces himself and foreshadows the crime to come, addressing Aegisthus as though he were present and could be spurred on to action. This is the typical short motivation, wavering between a conception of actual, tangible spirits and a symbolic representation of evil suggestions inherited or nursed by the imagination. He comes from the black home of Dis and he leaves suddenly, so as not to delay the course of Phoebus. Neither Dis nor Phoebus is more than a figure of speech.

SUPERHUMAN ELEMENT

The chorus that follows carries out the general tone of the prologue, shuddering at the horrors to come. But significantly, I think, there is no thought of a god's punishment on the house of Atreus. It is Fortune, with her love of bringing low the mighty, before which the chorus trembles. They shudder at the thought of fickle Fate which they liken to the storm that blows down the highest towers, the too favoring breeze that wrecks the ship.

Clytemnestra, with the familiar nurse, always useful to avoid the appearance of too much monologue, appears flogging her wrath into action, goading herself to face the murder of her husband. The nurse furnishes the necessary halfhearted arguments against her act until the Queen has risen to sufficient heights of fury. Just then Aegisthus arrives and Clytemnestra, at once becoming fearful, reverses her position and takes up the argument against the crime. Little enough progress has been made when they finally withdraw to make further plans. Two incidental references to the gods occur in this act. Clytemnestra (who does pride herself on divine ancestry) scoffs at the idea that the gods gave a fair breeze from Aulis.

> O House of Atreus, still surpassing crimes
> Of old with crimes new fashioned, bought we these
> Winds with foul bloodshed, war with butchery?
> And was it this that loosed the thousand ships?
> Nay 'twas no favoring god sped them from Greece,
> 'Twas Aulis drove the accursed hulls from port.

And when Aegisthus claims a divine father, even his consort Clytemnestra bids him not besmirch the gods.

The second choral interlude is the hymn—first to Phoebus, then to Juno, Pallas, Trivia, and finally Jupiter. The object of the ode seems to be largely to furnish contrast to the gloom that has preceded. The address to the gods is little more than a summary of conventional attributes, with a suggestion of the ceremonial dance of the Argive maidens into the midst of which Eurybates plunges with his message of Agamemnon's return. He uses religious phrases:

> Ye shrines, ye altars of the gods above,
> Ye lares of my fatherland: after
> Long weary years, and well-nigh skeptical,
> I greet you now a suppliant.

This has little more religious significance than his way of telling about the return of his chief:

> Now pay your vows unto the gods of heaven,
> For lo the glory of our Argive land
> Returns: victorious Agamemnon comes.

The phrases are partly conventional, partly the attempt of Seneca to give some local color to the scene (and even this is marred by the intrusion of the Roman lares).

Eurybates tells the story of the return after the fall of Troy. In the stormy convulsion of nature, Pallas is said to have hurled her father's thunderbolts at the struggling Greeks. This leads up to the striking of Ajax and his defiant speech and death. This is another interesting passage; it has no bearing whatsoever on the plot; the messenger speech is disproportionately long even without it. But here was a magnificent opportunity for the most melodramatic narrative imaginable: Ajax, flung burning into the sea to rise enveloped in flame, swim to his ship, then mount a rock to thunder his defiance at Athena until Neptune with his trident splits the rock and hurls him forever into the depths. The divine machinery is all there, but there for the obvious reason that the purple patch is borrowed with all its technique from the epic cycle.

The announcement made, Cassandra and her maidens enter, mourning their fate, followed by Agamemnon who proceeds into the palace after a few words with Cassandra. He speaks of her as possessed by the god. This seems to be a somewhat conventional euphemism for her madness, which performs no essential function in the way of motivating the plot but enables her to describe the murder of Agamemnon, taking place within the palace. She takes full advantage of this opportunity, making the most of the bloody details.

Elektra enters, bringing her small brother Orestes, seeking to send him away in safety as his father's avenger. How she has learned of the crime and come is not made clear! But opportunely Strophius with young Pylades arrives in a chariot and, on learning the situation, speeds off with Orestes. Elektra remains to be berated by Clytemnestra and Aegisthus and is dragged off to prison, Cassandra is condemned to die, and the hurried last act ends with her prophecy of doom to come.

Such a summary makes it clear, I think, that in the general course of a play as well as in the specifically supernatural parts, there is little enough of religious feeling. The gods, as casual symbols or even as the realities of another age still intruding, are bound to occur constantly but not religiously. It is not the gods who control the world of these dramas; it is Fortuna, the fickle Fate that casts down the mighty and strikes always without warning. Even when a chorus in the *Phaedra* (959) starts out to sing an ode to a god, it develops into a protest against Fortune. Medea is an apparent exception. She calls on all the infernal gods again and again but obviously this is a part of the tone background of her lethal magic. The supernatural in Seneca is one of the tools of his trade, and it passed on as such to Elizabethan drama when the ritual of an alien religion would have been wholly ineffectual.

CHAPTER IX
PHILOSOPHIC CONTENT

DRAMA, by tradition a religious function, would seem to have suffered a major operation when the religious element was largely removed. And so it did. Even Euripides necessarily compensated such loss as had already occurred in his drama with the interest in psychological studies of individuals, in minor conflicts, and with the rhetorical arguments that appealed to his time. Seneca was hardly a subtle psychologist, and only in part could the rhetorical flourishes and the melodramatic parade of the supernatural take the place of the more substantial religious appeal of his forerunners. Nor had he new plots to present. What he sought to use, to give more body and tone to his plays, was a certain philosophic atmosphere.

Long since, the competition between the ethical sects had ceased to be a struggle. The Epicurean who had once been an earnest materialist was little more in the time of Nero than the nonreligious man of the day. Stoicism had first of all combined with sturdy Roman conservatism and in the modified form in which Panaetius presented it, with the Aristotelian mean as a cardinal doctrine, had become the orthodox creed of Rome. With the vast influx of foreigners into the citizenry of the metropolis in the first century, whether by immigration or emancipation, Stoicism took up the fight for a decent standard against the superstition, ignorance, immorality, and indifference of the rest of the population. The Stoic felt a moral urge, a missionary sense of responsibility, for, if there was a divine order of reason in the universe, happiness for all could result only in the universal will to conform with that order. Therefore, whether in the person of the humorous, never too serious Satirist or the intense and rather raucous sidewalk preacher, or at his best as the intellectual essayist, the Stoic had always a burden of responsibility as the reformer of the world's morals. Seneca in his essays was a Stoic, and it is largely the tone of Stoic doctrine that gives to the plays a certain unity of atmosphere. He is not, however, in the tragedies what we are apt to consider the orthodox Stoic.

In this respect there is an interesting parallel with Horace. Horace the Satirist, especially in the *Epistles*, is a Stoic; in the *Odes* he is first and always a lyric poet. The result of this divided personality is much apparent contradiction in the *Odes* because of the fundamental Stoic belief which emerges not infrequently, apparently unoffended by the *carpe diem* attitude of the poet. The Seneca of the moral essays is a Stoic philosopher: in the tragedies, he aims at being a dramatic poet. Being less of a poet than Horace, Seneca allows much more of his philosophy to emerge in his plays and, as a matter of fact, this Stoic tone is well-nigh predominant. But as a poet, speaking to a wider public than any philosophic coterie, he allows himself the luxury of some of the more popular beliefs, especially the belief in Fortuna. He feels free to use much that is *not* Stoic, as a Christian poet, even with a predominantly religious tone, might often express an entirely un-Christian attitude toward Fate. Seneca the philosopher believed in predestination; the poet Seneca saw constantly in the world the caprice of Fortune.

This inconsistency of point of view in the tragedies is of course due in part to literary tradition. Seneca was a constant borrower from Horace, and Horace was by no means a systematic philosopher, even in the *Epistles* and the *Satires;* in the *Odes* he was almost wholly the poet. His treatment of Fortuna is illuminating. In the thirty-third ode of the first book he seems to be writing a recantation of "mad philosophy." That this was materialism, Epicureanism, is implied by the reason he gives for recantation, that Jupiter, by a lightning bolt from the blue, has upset his philosophy. In other words, there is a power outside of the material universe that can interfere with the scientific order. In the next stanza this power becomes *deus*, and finally, at the end of the poem, Fortuna. The poem is short and addressed to no one; it seems to be in a sense a prologue to the following ode, a prayer to the Fortuna of Antium, the familiar goddess accompanied by Spes and Fides. Throughout the poems of Horace, Fortune has as her chief attribute the sudden reversal of the existing state of affairs, the raising of the humble, the smiting of the great. And it is interesting to hear Horace, in the third book (*Ode* 29.49), say that while Fortune remains with him, he does her homage, but when she goes he wraps himself in his philosophic *virtus* and enjoys his upright poverty. The tradition was strong: it is sufficient to note that the history of Asinius Pollio presented the *ludus Fortunae* (*H.O.* II. 1.3) and that, in the epic of the Stoic Lucan, Fortune as an abstract entity is second only to Fate. It is, therefore, not surprising that in Seneca's plays there are four choral odes on Fortune.

There is one more caution to be observed. "Philosophic" to the Roman had a different meaning from that which it held for the Greek. The Roman was never much of an abstract philosopher. In early times he looked askance on philosophy as an alien influence from Greece, boding no good to the Roman state. When it could not be barred out, he made, with customary shrewdness, a compromise which served his purpose: modified Stoicism he merged with his own tradition and gradually Romanized. At best, only a few Romans were ever interested in abstract philosophy; it was only the practical, concrete branch of ethics that was generally tolerated and, in the first century, a philosophic tone means rather a moralizing tone, the atmosphere of wise maxims. In a play, this atmosphere is produced chiefly in two ways: those choral odes, which are not knit in with the plot, deal for the most part specifically and at length with "philosophic" questions, just as, in the Greek drama, the tendency was to devote such odes to prayers or hymns, to *religious* expression. In the second place, and perhaps in the long run this is essentially the more fundamental, there appear throughout the dialogue parts, that is in the plays proper, so many moral maxims, so many *sententiae* of a philosophizing tone as to give color to the whole.

One of the most characteristic tenets of Roman Stoicism was

that of moderation, Horace's golden mean. It is not always so wisely presented as it was by Horace and it often appears rather as a warning against excessive greatness or overweening ambition. This is quite proper for tragedy which traditionally pictures the fall of the great, and it is natural too; few people have enough of the Diogenes in them to need a warning in the other direction. Even such poems as Horace's *Aequam memento* and *Rectius vives* have the natural stress placed on the danger of too high flights. Very close to these, and reminiscent of the latter in phrasing, is the short fourth ode in the *Oedipus*. "If I could guide my own life, I should trim my sails when the winds were favorable and always keep to the *media via* in life." This is the theme illustrated by the fatal flight of Icarus and the safe moderation of Daedalus. The first ode of the *Hercules Furens* is also essentially an ode to moderation, complicated in various ways. For one thing, the picture of the simple country life obviously makes a strong appeal to the writer and he elaborates it. Then, when he swings into the contrast, the ghastly artificiality of city life, the influence of Satire grips him just as strongly and, for some lines, he presents us Horace in paraphrase. This Horatian mood evidently holds, for it leads him to the somewhat inappropriate sentiment by way of conclusion: While Fate permits, live joyously, for life is short and death is sure. This again leads him on to a third Horatian theme, the daring of mankind which tempts Fate continuously. The whole ode is perhaps more Horatian than philosophic but the leading theme is moderation.

Odes on moderation, with the added theme of the daring of mankind which is a violation of the Panaetian creed, outnumber all others in the eight plays. The second chorus in the *Hercules on Oeta* contrasts the happy safety of the poor man in his moderation with the unhappiness and danger of the dweller in marble halls. The familiar illustration appears again here. Icarus the immoderate, Daedalus, safe in his conservatism. With it comes also the conceit which appealed strongly to Juvenal later, that poison is drunk from *golden* goblets. So too Thyestes argues when he is returning fearfully to the court of Atreus and eulogizes the life of simplicity. "O happiness," he cries, "to eat one's food in safety, stretched on the earth! Crimes do not enter hovels; the food on simple tables is safe to eat: poison is drunk from golden cups." This is followed by a thoroughly Horatian paragraph.

> My home stands not upon the mountain peak
> To overawe the humble, in my house
> No coffered ceilings shine with ivory,
> No watching slave defends me while I sleep.
> I speed no argosies to bring me fish,
> Nor thrust the sea back to accommodate
> Foundations measureless. I do not feed
> My arrogant belly on the tribute paid
> By tribes without the law, nor garner tithes
> From lands beyond the Parthian boundaries.

The same general idea had just been expressed by the chorus, indicating that it is not a personal characterization of Thyestes:

> Let who will incontinent
> Seize the dizzy height:
> Me, with simple peace content,
> Homely joys delight.
>
> Known to none, by none distraught,
> While my hours fly;
> When my hours have come to naught,
> Old in peace I'll die.
>
> But to him comes many a fear
> Who, as looms his goal,
> Known to all men far and near,
> Knows not his own soul.

The opening ode of the *Agamemnon*, while it is practically concerned with kings, deals with them largely from this same point of view and uses the Horatian figures of the lightning striking the highest mountains and the safest course being well in shore. The best example of the other phase, the daring of mankind which brings destruction in its wake, is the second chorus of the *Medea*, in its very opening word reminiscent of Horace's *Audax omnia perpeti*.

These more extensive passages presenting the advantages of the golden mean might be amply supported by the quotation of sententious lines from all the plays; some of these have appeared in other connections. For the present, it is clear that the value of moderation is a prominent thesis with Seneca. Another is the essential quality of *virtus*. This is less prominent, for the reason, I suspect, that Seneca, like the Satirists, is more interested in the reverse side, the darker picture of vice. In the case of Hercules too, virtus has an admixture of physical bravery, though even with him it is primarily a moral quality, for it is because of his benefits to mankind that his "virtue shall find a place among the stars." Elsewhere it constantly verges on the meaning of courage, good or bad. Medea seems to take it so. The nurse tells her that Fortune should be tried only when there is a chance for virtus, and Medea, whose plans are hardly virtuous even from a pagan point of view, tells her proudly that there can never fail to be a chance for virtus. There is much more of the moral content in the bitter comment of sad old Amphitryon, worded by Marston in the *Malcontent:* Mischief that prospers men do virtue call.

The number of Stoic maxims which are used to enable speakers in the play to make striking utterances is too great to be an accident. Furthermore, they are not used by Seneca to build up the pictures of this or that character. It is perfectly evident that, while there is character drawing to a limited extent especially of the more exaggerated, melodramatic sort like that of the wily Ulysses who has become almost a comic detective, the majority of characters are merely mouthpieces for the lines that would go well with Seneca's hand-picked audience. It is not, therefore, doing any injustice to the poet to gather isolated lines here and there to illustrate the point. Seneca himself in many an instance leaves his sententious lines isolated.

That the first hour of life determines the last is epigrammatically stated more than once. (Cf. *H.F.* 874; *Oed.* 988.) Death is a refuge when all else fails. (*H.F.* 426; *Tr.* 329; *H.O.* 117; *Pb.* 878, etc.) The good man finds in suffering a worthy antagonist whom he rejoices to fight. (*H.F.* 433.) Tranquillity produces happiness. (*H.F.* 139 ff.) The power of kings is not a "good." (*Agam.* 57 ff., etc.) Riches are not a good. (*Med.* 204 ff., *Ph.* 518, etc.) Wealth provokes crimes. (*Th.* 453.) Poverty is not an evil. (*Med.* 211 ff., etc.) Beauty is not a good. (*Ph.* 761 ff., 820 ff.) Death is not an evil. (*Tr.* 371 ff., 954.) Nobility and birth are not goods. (*H.F.* 340.) The brave man cannot be miserable. (*H.F.* 463.) The true king is not the man supported by force on a throne, but the man who has raised himself above all fears and desires by virtue of his own reason. (*Th.* 348, 390.)

Such are some of the Stoic maxims that find emphatic expression in the plays. Even when Phaedra's nurse urges Hippolytus to abandon his life of austerity she feels it necessary to use the terminology of Stoicism and to pretend that she is *not* violating its tenets. She bids him follow a life according to Nature. (*Ph.* 481.) Still other points of Stoic doctrine will appear in a discussion of the Satiric elements of the plays. But first there are at least two elements of the Senecan background that must be noted which are not consistently Stoic.

The literary tradition of Fortuna has already been noted, but it must be emphasized. The Seneca of the moral essays is not in spirit the Seneca of the tragedies. The Stoic dogmas of the former have largely impregnated the work of the latter, but the latter is also a poet and a poet of his own generation. That generation had inherited and greatly enlarged the tradition of the play of Fortune even in a conventionally Stoic universe. This popular belief in chance, or rather in something halfway between blind chance and canny Nemesis, was just what Seneca wanted for his melodramas and if as philosopher he was constrained to forego the luxury of fear he could as poet compensate his more human nature.

Fortune therefore becomes one of the greatest figures of the tone background of the tragedies. Five choral odes, as we have seen, are devoted largely to the presentation of the vagaries and injustices with which chance or Fortune rules the world. That it is not wholly blind chance seems to be indicated by its tendency

PHILOSOPHIC CONTENT 159

to strike down the highest. The lightning rarely strikes the lowlying valley (*Ph.* 1132) and so Fortune does not interfere with the humble. (Cf. also *Ph.* 11, 29; *Agam.* 96.) But this is not a wholly constant attribute. Although one of the greatest of the Fortuna odes (*Agam.* 57 ff.) dwells entirely on the threat against the monarch who can never wield a tranquil scepter, another equally impressive (*H.F.* 524 ff.) is more concerned with the general unfairness of Fortune's favors:

> O Fortune ever jealous of the brave,
> The good man knows no justice at thy hand.
> Eurystheus shall be King in slothful ease,
> Alcmena's son wage endlessly his wars.

And in the same play (325) "uneven Fortune" is said never to spare the highest virtues. The clearest expression of this feeling, that Fortune is blind and yet in some way manages to do pretty thorough injustice, is found in the *Phaedra*. The chorus addresses Nature, the great parent of the gods, and Jupiter the lord of fiery Olympus, and asks why they take such infinite pains to make an ordered universe in which the seasons are regular and a plan evident and yet pay no attention to the injustices to which mankind is subject.

> For Fortune rules the affairs of humankind,
> Knowing no order, scattering with blind chance
> Her favors kindliest ever to the worst.

As a philosopher, Seneca must needs make a brave if hopeless attempt to explain the problem of evil in a god-governed universe: it must have been a relief to him to be able as a poet to express his very human bewilderment and rage. It is in this role of poet that he can speak of Fortune as exhausting its own strength (*Agam.* 698); it is partly as poet but partly as philosopher that he finds a different limit to the power of Fortune. "Fortune fears the brave, destroys the coward" (*Med.* 159), or again: "Fortune can take my wealth but not my heart." (*Med.* 176.) Because, perhaps, of the natural pessimism of human nature, Fortuna had gone through the same evolution in the

Roman world that the conception *casus* went through. At first, each represented an idea neither good nor bad but in the end (like the concept *tempestas*) they emerge with scarcely a remnant of their better natures. For Seneca the playwright cruel Fortuna was a congenial spirit.

But if he made much of the sardonic god of chance, the greatest and most omnipresent patron of his art is Death; Death can give the somber touch to the atmosphere of a drama most effectively, whether it be Death the reaper or Death the final harbor of peace. For it is in contrast with fickle Fortune and as the only sure port for the weary that Death gives the ultimate touch of blackness to the theater of Seneca. When everything in life is so hostile that Death becomes a friend, and that too without the lure of future bliss in paradise, then the isolation of misery is about complete and the playwright has accomplished his purpose.

> And what a luring curse to humankind
> Is this mad love of life when from all ills
> Escape lies ready and the free gift of Death
> Calls to the wretched, Death the placid port
> Of everlasting peace. No terror there
> Intrudes, no stormy blast of arbitrary
> Fortune nor lightning flame of unjust Jove.

This is the cry of the Trojan captives that attend Cassandra (*Ag.* 589) and another captive, Iole (*H.O.* 215) has the same attitude when she checks herself from mourning for her parents, for even-handed Death has put them where they are safe, while her own fortune, still insecure, is what really calls for tears. And Deianeira too (*H.O.* 1021) finds Death the only harbor of refuge (*portus*) from her troubles. Death is the last weapon of defense against Fortune: "No man but has the power to rob us of life but none may rob us of death" (*Phoen.* 152); "Death alone saves the innocent from Fortune" (*Oed.* 933); "Death can never fail the man with will to die" (*Phae.* 878).

On the other hand there is of course another aspect of Death:

death as a threat, the melodramatic weapon, as well as the heroic defiance that meets that threat:

> Let chains drag down my body and with long
> Slow hunger let my death be meted out:
> No force shall break my faith, Alcides. Thine,
> Thine shall I die. (*H.F.* 420, Megara speaking.)

However, this side of the picture, the horror of death, does not lend itself so well to sententious remarks and rather serves as the implied background of every play, a part of the atmosphere of cruelty, hate, treachery, and misery in which all of the plays proceed.

Seneca must have thought much of the imminence of death. Good Stoic doctrine recommended suicide when the bad in life overbalanced the good. But Seneca was not entirely sure that the afterlife was more desirable. On this point Stoic doctrine had never been very definite or clear. The soul rose as far through the strata of the atmosphere as its condition of purity allowed. It might rise only so slightly that it could be caught back into another earthy prison or it might rise to the supreme heights whence, till the final conflagration, it could contemplate the perfection of the divine. But Roman Stoics had never been given to speculation. Their function was to express effectively the rules of ethical conduct which must guide man in his struggle toward virtue and to exhort him as he struggled. The theory of afterlife, never satisfactorily formulated by Greek Stoics, had scarcely been touched on by the Roman. Seneca seems to have accepted the general proposition that the stories of punishment in the next world were inventions of the imagination (*Ad Marciam*, 19.4). Death is neither good nor bad in itself for it is really nothing but a boundary. But so far as I know, he never completely convinced himself that there was no afterlife at all. His desire to do so is clear and it contributed to the tragedies the best of all the choral odes, the second in the *Troades* (371 ff.). It is perhaps the most optimistic utterance in the plays and by this very fact emphasizes the blackness of the general tone atmosphere.

OUR SENECA

Is it truth or an idle tale,
To frighten the timid soul,
That our spirits live beyond the vale
And the grave is not the goal?
When our eyes are closed in death
And our last day's sun is set,
When we cease to draw this troublous breath,
Is there no respite yet?
Or shall the torch of our funeral pyre
Blend body and soul in releasing fire?

All that the rising sun beholds
Or, sinking, sets aglow,
All that the ocean stream enfolds
With its tides that ebb and flow,
All, all, with the speed of heaven's steed,
Shall Time the reaper take for his meed.

As each bright constellation
Speeds through eternal space,
As the master of all creation
Guides the centuries' mad race,
With the speed of Hecat turning
On her downward way to press,
So we seek with breathless yearning
That far goal of nothingness.

And the soul that reaches Death
Is gone for eternity.
As a dying fire's vaporous breath
Or a cloud against the sky,
So the soul that has ruled our life
Is gone with the speed of thought:
There is naught when Death has ended strife
And Death itself is naught,
Only the last line gleaming white
Of a race that is run in a single flight.

Fling off each fear, each hope forlorn,
For Chaos and Time shall win:
And Death that leaves the body shorn
Shall shatter the soul therein.

Where shall ye rest when life shall close?
Where the souls that are yet unborn repose.

One phase of the philosophic atmosphere or background of the plays is distinct enough to be treated separately although it is not in reality either wholly independent or even always distinguishable. That is the satiric element. Roman Satire was a type of literature, not a figure of speech related to irony. In England, Johnson and Pope imitated it to a certain extent but it never established itself thoroughly outside of Italy. Its earliest exponent at Rome was Lucilius who made Satire the vehicle for the most variegated comment on life and manners. Horace inherited the tradition of variety, confirmed the use of the hexameter meter and became the most distinguished writer of Roman Satire. To Seneca, Satire must have been the type of literature written by Horace rather than that which came later and appealed to English imitators, the more materialistic Satire of Juvenal.

The Roman Satire seems to have had its origin in one of the offshoots of the Platonic dialogue and therefore to have come honestly by its philosophic characteristics. For even after Lucilius had given it the stamp of miscellaneous criticism, the criticism always retained a considerable element of ethical tone. This tone was in general Stoic. Epicureans would never have developed a vehicle for criticism and improvement, for they were not particularly interested in conversion or reform: it requires a dogma of duty to a supreme power to develop the missionary zeal of the reformer, and anyone whose sincere ideal is personal pleasure and freedom from pain can hardly undertake seriously to improve his neighbors. An Epicurean, like Lucretius, might offer joy and release from fear to anyone that cared to accept, but he could never have attacked those who failed to listen. The Stoic not only taught virtue but tended to demand an audience.

The Stoicism of the Satire was of course the modified Roman Stoicism of Panaetius with its stress on the principle of moderation. Virtus was the goal held up by the Satirist as by the more legitimate philosopher, but both had a tendency to dwell on the *vitia* which must be removed or avoided in the attainment of virtue. This was especially true of a popular type like Satire which diverged far from its original philosophic tone and came to be looked upon primarily as a vehicle of criticism. As exemplified by Horace, Satire in its philosophic function presented virtue as a general goal and moderation as its greatest element and it held up to scorn the vices which hindered moral progress, stressing particularly luxury, ambition, avarice, superstition, and lust. Horace treated these with urbanity and charm, Juvenal with rhetorical brilliance and intensity. Juvenal was more inclined to see their external manifestations. Seneca lived and wrote midway between the two great Satirists. He was a philosopher and a dramatist. But, by his day, the spirit of Satire had permeated Roman literature to a remarkable degree and it must always be remembered that Satire was originally philosophic in its function. Furthermore Quintilian (X. l. 129) distinctly says of Seneca that he was *"in philosophia parum diligens, egregius tamen vitiorum insectator."* It should not therefore be surprising to find the Satiric quality strong in the dramas which have already shown a considerable touch of philosophic atmosphere.

Perhaps the most obvious instance of this Satiric element is the speech of Hippolytus in the *Phaedra* (483 ff.) in answer to the appeal of the nurse who would have him abandon his chaste country life. His first answer is that no life is so free from vitia as the life of the country and then he follows this up with a specification of the vices of the city which are unknown in the country.

> No life there is so free from every vice,
> More kin to days of old, than that which leaves
> The city walls and seeks the woodland's peace.
> No frenzied avarice besets his life
> Who gives himself unto the mountain heights.
> He cares not for the favor of the crowd,
> Its fickle popularity, nor yet
> Its poisonous jealousy. Content he lives,
> Fawns not on power nor, seeking power himself,
> Bows before office or illusory wealth.

Ransomed from hope and fear, no venomous tooth
Of envy reaches him, he never knows
The manifold crimes that haunt the city streets
Nor shudders at each tumult, does not live
A life of pretense. Never does he strive
To deck his mansion with a thousand piers
Upholding gilded rafters.

Later on in his speech, after eulogizing the positive value of simple outdoor life, he returns to attack luxury (with the epigram *sollicito bibunt auro superbi*), greed, and lust.

The opening chorus of the *Hercules Furens* presents another eulogy of the simple life and even more vividly arraigns the evils of the city. Unlimited desires and dreadful fears attend that life. One man gives up his sleep to make his morning call at the proud door of some nabob; another piles up useless wealth, "poor in the midst of hoarded gold," for he can only gaze upon it impotently; another is ambitious for public office and still another for the fame of an orator. This passage is particularly interesting. The *ille . . . hic; illum . . . hic* is a usage by no means confined to Satire but very frequently employed by the Satirists. The phrase *gazis inhians* used of the miser must almost surely come from Horace: *congestis undique saccis/indormis inhians* (*Sat.* I. 1. 70) and there is much Horatian reminiscence throughout the ode. But the item of the ambitious social parasite who hustles around to morning calls is one unknown to Horace. Juvenal and Martial railed at the custom and this passage is evidence that it was already a sufficiently widespread nuisance to be the object of Satiric attack in the Age of Nero.

In the impressive ode of the *Thyestes* (336 ff.) that draws the contrasted picture of the Tyrant and the King, a splendid exposition of Stoic doctrine, the conventional subjects of Satiric attack come forward again: *ambitio impotens, favor vulgi, opes*. A little later in the same play (453), Seneca tries to improve the epigram he had already made: *venenum in auro bibitur*, and follows it up with a thrust at ivory ceilings and at the presumption of the rich in pushing out their building foundations into the sea.

Horace's forebodings in this last respect seem not to have been groundless.

To return to the *Phaedra*, the nurse pleads with her mistress in the tones of a true Satirist and arraigns the man who glories in success. To him who exults overmuch in his prosperity there enters in that comrade of good fortune, lust for more. No ordinary meals, no common house or service of pottery can please him any more. Such is the fate which brings doom to the rich.

Moderation and the *media via*, the mean between two extremes, were prime tenets of Horace's *Satire* which became even more strictly associated with Satire than with Stoicism which, in Seneca's day, had a tendency toward the extreme even as it had had in the days of the younger Cato. In his early poems, written in Corsica, Seneca had eulogized moderation and he does the same thing in one of the last two short choruses of the *Oedipus:* Could I forge my fate to my own taste, I would trim my sails to a light breeze, nor ever let the masts strain under a heavy wind. The figure comes from Horace whose nautical accuracy was greater. Seneca winds up the stanza also with another Horatian reminiscence: *tuta me media vehat / vita decurrens via*. In good Satiric fashion, the truth is driven home by means of an illustration: Icarus, flying too high, was wrecked, while the conservative Daedalus awaited him in safety. The conclusion is wholly characteristic of Horace: *quicquid excessit modum / pendet instabili loco*. The myth of Icarus would have been wholly in place in a Greek chorus but, as has already appeared, Seneca did not follow the Greek model in his choruses so that it is easier to see in the Satiric method of illustration the model for such a bit as this.

The *media via* appears again in the second choral ode of the *Hercules on Oeta*. At line 675, a summary stanza begins: *quisquis medium refugit iter / stabili numquam tramite currit*. Icarus and Daedalus once more serve as illustrations and the ode winds up with the familiar observation that Fortune overlooks the modest and strikes down the outstanding. But the earlier part, too, of this choral passage had had much that was reminiscent of Horace in his Satiric role. Such an epigram as *nam rara fides / ubi*

PHILOSOPHIC CONTENT 167

iam melior fortuna ruit has a Horatian quality and is followed up with an exposition of the unenviable position of the monarch. *Pauci reges non regna colunt* strikes the keynote and details are added with familiar references to mythology characteristically overdone. Horace is recalled in the conceit that the poor man does not fear the threatening sword and Juvenal is anticipated in the sententious remark, *aurea miscet pocula sanguis*, which was simply another version of his own: *venenum in auro bibitur*. (*Thyestes* 453.)

One matter of form rather than substance should be noted in this connection. In *Hercules Furens*, in the prologue (l. 89), Juno says with bitter irony: *I nunc, superbe, caelitum sedes pete / humana temne*. The same tone of scornful irony sounds in the words of *Medea* (l. 1007): *I nunc, superbe, virginum thalamos pete, / relinque matres*. This ironical exhortation to do something which has proven disastrous is perfectly familiar from Juvenal (VI. 306; X. 166; X. 310; XII. 57), especially from his exhortation to Hannibal: *I nunc demens et saevas curre per Alpes / ut pueris placeas et declamatio fias*. But Persius had already used it effectively (IV. 19)[1] and Horace too. (*Epist.* I. 6.17; II. 2.76.) It is true that the same sort of ironical imperative is used by Vergil (*Aeneid* IX. 631) (without, however, the characteristic *nunc* and *et*) but it was chiefly associated with Satirical thought. Witness the five instances in Martial.

Altogether the evidence of Satiric influence on Seneca is not at first glance impressive. On the other hand it is rather remarkable that the drama should have absorbed even so much of the spirit of moral criticism. It would not have been in place in Greek tragedy save insofar as it might be typical of some particular character. Into the Latin tragedy it intrudes in two ways, first, through the *sententiae*, which have been seen to be highly characteristic of Seneca, and second, in more isolated passages of sustained Satire. These latter are either choral odes or long purple patches created for recitation purposes. Such obviously is the speech of Hippolytus. This is in every way the most mark-

1. See Jahn's note on this passage for list of cases.

edly Satiric passage in the plays, following almost in detail the outline of a Stoic argument. It starts abruptly after the nurse's speech, not really meeting her immediate appeal to him to yield to the claims of love. To this appeal he returns, also abruptly, at the end of his long sermon, and the nurse responds only to his last remarks, leaving the Stoic passage entirely isolated. This of course is not surprising; it is the method that appears throughout the plays and is shared by the other literature of the day: the importation of whatever could be made to give rhetorical adornment for recitation purposes. By way of this particular importation there entered into the tragedy much of the sententious moralizing tone, which is obvious always in Seneca even when it is impossible definitely to assign a Satiric source.

CHAPTER X
STOCK CHARACTERS

THE great plays of Greece—the remark is really a platitude—depended for their interest on the development of the plot in harmony with the characters as presented. In some of the earlier plays the plot is hardly more than a situation, not quite static but at the same time not exhibiting any great development. The change wrought by Sophocles consisted in part in the development of a more intricate and more mobile plot. In Euripides, situations, within the framework of a less compact plot, were the object of the poet's chief concern. But throughout the whole great age of Greek drama the characters were pretty generally individualistic: except perhaps for the messengers, the chorus, and various attendants like Phaedra's nurse, there was scarcely any tendency to make stock characters out of any of them. They are not interchangeable. It is true that Euripides was inclined to make all of his characters follow, to at least a moderate extent, the laws of rhetoric, but in spite of the tendency toward forensic oratory all of the important characters retained individualities distinct from each other.

There is a general belief that the same is not true of Seneca, that his characters are not individuals but types; in other words, that he deals with stock characters. Analysis, however, tends somewhat to dispel this impression. In the *Oedipus*, for example, it is hard to name any stock character except the messenger. Tiresias is not the mere lay figure of a seer like Calchas in the *Troades*, nor an inspired prophet of evil like Cassandra. Nor is he the mouthpiece for the gods like the ghosts or Furies of other plays. He is perhaps more a piece of stage machinery than he should be. His blindness is emphasized, not as bringing him nearer to the unseen, but merely as an inconvenience. Insofar as he has an individuality it is that of a Roman priest rather than that of a Greek seer. Nevertheless he cannot be duplicated from the other plays. His *function* (that of giving information) is not wholly unlike that of Calchas who, if further developed, might very likely have been a fairly close parallel to Tiresias. But they are not, as they stand, alike: both are wooden, but they are not the same.

Oedipus too is neither a stock king nor a stock tyrant. He is not a strong and appealing hero and certainly not merely a pathetic old man. He is Oedipus and no one else, even if a far less convincing Oedipus than Sophocles'.

With the messenger, the case is different. He has no personality whatever of his own: he tells his tale without any conversation either preceding or following it and without any attempt on the part of the author to present an individual character. He exists only as the mouthpiece of the poet to tell what has happened off stage. But, even so, he is hardly a stock character for the very reason that he has no character at all. To this extent he differs from the other messengers in Senecan plays who, borrowed by Seneca from the Greek, became in his hands more stereotyped. So far as the *Oedipus* is concerned, Kreon, when he is used to report the results of Tiresias' necromancy, fulfills, far more than the actual *Nuntius*, the requirements of a typical Senecan messenger. He hesitates and finds excuses not to speak and finally, when persuaded to begin, deliberately recounts the setting of his story and develops it slowly and at great length. His function otherwise in the play is much reduced from that which Sophocles gave him and in the short quarrel scene with Oedipus he does not really appear as an individual.

In taking a great plot then from Sophocles, Seneca would seem not to have had recourse to stock characters except for the most familiar of all, that of the messenger, and even this he used in a somewhat exceptional manner. Of none of the other plays can the same be said: each one has at least one character to which the term "stock" may reasonably be applied.

The messenger appears in all of the Senecan plays. The reason for this has been already discussed, the necessity for extending the action in a play which preserves the unity of place and deals with incidents that cannot be very well presented on the stage. Seneca's contribution to the part of the messenger lies largely in the rather fixed rhetorical character of the speeches. At the moment, the interesting point is not the nature of the messenger speeches but the type of character of the messenger. The *Phaedra* will serve to illustrate this. In the preceding scene Hippolytus has departed under the curse of his father. The chorus gives the first hint of the character of the man who enters to tell of his fate:

> Why comes this messenger with hurried step,
> With saddened look and tear-washed countenance?

Then the messenger himself gives proof of his own agitation:

> O bitter lot and hard, duty unkind:
> Why did chance give to me this hateful task?

The introductory conversation that follows reveals a man hesitant to repeat his story, excited and timorous and concise.

> *Theseus.* Fear not to speak disaster openly;
>   This heart of mine is not undrilled by woe.
> *Messenger.* My tongue refuses mournful speech to grief.
> *Theseus.* Speak out: what Fate besets our shaken house?
> *Messenger.* Hippolytus lies slain in grievous wise.
> *Theseus.* His father knew before his son was lost;
>   The adulterer now is dead. Tell how he died.
> *Messenger.* When first he left the city, stretching out
>   A quickened pace, with angry step and swift,

and so on for over a hundred lines of rhetorical description. In this particular case there are some eight-and-a-half lines of conversation at the end of the recital but they serve only as a framework and not to characterize further the messenger who has spoken his account of Hippolytus' death without, for example, a single phrase or word or idea that would present him to the reader as a servant. Such lines as these, suitable perhaps to epic but not to a slave's account, are typical:

> A mighty sea came thundering from the deep,
> Rearing to heaven. No breeze stirred o'er the surge,
> No quarter of the quiet sky gave sound;
> Self-roused the portent of the peaceful sea.

Learned allusion is used to enhance the picture, such as no slave would be expected to employ.

In the *Troades* the messenger enters with the same agitation.

> O cruel Fate, o horrid, cruel Fate,
> What crime so terrible these twice five years
> Has Mars beheld? What shall I groan for first?

Once quieted, he too becomes a skilled raconteur, beginning:

> One mighty tower survives of what was Troy
> Where Priam used to stand.

In this play the messenger has a function of his own, namely, to shepherd the Trojan women to the ships, so that the close of the speech is unlike the others but again does not serve to develop any individuality in the messenger. It should be noted that in the *Troades* Talthybius the Greek herald is also used as a messenger. He enters, exclaiming against the Fate that keeps the Greek ships from sailing. When pressed by the chorus, he tells his tale in the fashion of a messenger. There is no reason except the manuscript reading to give this particular messenger a name. Even Andromache's account of her dream tends to slip out of character as it approaches epic narrative, but it has some touches of characterization when she speaks of Hector with real emotion.

Eurybates in the *Agamemnon* has not the pitiful agitation of the typical messenger but his reluctance to speak has to be overcome by Clytemnestra and his epic style is above criticism. The messenger in the *Medea* cries out at his entrance:

> All, all is lost, the kingdom fallen quite:
> Children and sire lie one commingled ash.

In face of his grudging responses the chorus urges him to tell the story, but this never comes. Just when it should follow, the nurse bids Medea flee and the heroine makes a very long and fiery speech. The suspicion can hardly be avoided that something has been lost from the text although it is of course possible that Seneca simply chose to give Medea the chance for rhetoric here and actually did introduce a messenger to utter less than ten lines. The messenger of the *Thyestes* enters with frenzied exclamations, is at last quieted by the chorus, and tells his story at the usual length and in the usual manner. A slight element of variety is introduced by promptings and exclamations by the chorus interspersed through the narrative. Beyond one such interruption, there is little out of the ordinary in the messenger scene of the *Hercules on Oeta*. This messenger, however, does not twitter. He answers the first questions laconically and is then drawn into the usual narrative. In the early part of the same play, Hyllus has the role of messenger and does evince rather panicky excitement before beginning in deliberate epic style a long narrative. There remains the *Hercules Furens*, which has no messenger appearing as such. But Theseus performs the function in what is in one way the most extreme instance of undramatic narrative. He does not play the excited messenger but at the same time he is not an individual. A conversation with Amphitryon furnishes the introduction and inserted questions by Amphitryon keep the narrative alive. The noteworthy point is that this narrative tells solely of the past history of Hercules and has no bearing whatever on the plot. It serves to occupy the time while Hercules attacks Lycus, a rare instance of any such concern on the part of Seneca, but in reality it is purely and simply a purple patch, the messenger's speech without use or excuse, spoken by one of the most individual characters of the old tradition with no more individuality than if he had been a stock messenger.

Such is the messenger in Seneca, a piece of stage furniture, used to present to the audience an account of what cannot well be assumed to take place before their eyes. He is a character but without personality.

In sharp contrast with these messengers of Seneca is such a one as brings the news of Hippolytus' disaster in the play of Euripides. He is announced by the chorus as a groom of Hippolytus. In serious fashion he asks for Theseus. Confronted with the King, he tells him that he has bad news and, when told to proceed with his report, states the bare fact that Hippolytus is as good as dead. Theseus asks to know what happened to him and the messenger answers him at length. But the story is not the conventional narrative in which the Senecan messengers indulge. The character of the loyal groom is evident throughout; the language is suited to the character; and the facts are plainly the result of observation at first hand with no suggestion of the intervening artistic touch.

> We on the headland where the seas wash in
> Were currying the horses, all in tears.
> For one had come that told us how no more
> Hippolytus might live within this land,
> A wretched exile by thine order; then
> He came, weeping himself, and joined us there
> Upon the cliff: ten thousand faithful friends
> Came with him. When at length he checked his tears,
> "Why should I mourn?" he said, "I must obey
> My father's word. Come then, ye slaves,
> Harness the horses to my chariot;
> This city is no longer home of mine."
> Then every man turned briskly to his task
> And quicker than a word we brought the team
> Straight to the master. From the rim he seized
> The reins and stepped, still in his hunting boots,
> Into the car.

The same simple narrative describes the whole scene; at times it is highly poetic but the poetry is in large part at least the result of clear, direct, almost naïve storytelling.

> When we had reached the more deserted spot,
> There is a cliff that lies a bit beyond
> Our land and fronts toward the Skironic Gulf.
> Then from beneath the earth a sound most like
> The thunderbolt of Zeus sent forth a roar
> Most terrible to hear. The horses tossed
> Their heads, pricked up their ears, and a new fear
> Was ours: what was the sound. And as we looked
> We saw a wave prodigious, stretching up
> To touch the sky, that hid the very sight
> Of Skiron's cliff and hid the Isthmus too
> And all the headland of Asklepias.

STOCK CHARACTERS

At the end of his speech the loyal groom risks his very life in declaring his belief in the innocence of his master and begging Theseus to relent.

The herdsman in the *Iphigeneia* is another good illustration of a highly individualized messenger. The chorus announces him as a herdsman and there is no doubt as he tells his tale that such he is. The characterization goes so far as to present even the ludicrous side of his simple nature.

> There is a cave washed out by constant waves
> Where purple fishers go for shelter. There
> One of us herdsmen saw two strange young men
> And came on tiptoe to us. And he said:
> Do you not see them—gods they are that sit
> There on the headland. Then one pious soul
> Out of our crowd, lifting his outstretched hands
> Prayed to the two. Another feckless fellow,
> Godless and bold, laughed at his prayers and said
> That these were shipwrecked sailors scared by our law
> That sacrifices strangers.

The battle between the herdsmen and Orestes and Pylades is told in all simplicity, presenting unblushingly the ludicrous cowardice of the herdsmen and giving a vivid picture of the madness of Orestes as it appeared to a much perplexed yokel.

It would certainly not be fair to represent Euripides as always drawing each messenger as an individual. The ones that have been described are clearly pictured and make a vivid impression, but there are many messengers throughout his plays and these do not always measure up to the standard of the herdsman and the groom. In the *Medea*, for example, at line 1116, the heroine announces the approach of one of Jason's grooms. The manuscripts call him a messenger. He enters with exclamations urging Medea to flee. Questioned by her he tells everything in two lines. When pressed he tells his story at considerable length. There is some characterization, for he remarks that when "we heard that the quarrel between Medea and Jason was settled we were greatly delighted." He pictures one of the servants stroking the children's heads while he ran along with them to see the happy conclusion. He has a number of platitudinous remarks filled with superficial wisdom at the close of his speech sounding much like a chorus leader or an old nurse. At the end of his long speech, however, there is no conversation in which he joins and he does not appear again although no exit is provided. He is dropped like a piece of machinery.

Even more mechanical perhaps is the messenger in the *Andromache*. There is no announcement of his arrival whatsoever except as he makes it himself as he begins, "The news I bring." There follows what became a familiar piece of technique, a summary statement, questions, and a long story. There is no characterization. The speaker might be anybody and there is no exit provided.

In the same manner, in the *Suppliants*, the messenger announces himself to the chorus at 634. No one else is present and there has been no warning of his arrival. There is not, to be sure, any exclamatory entrance for he has no tale of disaster to tell as is usually the case. He has a cheerful story. Adrastus appears somehow at the end and converses with him. There is no general characterization of the messenger and no adequate exit provided for him.

The messenger of the *Herakles*, 910, does come in with violent exclamations without introduction, with concise statement of the facts, with questions by the chorus and a long story following. Toward the end there is some slight attempt at individualization, but not a great deal. No exit is provided.

In the *Elektra* (l. 761) the messenger is expected by the chorus and Elektra. He is not actually announced. Elektra says, "Where are those that can give us news?" and the chorus assures her they will come. In the very next line the messenger appears saying, "Ah maidens, I am come to report that Aigisthus is dead." There are a few comments and then a long story. No comments follow and no exit is indicated.

The situation in the *Helen* is complicated by the difficulties of the play, but at 597 a messenger bursts in unannounced stating his own arrival and at 1512 another does the same thing, but in

STOCK CHARACTERS

this case the technique is more conventional. He bids Theonoe listen to him and states that Helen is gone. After a few questions and answers he gives a long story which presents no characterization and does not motivate an exit.

In the *Phoenissae*, at line 1062, the messenger enters asking if anyone is at home. Iokaste comes out and, after a short and rapid conversation, the long story follows. Again there is no prepared exit. Very similar is the messenger in the *Orestes*, although at 852 he is announced by the chorus as coming. He enters with exclamations and after questioning gives his long story with some slight characterization but with no prepared exit.

The messengers in the *Bacchae* are like almost everything in that play, somewhat out of the ordinary. The first one is announced by Dionysus at line 660. He does not exclaim on entering but makes a brief statement and after a few lines of conversation gives his long account of his doings on Kithaeron. The story is poetic to a greater extent than would be expected from a rustic character but there is evident attempt to give character detail. There is no motivation of the messenger's exit. The second messenger arrives at line 1024 and makes announcement of his own entrance. The chorus only is present and the messenger first makes the concise statement that Pentheus is dead. He is briefly questioned and tells his long dramatic story which again is too brilliant for his character and, with no conversation at the end, makes his exit without any dramatic explanation.

It is clear that Euripides' practice was to accept the tradition that happenings off stage should be reported in epic form by some messenger. In some cases the messenger was a character and in such cases his entrance and exit were easily motivated. On the other hand he might be merely a piece of stage mechanism, in which case some attempt was made to motivate his entrance but practically none to remove him from the stage convincingly. The speeches by the messengers are occasionally adapted to the character of the speaker but at times this is entirely overlooked and the narrative is not in character. The messenger in such cases approaches closely to the messenger of

Seneca who simply carried the tradition to the final point at which the messenger ceased to be an individual at all and became merely a conventional mouthpiece. The variety of Euripides' plays more than anything else accounts for the variety of the messenger speeches, although it is true that he showed interest at times in creating a really individual character for the part. Seneca's messengers might readily be interchanged, so that we think of them not as so many different characters presenting something that has happened out of sight, but merely as a typical character, always the same, serving this particular function.

The messengers of Euripides are certainly no stock characters. Nevertheless the assumption that Euripides' treatment of them was typical of Greek tragedy would not be justified. The question is by no means so simple as that.

In Sophocles, for example, there are messengers who are fully as colorless as those of Seneca. The messenger who announces the blinding of Oedipus has no particular individuality. The exclamatory entrance is there and the quick summing up of the whole report, to be expanded later at length with all the proper setting of a short narrative. It is interesting that no exit is prepared for him and that, in spite of the careful technique of Sophocles, there is no indication of how this messenger ever leaves the stage. In the *Oedipus at Colonos* the messenger enters abruptly after a choral ode and tells first in a few lines and then in a long narrative the story of Oedipus' translation. He is merely the spokesman of the playwright and again it is interesting that there is no exit prepared for him. In the *Antigone*, the real messenger toward the end begins with ten or twenty lines of philosophizing until interrupted by the chorus. The narrative follows and again there is no prepared exit. In this play a contrast is furnished by the role of the guard in the early part of the play acting in reality as a messenger. This guard is thoroughly individualistic and has something of the mildly comic character of the herdsman in the *Iphigeneia*. He does, however, pass from the brief to the extended narrative just as the ordinary messenger does, but it is a striking fact that his exit is carefully prepared. There is a final messenger in the *Antigone* who has no long speech, no character, and no exit. In the *Philoktetes*, there is no messenger and in the *Elektra* only the old Paedagogos who has the function of a messenger with his false narrative. He is, however, a real character and the technique is handled with care. On the contrary, in the *Ajax*, the messenger has a short announcement followed by questions and a long narrative, but has no individuality and no exit.

In general then, it is clear that Sophocles at times used characters as messengers, drew them with care, and worked them successfully into the technique of the play. At other times he used them as mere pieces of the stage machinery to report something happening off stage. And in such instances his regular procedure was to disregard the dramatic demand for a motivated exit. In this more mechanical function the messenger has a definite role which is that of a messenger only and not at all that of a character. As such he reappears in Euripides, later to be more mechanically employed by Seneca. But Euripides with his interest in lesser characters and more ordinary people could not resist the appeal of developing a messenger here and there into an interesting and real character. Just as the porter in *Macbeth* becomes one of the most striking features of the play, so the messenger in the *Iphigeneia* remains in the memory after many another more important character has vanished. This was, however, a development which did not apparently carry over into Seneca. The Senecan messenger has no individuality.

It is perhaps a foolish thing to try to find the origin of the messenger in Aeschylus. The play in his day was still very close to the choral performance and yet, for this very reason and because of the simplicity of the structure, a messenger of some sort was perhaps the most natural method of extending the field of action. Furthermore, by the time of Aeschylus' death most of the characteristic lines of dramatic construction had been at least defined.

In the *Suppliants* there is no actual messenger. The action which takes place at a distance is reported by Danaus who is a regular character with clearly drawn characteristics, who leaves the stage for a purpose and comes back to report his success in the town. He is a messenger, but he is not merely a messenger, and so far as is noticeable there is no special technique for introducing his report. He is not unlike Kreon in the *Oedipus* of Sophocles except for the fact that he has been in the play before he makes his report and that his reëntry is therefore simple.

In the *Persians* there is a case of action reported when Atossa tells the chorus about her dream. Here again, however, Atossa is a chief character in the play and there is nothing to suggest the technique of the messenger of later times. At line 249, however, there is a messenger who enters, introduced by the chorus with brief remarks. He addresses his country immediately on entrance and announces concisely that the host is lost. The chorus wails but does not ask questions. Atossa, however, breaks in and asks who is dead and who is not. With more interspersed questions by the Queen the messenger talks at great length. The scene is a long one and one phrase of epic character was destined to have long-lived influence in the tragedy: "There is an island hard by Salamis." This, I should say, was the first messenger, the ancestor of an extensive progeny. In the *Seven Against Thebes* there are two messengers. After Eteocles has made his speech to the people, opening the play, a messenger enters, at least reasonably prepared for by the last lines of Eteocles' speech. He addresses the King, explains himself, and reports on the army. There is just one speech and at the end he goes back to his job. He is reasonably in character as a soldier, but no particular effort is made apparently to picture him vividly. His main purpose in the play is to present the information which he gives. At line 371 the chorus announces the return of this messenger and there follows the long scene in which he tells of the seven heroes while Eteocles tells of the Thebans who oppose them. In this scene of course lies the central element of the play. The messenger has no particular characterization, but this seems to be hardly due so much to the fact that he is a messenger as to the general construction of the play which is largely a vehicle for these descriptions and others. No exit is provided for the messenger.

The second messenger of the *Seven* comes in at line 792, abruptly and unannounced. He addresses the chorus, thus furnishing his own technical entrance. He has no long story but simply announces the victory. No exit is furnished him. Similarly, at line 1010, a herald announces Kreon's decree with regard to the brothers. He has no exit and like the messenger is not a carefully drawn character.

In the *Prometheus*, Hermes might be considered to a certain degree a messenger, bringing the command of Zeus to Prometheus. He is, however, remarkably well drawn and his exit well motivated. He is in reality a character used to perform part of the function of a messenger.

In the *Agamemnon*, the chorus announces the entrance of Clytemnestra at 257 and asks her about the news. She is at first concise and then in answer to questions tells about the beacon message from Troy. It is not unlike a messenger's report, but the Queen is a chief character of course in the play and is much more carefully presented than any messenger. Later on, at 489, the chorus announces a herald who after a long preamble and some slight conversation produces his report at length with two interruptions by the chorus. No exit is furnished him and no particular character.

This is the extent of the messenger service in Aeschylus. The function of a person to report something from a distance has been established, but the delight in epic narrative and the fact that careful depiction of the different characters has as yet hardly become a recognized necessity in the tragedy are sufficient explanation for the fact that the messengers are sometimes not clearly presented as individuals. There is no feeling of a recognizable bit of machinery.

A second character which reappears more than once in Seneca is the out-and-out villain determined to do harm, usually in the nature of revenge. The characterization in such a part is ordinarily accomplished by monologue, the speaker goading himself to fury in order to accomplish his desire. Such are Medea's self-lashings (l. 40):

> Within his very vitals seek thy way
> And if thou livest, soul of mine, if aught
> Of former vigor still remains, drive out
> All womanish fears and make thy hardened mind
> A Caucasus indeed.

Or again (l. 54):

> End all delay, the home I won by theft,
> I'll leave with crime.

Medea is not, however, portrayed solely in monologue. The effect is reinforced by conversations with her nurse who acts as a foil and urges restraint.

Nurse. Kings must be feared. *Medea.* My father was a king.
Nurse. Dost not fear arms? *Medea.* Not though they're born of earth.
Nurse. Thou'lt die. *Medea.* I wish it. *Nurse.* Flee. *Medea.* I'd blush to flee.
Nurse. Medea. *Medea.* I'll be Medea. *Nurse.* And yet thou art
 A mother. *Medea.* To whom thou seest.

This helps distinctly in building the picture of Medea, but she adds to it by further monologue, as for example, at line 397:

> And if thou askest, wretched soul, what bounds
> To set to hatred, imitate thy love.
> Shall I without revenge suffer these rites
> Of royal marriage, shall this day slip by
> In idleness?

Finally, the report of Medea's incantations delivered by the nurse supplements the picture which is consistent throughout. The elements of importance at the moment, however, are the monologue and the rapid dialogue.

The first entrance of Clytemnestra in the *Agamemnon* is accomplished with the words:

STOCK CHARACTERS

> Come, slothful soul, why ponder safe designs?
> Why hesitate? The better way is closed.
> Time was thou couldst have guarded with thy faith
> The royal couch and scepter still unstained.
> Now faith is dead and piety and right,
> And since that dead can never know return,
> Give rein to crime and spur on villainy.
> By guilt alone is guilty way made safe.

The nurse argues with her in a conventional way urging every point that standard morality could suggest while Clytemnestra has a cynical response to each, and finally addresses her soul once more with even more violent castigation.

Atreus is almost the male counterpart of Clytemnestra. He appears in the *Thyestes* with his satellite but addressing himself:

> Coward, inert and nerveless, and (worst charge
> Against a mighty tyrant) unavenged
> In spite of wrongs. Up, up my soul and do
> What no posterity shall e'er approve,
> Yet none keep silent. Some unholy act
> Thou must devise, cruel and bloody, such
> That even Thyestes' self shall wish it his.

The satellite makes the same conventional protests that the nurses made to the female villains and with the same result.

The *Hercules on Oeta* furnishes a variation in the technique of presenting the villain. In the first place, the nurse speaks a monologue declaiming on the hardness of a woman scorned. Deianeira substitutes a prayer for vengeance to Juno for the familiar monologue addressed to the villain's soul. But this is not so different as at first it seems, for part of her prayer is this:

> If beast cannot be found to attack him, then
> Guide me I pray until my soul conceive
> Some proper vengeance. I myself can be
> All that is needful.

The nurse makes all the conventional protests. There is less rapid interchange between the heroine and the nurse than in some of the other plays, but it is no different in content and the longer speeches of Deianeira serve the purpose of the more usual long monologue; she is lashing herself to action.

Each of these four characters, Medea, Clytemnestra, Atreus, and Deianeira, is conspicuous for a deliberate attempt to rouse himself or herself to sufficient fury to act in a way admittedly villainous and inhuman. Each is accompanied by a confidante, a foil intended to put forward a weak, conventional, ineffective protest, and the more to emphasize the character of the villain.

In the case of Atreus, there is an element not present in those of the three women. Atreus is a man of power, a tyrant. This he admits himself in his second line and he glories in being in the fullest sense of the word a tyrant.

> This is the greatest boon of royal power:
> A people must endure its master's deeds,
> Endure and also praise.
> True praise may happen to a humble man,
> The false but to a tyrant.
> Honor and loyalty and faith are best
> Virtues of private men, kings may proceed
> By whatsoever way they will.

The character of tyrant is not in this instance very sharply distinguished from that of an ordinary villain although the point is emphasized by the chorus that follows this particular act, developing the Stoic contrast between the king and the tyrant. In the next act, too, Thyestes develops the Stoic thesis of the futility of high position and the blessings of humility. The role of Atreus takes on, therefore, a little more significance. His entrance in the following act, gloating over the imminent fall of his victim and his even worse ecstasy over his fiendish accomplishment, together complete the picture, especially the incredible jeering at Thyestes after the latter has been duped into eating his own children, culminating in Atreus' last word, the final line of the play:

> I leave thee to thy sons for punishment.

Lycus in the *Hercules* is another tyrant. His credo is this (511):

> Who uses death for every punishment
> Knows not the role of Tyrant; better far
> To bid the wretched live, the happy die.

This dogma he lives up to by refusing death to Amphitryon while he joyously prepares a pyre for Hercules. But Lycus is only a very minor tyrant, destined to fall before the hero on his return. The characteristics are there: disregard of justice, utter absence of human sympathy, self-aggrandizement, brutality of word and deed.

We are almost led to expect another tyrant in *Agamemnon* by the remark of Aegisthus (l. 250): King of Mycenae once, he shall return a tyrant. But Agamemnon has one scene only in the whole play that bears his name and that is a short scene with Cassandra in which he greets his home, comforts his captive, and expresses his homage to Jupiter and Juno. There is nothing of the tyrant in this scene. Furthermore, the character of Aegisthus is the villainous one of the play and yet he is not in a position to become a true tyrant.

In view of the general belief that the tyrant is a favorite role of Senecan tragedy and that Seneca gave to it its conventional characteristics, this is a very small crop of tyrants. The curious fact is that there is one tyrant only drawn at all in full and he, Atreus, is not *primarily* a tyrant, but a villain seeking revenge. Lycus is introduced by Amphitryon as "grim with a countenance that threatens ill, alike in heart and gait, in his right hand wielding another's scepter." And Lycus himself enters boasting to no one and to no purpose his wide possessions and the fact that he holds them by force, and he threatens Megara with this power, but, as we have seen, he is a short-lived and unimportant tyrant. Kreon and Jason are even less complete as types. The fact is that the accepted feeling that Seneca developed the stock melodramatic tyrant rests in part on the casual references to the tyrant throughout the plays and only in part on the actual character as presented. Atreus is without doubt a model but he is almost alone and not, like the messengers and villains and confidantes, one of a uniform series.

Incidental mention has been made of the nurse or confidante as a recurring character in the plays. Only the *Hercules Furens* and the *Oedipus* entirely lack such a character. The nurse in the *Phaedra* is perhaps the most complete example. Her mistress in the first act has spoken a long monologue filled with horror and self-pity. At line 129 the nurse addresses her and urges her to check the flame of love, herself making a long speech with an occasional rather superficial, commonplace epigram. Medea answers at length and the argument finally comes down to shorter speeches and even broken lines. The nurse urges moderation until she finds that Phaedra is determined to die, when the nurse's easy morals permit her to change her tone and advise yielding to love and winning Hippolytus. Later when the hero enters she urges him to relax his austere life. When Phaedra fails to win Hippolytus, the nurse rouses herself to action by the device of lashing her own soul—a device particularly appropriate to the villain but not uncommon elsewhere—and carries out her unfortunate inspiration of calling on the citizens and accusing Hippolytus of assault on Phaedra.

Except for the length of some of the speeches and the violent action at the end, Phaedra's nurse might be Medea's. This latter protests in the first act against her mistress' violent emotion and advances every orthodox argument against it in epigrammatic platitudes. Later in the play the nurse acts as a messenger to report Medea's incantations. Unlike the attendant of Phaedra, she has no further action in the play.

The nurse of Clytemnestra in the same way tries to soothe her mistress, pointing out the wickedness and danger of violence. She makes one rather long speech and is a bit overlearned.

Thyestes' satellite is also no different from the other confidantes. He is there to offer a foil and to present the commonplace objections to violent action, fear on the one hand, virtue on the other. Reminded sharply of his own position, he promises silence and disappears.

In the *Hercules on Oeta*, the nurse has the first entrance and exclaims at some length and with no little learning before she announces the coming of Deianeira. The latter bemoans her lot and the nurse interrupts with a fairly long speech, then a shorter one and finally in lines and half-lines. At the end she comes perhaps closer than any other of the confidantes to showing an individual character of her own:

> By these gray locks I beg, a suppliant,
> And by these breasts that erstwhile succored thee:
> Expel these furious angers from thy heart
> Nor suffer horrid thought of dreadful death.

All of the confidantes are presumably old, a fact which makes this touch less striking.

The interesting thing about the three old women and two old men is the role they play, on the whole mechanical, of bringing out the grim determination or violent attitude of their superiors. Their own lines are regularly full of proverbial wisdom and conventional fears. They really take to a considerable degree the part of the chorus leader in the Greek tragedy. The Senecan chorus has degenerated into a lyric interlude and the chorus leader is scarcely a character any longer. In each play this leader does speak a few lines, either introducing a new character or giving audience to a messenger, but the character which furnishes the pedestrian opposition to a more important character is no longer the chorus but the confidante.

In the *Choephoroi* Aeschylus first presented a faithful old nurse. Like many of her successors in later drama, Orestes' nurse is loyal to her foster child in the midst of a hostile environment. She has no scruples about deceiving her masters, for her only ethical principle is loyalty to Orestes. She appears in one scene only, sent from the palace on an errand, and her conversation is solely with the chorus. In other words, while she is a nurse, she is not a confidante. She is a character in the play and does not serve as a foil for another character. She has nothing in common with the nurses in Seneca except the accident of her profession. Sophocles also has little to offer as a model. In the *Elektra*, the paedagogos is solely a prologue character and the nurse in the *Trachinian Women*, in addition to her function in the prologue, acts later as a messenger. These two examples, however, from Sophocles contain the germ of the stock character of the confidante, a character existing almost exclusively as a sympathetic audience for someone more important.

The extended use made by Euripides of such a character is accompanied by a development of the type. He does not to any great extent crystallize it into a stock type but there is a distinct family resemblance between Hermione's nurse in the *Andromache* and Phaedra's in the *Hippolytus*, between Medea's nurse and the old paedagogos who converses with Antigone in the prologue of the *Phoenissae*. And in the *Medea*, the device of an exposition by means of a conversation between two such characters is well developed. The nurse in the *Hippolytus* is perhaps the least attractive, but at the same time the most completely portrayed.

Seneca then found in the Greek drama the character of the confidante, usually an old and faithful servitor somewhat addicted to commonplace philosophy, serving a useful function as auditor but not devoid of individuality. Partly by too free a use of so convenient a device, partly by a failure to characterize to any extent the individual nurses and pedagogues, and perhaps most of all by giving them too heavy a burden of commonplace wisdom and unnatural rhetorical learning, he left to posterity a stock dramatic character, the confidante.

CHAPTER XI
CONCLUSION

IT is not for the classicist to trace the development of Senecan influence in English drama where he can at best be only an enthusiastic amateur. It would however be unsportsmanlike, after analyzing "Seneca, his style," not at least to indicate what to the classicist seems to be the most fruitful line of investigation.

First of all, it should be recognized that the question of "good" or "bad" literature is not involved. The present study has surely made clear that Seneca's plays could never rank with those of Sophocles in dramatic greatness, and most of the English plays of the late sixteenth century are dreary enough reading today. But that is not the question. Sidney, who found no model to compare with Seneca, and Symonds saying that "such being the nature of Seneca's tragedies, we must condemn them as pernicious models for incipient literature," are both, so far as the present problem is concerned, beside the point. Good or bad, the plays of Seneca *were* used as models and the important thing is to understand just what it was that they contributed and what effect that has had on the literature that did the borrowing.

That Seneca did exercise a great influence on pre-Shakespearean drama is generally admitted. Cunliffe and Brooke in recent times have pointed out the evidence and to a certain extent analyzed it. But it is essential, I think, to indicate more in detail the appearance of such elements as have been isolated in the present study.

George Peele might have been adapting Seneca when he began the prologue of the *Arraignment of Paris:*

> Condemned soul, Ate from lowest hell
> And deadly rivers of th' infernal Jove
> Where bloodless ghosts in pains of endless date
> Fill ruthless ears with never-ceasing cries,
> Behold I come in place and bring beside
> The bane of Troy.

Here is the external motivation in a detached prologue with the "I come" technique to explain the identity of the speaker. In Lord Brooke's *Alaham*, a ghost speaks the prologue, and in the *Spanish Tragedy* a ghost driven by revenge. The tone quality so evident in Seneca is the same in all of these. Perhaps the *Misfortunes of Arthur*, with Gorlois' ghost, furnishes as typical a Senecan atmosphere as any. *Gismond of Salerne* is interesting in having the divine motivation in the prologue, in this case by Cupid, while at the opening of Act IV a strong Senecan flavor is given by a supplementary prologue pronounced by Megaera. Discord, in *Caesar's Revenge*, has no Fury, but does not need any helper to spread a tone of horror through the prologue:

> Hearke how the Romaine drums sound bloud and death,
> And Mars high mounted on his Thracian steede
> Runs madding through Pharsalia's purple fields.
> The earth that's wont to be a tombe for men
> Is now entomb'd with carkases of men.

This last conceit would have won Seneca's commendation and jealousy, and he would surely have recognized the model for the astronomical and historical window dressing that follows. The author thought so well of his prologue device that he brought in Discord again before each act, a chorus or a repeated prologue as you will.

The prologue detached from the play proper and assigned to an otherwise extraneous character did not long survive in English drama, except as it carried still further the process begun by Euripides and, like the prologue of Roman comedy, became the mouthpiece of the author directly to address his audience about his play, not from within the piece but from without. This use is perfectly familiar, for example, in Chapman's plays.

Like the prologue, the chorus entered English drama abruptly and definitely, only to be abandoned later. In *Jocasta*, the chorus deals with Necessity and the golden mean, the familiar sailor furnishing illustration, a Horatian inheritance by way of Seneca. The choruses are regularly moralizing poems rather than songs and with the *Spanish Tragedy* the barest remnant of a chorus is left consisting of the ghost of Andrea and Revenge:

CONCLUSION

> Here sit we down to see the mystery
> And serve for chorus in this tragedy.

They serve as chorus by interjecting a few lines of comment between the acts. And such was in reality the most tangible service of the chorus to English drama: it emphasized the act division so important to a proper dramatic development.

Of the types of long speech in Seneca the most popular with his British emulators was the soliloquy. Videna opens the fourth act of *Gorboduc* with familiar question and exclamation:

> Why should I live and linger forth my time
> In longer life to double my distress?
> O me, most woeful wight, whom no mishap
> Long ere this day could have bereaved hence.

Her soliloquy fills eighty-one lines, is motivated neither at entrance nor at exit, and has no possible listener. Cleopatra, in the first act of Daniel's play, has more than twice as many lines, opening on the same key.

> Yet do I live and yet doth breath extend
> My life beyond my life? Nor can my grave
> Shut up my griefes to make my end my end?

It is worth noting too that this long speech ends with a foreshadowing of evil:

> That hereby yet the world shall see that I
> Although unwise to live had witt to die.

A Medean touch is evident in Alaham's soliloquy in the first act of Lord Brooke's play:

> You spirits there growne subtile by your age!
> Not you that doe inhabite Paradise
> Whose constant ioyes most unacquainted be
> With all affections that should make you wise!
> No, I invoke the blacke Eternity
> As apt to put in action as devise!
> Helpe me that have to do with princes' power
> To plucke down king, with king's authority
> And make men slaves with show of liberty.
> Free hope from evill lucke revenge from feare;
> Ruine and change adorne you every where.

Later in the same play, Hala is even more thoroughly Medean:

> Now Hala, seeke thy sex; lend Scorn thy wit
> To work new patterns of revenges in.
> Let Rage despise to feed on private blood;
> Her honor lies above where danger is
> In Thrones of kings, in universall woe.

Perhaps the best illustration of that type of monologue which opens with a sententious bit of moralizing is the opening speech of *Bussy d'Ambois* with its first line, "Fortune, not Reason, rules the state of things."

The Senecan monologue of this type had a longer career in English literature than some of the other elements of Latin drama. In the hands of Shakespeare it attained perhaps its greatest heights and produced many of his most famous passages. To illustrate the close relation between Shakespeare's great speeches and their Senecan prototypes it will be necessary only to recall the familiar monologue of Lady Macbeth:

> Come, you spirits
> That tend on mortal thoughts, unsex me here,
> And fill me, from the crown to the toe, top-full
> Of direst cruelty! make thick my blood,
> Stop up the access and passage to remorse,
> That no compunctious visitings of nature
> Shake my fell purpose, nor keep peace between
> The effect and it! Come to my woman's breasts,
> And take my milk for gall, you murdering ministers,
> Wherever in your sightless substances
> You wait on nature's mischief! Come, thick night,
> And pall thee in the dunnest smoke of hell,
> That my keen knife see not the wound it makes,
> Nor heaven peep through the blanket of the dark,
> To cry, "Hold, hold!"

Such soliloquies are perfectly familiar. There are also pronouncements such as Gorboduc addresses to his lords, there are arguments with choral lines separating the long speeches, as we find in *Jocasta*, and, as in Seneca, so in English plays, we find the same elongated members of dialogue which defy classification.

CONCLUSION

But of all the forms of long speeches the soliloquy and the messenger's speech are the two that found keenest response in the hearts of the Elizabethans and also the most practical demand on the part of English playwrights.

The messenger speeches are often astonishingly close to their Latin models. In the fourth act of the *Misfortunes of Arthur* the messenger enters with exclamations of a rather literary tinge:

> Thou Echo shrill that hauntst the hollow hills,
> Leave off that woont to snatch the latter word:
> Howle on a whole discourse of our distresse,
> Clip of no clause: sound out a perfect sense.

After some rapid conversation, in which he is urged to speak and during which he demurs with the Senecan conceit, "Small griefs can speak, the great astonisht stand," he begins his long and leisurely story as follows:

> Now that the time drew on, when both the camps
> Should meet in Cornwall fieldes th' appointed place.

Another typical messenger reports the battle in the fifth act of *Jocasta*. In *Cleopatra* and in *Philotas*, the messenger reports the catastrophe, in both cases to the chorus, while in the second act of *Arthur* he seems to have no audience. The *Spanish Tragedy* (Act I. Sc. 1) furnishes a perfect example of the messenger speech transferred to one of the characters. The Spanish king and his general have a short preliminary conversation in which the latter states succinctly the import of his message. The king is not satisfied but wishes more detailed account of the battle. Whereupon the general begins:

> Where Spain and Portingal do jointly knit
> Their frontiers, leaning on each other's bound,
> There met our armies in their proud array.

The story is dramatic, rhetorical, long. Chapman, in the second act of *Bussy d'Ambois*, produces a most orthodox messenger who bursts into our presence with learned classical allusions quite beyond his station:

> What Atlas or Olympus lifts his head
> So far past covert, that with air enough
> My words may be inform'd and from his height
> I may be seen and heard through all the world?

After five lines and the proper request from his auditor, he tells his tale at full length.

The rapid dialogue is often more extensive in the early English plays, as was natural from their origin, but it was reduced in the Senecan imitations, where it shows much of the rhetorical effect in epigrammatic repartee. In the third act of *Jocasta*, for instance, there is some thoroughly Senecan sparring between Kreon and Meneceus:

> *Kreon.* Thy wit is wylie for to work thy wo.
> *Meneceus.* Oh tender pitie moveth me thereto.
> *Kreon.* A beast is he that kils himselfe with a knife
>   Of pitie to preserve an other's life.
> *Meneceus.* Yet wise is he that doth obey the gods.
> *Kreon.* The gods will not the death of any wight.
> *Meneceus.* Whose life they take, they give him life also.
> *Kreon.* But thou dost strive to take thy life thy selfe.
> *Meneceus.* Nay, them to obey that will I shall not live.

One other illustration will suffice. In the third act of *Alaham*, Hala and the nurse are in conversation:

> *Nurse.* What force can princes forces overbeare?
> *Hala.* That force which makes their pride it cannot feare.
> *Nurse.* How enters malice where there is mistrust?
> *Hala.* With tribute into State: to kings with lust.
> *Nurse.* What way to these? *Hala.* Prosperity, successe.
> *Nurse.* These add more power. *Hala.* So much suspects the leese.
> *Nurse.* What can you add? *Hala.* Presents, obedience, praise.
>   They need not knock that enter in to please.
> *Nurse.* Flatteries are plain. *Hala.* To kings that see their ill.
> *Nurse.* Kings jealous are. *Hala.* Of truth not of their will.
> *Nurse.* Usurpers feare. *Hala.* Worth not humilitie.

It seems at first rather strange that there is not more trace of the epigrammatic conversation to be found in the tragedies of Shakespeare. As a matter of fact the rather sudden elimination of this element is significant. Shakespeare, making use of all that tragedy had learned under the classical discipline and applying a genius wholly comparable with the Greek, produced plays in which there was no longer need of the rhetorical and somewhat superficial attractions that were intended to hold the unwilling auditors of a recited drama. Once more, important plots returned to the stage and in the development of plot Shakespeare required an economy of means quite foreign to the genius of Seneca. As in Sophocles so in Shakespeare, the dialogue must be used thriftily to build up character and situation and there is little time for rhetorical fireworks. Such epigrammatic sparring as does occur in Shakespeare is to be found in the comedies where it is part of the entertainment and where the plot does not require the same tense development.

The passage quoted above from *Alaham* shows also the influence of the Senecan confidante, a character which, like the tyrant and the villain, is too familiar and persisted too long to require extensive illustration. It is sufficient to recall the old nurse of Juliet, who has, to be sure, become a real character but whose origin is clear, Saturninus in *Titus Andronicus*, and Lorenzo in the *Spanish Tragedy*. So too the ghost and the rest of the supernatural paraphernalia, the soothsayers and sorcerers, the dreams and prophecies, these have been much used and widely studied. The five ghosts in the *Revenge of Bussy d'Ambois* would have given Seneca pause. As to the straining after epigrams and the philosophic platitudes which these epigrams expressed, it is sufficient to remember Chapman's conception of the purpose of tragedy as he expressed it in the dedication of the *Revenge:* "material instruction, elegant and sententious excitation to virtue, and deflection from her contrary, being the soul, limbs, and limits of an authentical tragedy." Rather than multiply illustrations of Senecan reminiscence, I shall try to estimate the essential influence of Senecan tragedy as a whole on the English.

First of all, the classical form was imposed upon the native drama which had been rambling and formless in the extreme. The division of a play into acts was perhaps the greatest single factor in English dramatic development. It meant that the playwright could no longer simply tell a story beginning where he saw fit and ending in much the same manner. It meant that he must study his material, make proper selection, and distribute the material between five parts. Once this became necessary, it involved the study of what was to be done in each act, in what way each part furthered the plot as a whole. Mechanical as it seems, this division into acts was in itself a tremendous contribution to the English stage. It is the most essential part of the discipline which was classical tragedy's gift to England. The chorus, therefore, which soon died out was no negligible influence, for it marked definitely this act division and in addition, by its comments on the action, contributed to the discipline which required of the playwright a study of his own material.

But if the form was new and strange, so also was the subject matter. The abrupt introduction of almost alien plots, new characters with strange points of view, this too caused a more studied and deliberate composition. It discounted for the moment the facility which was destined to bring the morality to premature decay and enforced upon the playwright a second discipline. In this was involved, I should say, the care of expression, the passionate devotion to the effective word, the epigrammatic phrase, the imposing speech, in fact all the much-abused rhetoric of Senecan plays. The rhetoric may offend our supersensitive ears but its requirements were again an instrument of discipline against the slipshod colloquialisms of the contemporary stage in England.

Much has been said about the cosmopolitan tone introduced by Seneca. I have tried to indicate what was the cosmopolitanism of his age and I think, now that his product is before us as a whole, we can perhaps make a wider generalization. The tone which Senecan plays gave to Elizabethan came as a violent change from the tone of the Miracles and Moralities. It is sophisticated instead of naïve; it is rhetorical instead of plain, which perhaps implies an insincerity; it is pagan and moral rather than Christian and religious; it is of the nobility and gentility and not of the commonality; it is wholly serious and tragic, never injecting comedy or showing any hospitality to relieving humor. The whole tone of the new drama was different. It was not at first an influence but a substitution. And that was of course why at first the new was ignored by the populace and confined to university and court influence. But its disciplinary value was too potent and too obvious to shrivel in the cold of the cloister or become too rank in the hothouse atmosphere of the court. It eventually, though more slowly, brought popular tragedy under some discipline and thereby saved its life. Symonds grows lyrical over the muse of romantic drama that made English poetry great because it resisted the attacks of the artificial classicism of Seneca. It would in all probability have died prematurely without the discipline which made possible the freedom of a Shakespeare. The hard training was necessary first and Seneca was opportunely there to give it.

Nor was the pill wholly unsugared. The romantic in the drama, that element so hard to define, that which even though dispensable is injected into the play to appeal to the emotional interest of the spectator without detracting too much from the plot, this romantic element was by no means lacking in Seneca. His popular appeal was not that of romantic love, to be sure, but it was the appeal of romance nonetheless. Aeschylus, in the age of colonization, had introduced the strange features of life beyond the frontiers to feed the curiosity of his audience. That was romantic appeal. To Nero's courtiers there was little enough that was novel with which to win their attention. It required exaggerated effort of rhetoric and melodrama. These two combined in the accounts of horror which often had no honest function in the plot, but became too frequently the prominent part of the play because of their popularity. This type of romance Seneca bequeathed to England. Coming from a recited drama to an acted, it at once produced what Horace warned against, acted horrors on the stage. It was not because of fine feelings but of inadequate facilities that Seneca restricted his horrors. He would gladly have brought torture and murder on the stage had he had a stage, and his audience, far from disapproving bloody horrors, went to the pantomime and the gladiatorial show to sate their appetites as soon as they could hurry away from his duller recitations.

How rapidly the Senecan influence was absorbed and digested is obvious to every reader of Shakespeare, and the Senecan influences in Shakespeare's plays can best be analyzed and presented by Shakespeare scholars. The larger aspects are, however, obvious. The English translations of Seneca appeared from 1559 on, the collected volume by Thomas Newton in 1581. *Macbeth* cannot have been first produced later than 1610. Within the space of one generation, therefore, the Senecan influence had done its work.

It might seem at first glance that there is little enough in *Macbeth* to suggest any Roman influence at all. Yet it is necessary only to retrace the steps of the investigators through the plays of Marlowe and Kyd and Chapman and the rest and to recall the earlier, uncontaminated Miracle and Morality and Interlude to see how mistaken would be any such conclusion. The very unity of plot which marks the Shakespearean tragedy is foreign to the earlier plays, as is the concentrated tone of horror, the division into acts, the whole return to something of the Greek conception of tragedy.

In detail, too, the Senecan influence is obvious. The very opening lines, the first witch scene, which might at first seem wholly native, surely reflect the method of the Roman playwright, the use of a tone-setting prologue loosely attached to the play proper and by preference introducing a grim supernatural motivation. Shakespeare has given to the Senecan prologue much of the picturesque, and the witches are undoubtedly the product of genius rather than rhetoric, but the relationship is clear. Furthermore, with something of the effect of a chorus, the witches return from time to time, breaking the action dramatically and emphasizing the tone of horror and dread. In this respect they are reminiscent of the crude technique of the *Spanish Tragedy*, itself so clearly a legacy from Rome.

CONCLUSION 199

The bleeding sergeant who opens the action proper with his report from the battle is no Senecan messenger, but neither is he a realistic character. His rhetoric betrays him.

> As two spent swimmers that do cling together
> And choke their art.

A bleeding sergeant about to faint would hardly have thought of a series of fine figures of speech; certainly he would not have said, "Or memorize another Golgotha." This element of the rhetorical is perhaps most evident in the soliloquies in which the play abounds. It will be enough to recall Macbeth's speech in the second act, "Is this a dagger which I see before me?" ending with the lines that have a familiar ring of foreboding in them:

> Hear it not, Duncan, for it is a knell
> That summons thee to heaven, or to hell.

There are many details of *Macbeth* that derive ultimately from Seneca but which need be mentioned only: the ghost of Banquo, the witches' brew, the unworthy scene in which Macduff's son is murdered, the extensive use of the "aside." At the same time it should not be forgotten that Shakespeare has resolutely turned aside from any acceptance of a Senecan model. He uses a mixture of prose and verse; he changes his scene at will; he spreads his action over some nine days; he multiplies his characters; he reverts to the admixture of comedy in the porter scene. His play is not a Senecan play but the Senecan elements, largely absorbed, are still evident and it seems no exaggeration to say that *Macbeth* without Seneca would have been impossible.

It may cause surprise that the injection of a second-rate drama into one in the primary stage could have had so vital an influence. I think that again this tendency to classify as good and bad obscures the question. Seneca may be bad. For certain ages and tastes he was good. What matters it? He exerted a great disciplinary influence on a drama in swaddling clothes and the infant had a most phenomenal development. One thing the critics forget who vituperate the Senecan drama. It was the reproduction in another medium of a drama which they with their habit of evaluation would have to admit was good. The vitality of Greek tragedy was not lost even in the process of evaporation which was necessary to preserve it for two thousand years. Sophocles, presented directly to sixteenth-century England, would have in all probability been passed by. But the evaporated product was acceptable and Seneca by means of his own mediocrity, which was understandable and human, gave to the predecessors of Shakespeare as much as they could absorb of a far greater drama than either he or they could comprehend.

OEDIPUS TYRANNUS
of SOPHOCLES

PROLOGUE

Oedipus.
  My children, ancient Kadmos' newest brood,
  What is this embassy that waits impatient
  Bedecked with suppliant branches? All our town
  Is filled with sound of holy sacrifice
  And paeans too and wailing misery.
  These things, my children, I have deemed it wrong
  To learn from others: I went forth myself,
  I, famed on the lips of all men, Oedipus.
  But tell me, sire—for thou art fit to speak
  For these—in what mood stand ye there? In fear
  Or loyalty? Stony of heart the man
  Who finds no pity for such embassy.

Priest.
  O Oedipus, that rulest o'er my land,
  Thou seest us, how of every age we sit
  Before thy altars, some not yet endowed
  With strength for distant flight, and some
  Heavy with age who serve as priests (myself
  The priest of Zeus) and other some elect
  From all the tribes. Within the market-place
  Sits the whole populace in suppliant garb
  By Pallas' twofold shrine revered, or where
  Ismenus' sacred soil speaks prophecy.
  For, as thou seest too, our commonwealth
  Labors full sore nor yet avails to lift
  Its head above the billowing surge of death,
  Wasting alike in the rich crops of earth
  And in her grazing herds, while women suffer
  The pangs of barren childbirth. Through her midst
  The fire-bearing god, mad pestilence,
  Hurling his shafts, scourges relentlessly
  Our city till, beneath his hand, the home
  Of Kadmos is made void and Hades black
  With groans and lamentations is enriched.
  Not with the gods do I now make thee one
  Nor these thy children seated at thy gate,
  But first of all mankind we reckon thee
  In ways of men and in perplexities
  Haling from heaven above. 'Twas thou that camest

Loosing our Kadmeian city from the toll
We paid the singer of harsh harmonies,
Learning no clue from us: no other man
Instructed thee but by the lore of god,
Men say, believing, thou didst right our life.
Now too, o Oedipus, that rulest all,
Turning to thee we all petition thee:
Discover straight some remedy for us.
It may be thou shalt hearken to the voice
Of god or of some man, thou knowest whose.
For yesterday's experience methinks
Best validates the counsel of today.
Up then, and save thy city, thou who art
Best of mankind; up, gird thyself, for thee
This country calls its savior, honoring
Thy past devotion. Never let memory
Recall thy rule, how once erect we stood
Upraised only to fall. Nay save the state.
A happy rescue from the cursed Sphinx
Thou gavest us long since: be now the same.
And thou wouldst rule this city as thou dost,
Better to rule o'er men than emptiness.
Fortress and ship alike become as naught
Bereft of humankind to dwell therein.

Oedipus.
My children pitiable, not strange to me,
Familiar rather are the things ye ask.
Full well I know your anguish—yet, howe'er
Ye suffer all, there is no one of you
Whose suffering equals mine. Your several griefs
Touch each one man, no other than yourselves:
My spirit groans for all the city—ay,
For me and you alike. Ye rouse me not
From sleep, for, be assured, I have shed tears
Uncounted; many a path my mind has traced,
And that which I have found —one only means
To remedy our lot—that have I followed,
Sending Menoekeus' son, my brother Kreon,
Unto Apollo's Pythian shrine to learn
What word or act of mine might save the state.
Already with the loitering length of days
Time tortures me in wonder how he fares.
For well beyond what old experience

Bids us expect he still is absent. When
He comes, I shall not then be derelict
In my fulfilment of god's whole behest.
Priest.
Timely thy word, O King, for these but now
Point me to where already Kreon comes.
Oedipus.
O Lord Apollo, may he come endued
With bright good fortune, as his eye is bright.
Priest.
'Tis safe to hazard that his news is good:
Else not with fruited laurel were he decked.
Oedipus.
Soon shall we know for he can hear us now.
My lord and kinsman, son of Menoekeus,
What message dost thou bring us from the god?
Kreon.
Good news, for I declare that even ills,
If they but end aright, may all be well.
Oedipus.
What news is this? For neither bold of heart
Nor fearful am I at thy present word.
Kreon.
If thou wouldst hear in presence of these men
I am prepared to speak—or else within.
Oedipus.
Speak to them all. Heavier the grief I bear
For them than for my own heart's suffering.
Kreon.
Speak then I will my message from the god.
Lord Phoebus bade us all outspokenly
Drive forth the pestilence that's bred within
Our land nor fatten it beyond control.
Oedipus.
And with what exorcism? What is the means?
Kreon.
Exile or death, repaying ancient death.
For blood it is that overwhelms our state.
Oedipus.
Upon what man does god decree this chance?
Kreon.
Laius, my lord, was one time sovereign here
Over our land, ere ever thou didst come.

Oedipus.
    I know by hearsay, for I saw him not.
Kreon.
    And he being dead, comes clear god's high command
    Forthwith to punish those his murderers.
Oedipus.
    And they are where? Where shall be found the clue
    Hard to unravel of such ancient crime?
Kreon.
    Within this land he said. That which is sought
    Is found; the unconsidered vanishes.
Oedipus.
    At home or in the country or abroad
    Did Laius happen on his bloody fate?
Kreon.
    Faring upon a mission, as he said,
    Laius returned no more from his emprise.
Oedipus.
    No comrade of the road, no messenger
    Beheld the deed that one might learn from him?
Kreon.
    Dead are they all save one who terrified
    Fled with one word alone of all he saw.
Oedipus.
    And what was that? One thing may lead to much
    If we but gain some slight foothold of hope.
Kreon.
    Robbers he said encountered on the way,
    Not one but many, killed him ruthlessly.
Oedipus.
    How could a robber save by gold suborned
    From Thebes, attain to such bold arrogance?
Kreon.
    Suspicion spake as much but, Laius dead,
    No champion was there in our misery.
Oedipus.
    What dread disaster could restrain the state
    From learning all, its master so destroyed?
Kreon.
    The riddling Sphinx compelled us to resign
    Mystery remote for questions close at hand.
Oedipus.
    From the beginning then I'll prove it clear.

For just is Phoebus, rightly too thyself
Hast laid on me this duty to the dead.
So shalt thou find me rightly an ally
Unto this land obedient to the god.
For not alone as boon to distant friends
But for myself I'll scotch this pestilence.
Seeing that whoso slew him, he likewise
Fearing my venging hand, might slay me too.
Hence if I fail him not I benefit
Myself. Up then, my people, speedily
Stand from these altars, raise your suppliant staves.
Let someone gather here the citizens
Of Thebes, assured that I shall compass all
And we shall stand revealed all fortunate
Under god's guiding help—or fallen quite.

Priest.
My children, let us rise. It was for this
Which now he tells us that we gathered here
And so may Phoebus with his oracle
Be savior too and end the pestilence.

PARODOS

FIRST STROPHE

O thou Word, sweet spoken, of Zeus
    How shall I name thee?
Forth from the Pythian shrine
Gleaming with gold art come
    Unto glorious Thebes.
And my quivering heart is taut and I shudder with fear,
    Thou Delian God,
    As low on my knees I pray.
    Comes there a fate unknown
    Or again with the circling years
    Recurring woe?
Tell me, thou child of golden Hope, Word ever living.

FIRST ANTISTROPHE

First to thee, o daughter of Zeus,
    Deathless Athena,
Make I my suppliant prayer;

Artemis too I call
She who ranges the hills
And she sits on the throne high raised in the gathering place;
And Phoebus who shoots
Afar over earth his darts:
Threefold defenders, come
As of old at our city's need
Ye came to save,
Banishing far the flame of woe: come now to save us.

SECOND STROPHE

Woe, woe is me, countless the pains I bear;
All that is mine is doomed:
No shaft of wit
Brings me deliverance;
No generations new
To cherish my fatherland
No more do the mothers of Thebes, bearing their sons
Suffer the pain and live,
But soul on soul, like birds, ye may see them fly
Swifter than fire
On to the distant strand, home of the western god.

SECOND ANTISTROPHE

Beyond our ken, countless the city's dead;
Foul on the plain they lie
In cruel ranks;
Mothers bereft, gray haired,
In supplication bent
And wives by the altar side,
They groan for the ills that are ours: sorrows untold:
Paeans of woe that burst
From aged lips that moan for a city doomed.
Wherefore for these
Send us some bulwark fair, golden daughter of Zeus.

THIRD STROPHE

Ares too, god of the raging death:
Helmet nor shield are his
But the flame and the shouting.

OEDIPUS OF SOPHOCLES

> Back, turn him back, far from our fatherland,
> > Back on a favoring breeze
> > To Amphitrite's couch
> Or the harbor welcomeless of the Thracian surge.
> > For now if the night leave aught
> > Day comes apace to consume.
> > O, father above, on him,
> > Lord of the lightning flash,
> > Hurl now thy thunderbolt.

THIRD ANTISTROPHE

> Lord of light, god of the golden bow
> > Scatter thy shafts untamed
> > To defend us, we pray thee.
> Aye and the fire gleaming of Artemis
> > Which on the Lycian hills,
> > She flashes peak by peak;
> And the golden mitered god of our native land
> > Whose face with the wine is red,
> > Bacchus, I call, with thy rout
> > Of maenads attended, come.
> > Come with the flaming torch,
> > Smite thou the god disowned.

FIRST EPISODE

Oedipus.
Ye pray, and what ye pray for—if straightway
Ye hearken to my words and give me aid
Against the pestilence—ye may attain:
Deliverance and surcease from your woes—
Words of a stranger to this history,
A stranger to the deed. Not far alone
Could I without a hint pursue the quest.
Wherefore, your latest citizen, do I
Make proclamation to the Kadmeian land:
Whoso of you knows by whose hand assailed
Laius the son of Labdakus was slain
I bid him tell me all. But if he fear
For his own self, then let him none the less
Denounce himself, for he shall suffer naught
Save banishment. So too if any man

Knows that the culprit came from other lands
Let him not hold his tongue, for whoso speaks
Reward is his and gratitude beside.
But if ye will not speak, if dumb with fear
Ye seek to shield or friend or self from harm
Then hearken to the purpose that is mine.
No man soever from this sovereign realm
Whose rule is mine, by shelter or by word
Shall aid the murderer, or e'er admit
His presence at the litany or shrine
Of sacrifice or at the lustral fire,
But thrust him from his home, knowing full well
He is the accursed thing as now the god
By Pythian oracle hath made us know.
So do I purpose to ally myself
With god and with the dead. Here I invoke
This curse upon the guilty one or all
Wretched to plumb the depths of misery.
Likewise upon myself if knowingly
I harbor in my house the murderer
I imprecate the curses I have named.
So upon each of you I lay a charge
To heed these words—for my sake and the god's
And for our city in its barrenness
Abandoned of the gods and perishing.
For even if it were not sent from heaven,
This plague upon us, yet, 'twere unthinkable
To leave still unavenged the death
Of one so noble and your king withal
Nor track it down. Now since I hold the power
That once was his, and am the heir as well
Of his own marriage couch, possess the wife
That lay with him and would have borne to us
A common offspring had not fate ill timed,
Striking him down, forbidden, I pronounce
Myself his champion, even as his son,
And I shall leave no single thing untried
To find and seize that man who put to death
The son of Labdakus, heir to the line
Of Polydorus and of Kadmus too,
Ancient Agenor's latest progeny.
Meantime for such as see not eye to eye
With this my purpose, I invoke the gods

To grant them harvest neither in their fields
Nor in their homes, but with this pestilence
Or some more terrible, to end their line.
But citizens of this Kadmeian realm
That hearken to my words, on them I pray
May Justice smile forever and the gods.
Chorus.
O King, upon my oath as thou dost ask
I speak: I did not kill the man, nor know
The murderer. To say who did the deed
Was Phoebus' task who laid on us the quest.
Oedipus.
Right is thy judgment, but to force the gods
Unwilling, that may no man undertake.
Chorus.
Fain would I say what seemeth second best.
Oedipus.
If there be yet a third best, speak it out.
Chorus.
After lord Phoebus he who seeth most
In harmony, our lord Tiresias,
Might best reward our present questioning.
Oedipus.
Nor has this thought escaped me. I have sent
At Kreon's bidding twice to summon him,
Nor understand why he came not long since.
Chorus.
All other hints were vague and ancient tales.
Oedipus.
What hints then are there? I would know each word.
Chorus.
'Twas said some travelers had murdered him.
Oedipus.
So have I heard, but none saw him who saw.
Chorus.
Nor if he knows what fear is will he stay
When he has heard thy curses now invoked.
Oedipus.
Words may not frighten him who fears no deed.
Chorus.
But lo he comes who shall convict the man.
For these are bringing now the godlike seer
In whom alone of men is born the truth.

Oedipus.
>Tiresias, whose mind doth ponder all
>Things known and things unspeakable on earth
>And in the heavens above, though seeing naught
>Thou knowest in what plight our city stands
>Wherefrom, my lord, we find in thee alone
>Our sole deliverer. For Phoebus' word
>(Perchance thou hast not heard from messengers)
>Comes back in answer to our questionings
>Telling of one release from pestilence
>And only one, if we by searching out
>Should find and slay forthwith the murderers
>Of Laius or should drive them from our land.
>Wherefore begrudge us not thy counseling
>Whether from augury or from the lore
>Of other ways prophetic thou knowest aught.
>But save alike thyself, the city, me,
>And fend from all the taint of murder done.
>For we are in thy hands: man's noblest toil
>Is helping others to the uttermost.

Tiresias.
>Alas, alas, how frightful to be wise
>Where wisdom brings no gain. I knew this well
>But had forgotten. Else had I never come.

Oedipus.
>What sayest thou? How downcast art arrived.

Tiresias.
>Release me to my home. Most easily
>Shall we two bear our fates, if thou consent.

Oedipus.
>Strange are thy words nor friendly to the state
>That gives thee sustenance, if thou speak not.

Tiresias.
>Not so: for thine own words as I perceive
>Come not in season. Be not mine the same.

Oedipus.
>By all the gods I beg thee, leave us not,
>If thou knowest aught, me and these suppliants.

Tiresias.
>Aye for ye all are ignorant. Mine own
>Misfortunes shall I hide, to speak not thine.

Oedipus.
>What is this word? Thou knowest and wilt not speak
>But wouldst betray thy city unto death?

OEDIPUS OF SOPHOCLES 213

Tiresias.
> Neither myself nor thee shall I distress.
> Why ask in vain? Thou shalt not learn from me.

Oedipus.
> Basest of all base men, that wouldst enrage
> The hardest rock, wilt never speak, but still
> Present thyself unmoved in stubbornness?

Tiresias.
> My wrath thou blamest but thine own so near
> Thou seest not, and yet upbraidest me.

Oedipus.
> Who would not rage to hear such words as thine
> Wherewith even now thou dost outrage the state?

Tiresias.
> 'Twill come though by my silence hidden deep.

Oedipus.
> Then what will come thou too must speak to me.

Tiresias.
> I'll speak no further; wherefore if thou wilt,
> Vent to the full thy wildest storm of rage.

Oedipus.
> Truly I'll leave unsaid no single word
> Of all I think. Such is my rage. Know then
> What I believe: that thou didst plot this deed.
> Performed it too save only that thy hands
> Wrought not the act. And hadst thou now thy sight
> I'd say the murder too was all thine own.

Tiresias.
> Is't true? I charge thee then from thy decree
> Swerve not, nor from this day forevermore
> Speak unto these or me: thou art the man
> That bringest on this land the curse of guilt.

Oedipus.
> Thus shameless wouldst thou speak and still expect
> Somewhere to find a refuge from thy fate?

Tiresias.
> Safety is mine. I speak the all powerful truth.

Oedipus.
> Who taught thee then? 'Twas not thy priestly art.

Tiresias.
> I learned of thee, that forced my unwilling speech.

Oedipus.
> What speech? Lest I should err, speak it once more.

Tiresias.
 Hast thou not known or wouldst thou spread a net?
Oedipus.
 Unknowable it seems—speak it again.
Tiresias.
 I say thou art the slayer that thou wouldst find.
Oedipus.
 Not to thy joy hast spoken twice such words.
Tiresias.
 Shall I say more then that shall irk thee more?
Oedipus.
 Say what thou wilt, for thou shalt say in vain.
Tiresias.
 I say that thou hast lived most shamefully
 Unwitting with thy kin, nor knowest thy plight.
Oedipus.
 Dost think unharmed still to repeat such things?
Tiresias.
 Aye, if there be in truth protecting strength.
Oedipus.
 There is, for all save thee—but not for thee
 For thou art blind in ear and mind and eye.
Tiresias.
 These jeerings prove thee wretched for e'er long
 Each man of these shall hurl them back at thee.
Oedipus.
 Thou dwellest in continuous night, nor canst
 Hurt me or any man that sees the day.
Tiresias.
 'Tis not thy fate to fall by hand of mine.
 Apollo shall suffice, the charge is his.
Oedipus.
 Was't Kreon's thought or thine this treachery?
Tiresias.
 Kreon ne'er did thee harm but thou thyself.
Oedipus.
 O Wealth and Power and Craft outreaching craft
 Throughout our jealous life. What envious thrust
 Can we be safe from if for this throne's sake
 Whereof by gift I ne'er solicited
 Thebes made me master, if for this my lord
 Kreon the faithful, friend since first I came,
 Secretly plotting seeks to thrust me forth,

Suborning for his end this muddling priest
That knows the wiles of wealth, sees faultlessly
Where gain is for the getting, yet straightway
Sought for his priestcraft stumbles and is blind.
For tell me when hast thou shown prophecy?
Why when the riddling bitch bedeviled us
Didst thou not speak some safety to the state?
'Twas hardly for a chance arrival then
To spell that riddle, prophecy forsooth
Was needed then. Yet from thy twittering birds
Thou spakest naught, nor knewest aught from god.
'Twas I who came, I, Oedipus, that had
No knowledge of it all, and yet prevailed
By simple wisdom with no lore of birds.
Whom thou wouldst exile in the expectancy
Of high position close to Kreon's throne.
Sorrow shall be the harvest—thine and his—
Of this prophetic sowing. Wert not old
Such thought as thine should bring thee violence.

Chorus.

Oedipus, both his words and thine appear
Spoken in anger, so at least I judge.
Such words we need not: be it our concern
How best we may fulfill god's oracle.

Tiresias.

Tyrant thou art—yet cannot so refuse
The right to answer. That much lies within
My power. No slave am I to thee or any man
Beside—only to Loxias. Wherefore
Write me not down to Kreon's patronage.
Thou chidest me with blindness. Hear me say
That eyes thou hast but seest not thy plight,
Not even where thou livest nor with whom.
Dost know from whom thou'rt born? Nay, ignorant,
Thou hast made thyself the foe of thine own kin
That dwell with Hades or yet tread the earth.
Thee shall thy mother's curse, thy father's too,
Swift footed, two edged, drive from out this land
With eyes that see now, seeing then no more.
What refuge there that shall not echo back
Thy piteous cry—what haunt of desolate
Kithaeron—when thou seest the anchorage
Whither on favoring breeze, into this home

Thou hast sailed in to shipwreck. Other ills
Countless (thou seest them not) shall level thee
With thine own self and thy begotten seed.
Revile thou as thou wilt the word I speak
And Kreon too, for in the whole wide world
No man shall be so smitten as thyself.
Oedipus.
Can such things then be borne from such as he?
Begone to thy perdition—get thee gone—
Out of this house—begone I say, begone.
Tiresias.
I had not come hadst thou not summoned me.
Oedipus.
I knew thee not, that thou wouldst speak the fool
Or I had never brought thee to my house.
Tiresias.
I am but as I am—to thee a fool,
Yet wise indeed to those that gave thee birth.
Oedipus.
Who? Stay. Canst say who 'twas that gave me birth?
Tiresias.
This day shall give thee birth and give thee death.
Oedipus.
Forever riddles, riddles, dost thou speak.
Tiresias.
And art not thou the best to answer these?
Oedipus.
Chide me with that. Thou'lt find me fortunate.
Tiresias.
That was the fortune that hath ruined thee.
Oedipus.
I care not if the city so be saved.
Tiresias.
Then do I go—come boy and lead me home.
Oedipus.
Aye, let him lead thee, lingering here thou art
A nuisance, 'twere relief to have thee gone.
Tiresias.
I go for I have spoken that for which
I came, nor feared thy face; thou hast no power
Over my lips. But hark to what I say.
He whom thou seekest issuing thy threats
And heralding the death of Laius—he

OEDIPUS OF SOPHOCLES

Dwells here within—an alien visitor—
So is the tale—but shall appear at last
Native born Theban—yet no joy be his
At that discovery. For blind where once
He saw, a rich man beggared, he shall go
Forth to a foreign land feeling his way
With helpless staff, proving at last to be
Brother and sire to his own progeny.
And unto her that bore him in the womb
Both son and husband, to his aged sire
Betrayer first and then his murderer.
Go thou within and on these prophecies
Think well—if in one single circumstance
Thou find me false, denounce my prophet's role.

FIRST STASIMON

FIRST STROPHE

Voice, god-sent from Delphi's rock,
    Whose was the deed
    Ill-wrought with blood-stained hands
    Unspeakable? To lands
Afar with the speed wind-swift of the winged steed
    Now must he take his flight nor longer mock
    The embattled son of Zeus that leaps
       Swift following
    With the brandished flame that never sleeps
    And Fate insatiate unpitying.

FIRST ANTISTROPHE

Flashing from Parnassus' peaks
    Gleaming with snow
    Behest imperative
    To find the fugitive
That far through the trackless wood and the caves below
    Wanders alone distraught and ever seeks
    To avert the doom whose heartless Fate
       Relentlessly
    From Apollo's shrine immaculate
    Pursuing shapes unmoved his destiny.

SECOND STROPHE

Dread is the word, dread is the augury
    And the truth who knows?
Words have I none: fluttering hopes I see
    And anon fear in their place. For the morrow shows
    Darkness deep as today.
    What old grief can I say
    Breeding hate of our royal line
    Now might sully the fame long won
    By Polybus' son
Or fasten on him the doom of the word divine.

SECOND ANTISTROPHE

Zeus knoweth all, Zeus and the Delphian lord
    With all-seeing eye.
Yea, but of man, priests with prophetic word
    Why unto them yield we credulity?
    Though in wisdom of mind
    Man may humble mankind,
    Never shall I till the truth be clear
    Grant his guilt who released our state
    From ruinous Fate
Outwitted the riddling monster and banished fear.

SECOND EPISODE

Kreon.
    My fellow citizens, I am informed
    That Oedipus the King hath uttered here
    Grave charges against me. And so I come
    Resentful, seeing that in our present plight
    If he believe that aught in word or deed
    From me hath injured him, I have no will
    Under suspicion to prolong my life.
    Not simple is the harm that such a charge
    Does me but manifold if I am thought
    False to my city and to you, my friends.

Chorus.
    Such was the charge he made perchance
    Not in cool wisdom but in bitter wrath.

Kreon.
    And said he also that by my advice
    The seer put forth his lying prophecies?

Chorus.
   So spake he but with what intent, who knows?
Kreon.
   But with a mind unclouded and clear eye
   Brought he this charge against me? Tell me that.
Chorus.
   I know not. For I am not wont to see
   What kings perform. But look, he comes himself.
Oedipus.
   Thou? Thou? How art thou come? Such brazen front
   Of daring hast thou as to approach my house,
   The murderer proven of this man and now
   Usurper manifest of this my throne?
   Come tell me by the gods, was't cowardice
   Or folly seen in me that tempted thee
   To such a plotting or didst think the act
   Would not betray thy stealthy treachery
   Or even perchance that I might wittingly
   Ignore it? Is it not a fool's attempt
   With neither force nor friends to seek a throne
   That only numbers and great wealth can win?
Kreon.
   Knowest then what must be? Hearken thou shalt
   To answering words: and so with knowledge judge.
Oedipus.
   Trickster with words I know thee—yet am I
   Not quickly taught, knowing thy deadly hate.
Kreon.
   First hear from me one word that I shall speak.
Oedipus.
   So be thou'lt not assert thou art not base.
Kreon.
   And thou conceive some gain in stubbornness
   Unyoked with wisdom, then thou art not wise.
Oedipus.
   And thou conceive escape from punishment,
   Doing a kinsman ill, thou art not wise.
Kreon.
   Therein thou speakest true, I grant it thee;
   Yet show what wrong from me thou hast endured.
Oedipus.
   Didst thou advise or not that I must send
   To fetch forthwith this prophesying priest?

Kreon.
 Aye and now too approve such policy.
Oedipus.
 How long ago was it that Laius hence—
Kreon.
 Did what? I follow not thy questioning.
Oedipus.
 Was spirited by fatal violence?
Kreon.
 Long span of years must fill that reckoning.
Oedipus.
 And was this priest a priest in those days too?
Kreon.
 As wise as now and honored equally.
Oedipus.
 Made he then any mention of my name?
Kreon.
 He did not—or at least when I was nigh.
Oedipus.
 And of the murdered king—made ye no search?
Kreon.
 Assuredly we searched but learned no clue.
Oedipus.
 Why then did not this wise man speak these things?
Kreon.
 I know not; knowing not I hold my tongue.
Oedipus.
 This much thou knowest and wouldst be wise to speak.
Kreon.
 What thing? For if I know it, I'll not deny.
Oedipus.
 That had Tiresias not conferred with thee
 He had not named me Laius' murderer.
Kreon.
 If he says so, thou knowest. I too have right
 To question thee as thou hast questioned me.
Oedipus.
 Ask what thou wilt: thou shalt not prove my guilt.
Kreon.
 How then, hast thou my sister for thy wife?
Oedipus.
 That question surely may not be denied.
Kreon.
 And dost thou rule on equal terms with her?

Oedipus.
   All that her heart desires she has from me.
Kreon.
   And am I not a third with equal power?
Oedipus.
   Thou art in truth and so art proven base.
Kreon.
   Nay, if thou usest reason with thyself
   Consider first: would any choose to rule
   Encompassed round with terror if the same
   Authority might rest in perfect peace?
   For I at any rate have never sought
   To be a king rather than have the right
   Of kingly powers—nor any man of sense.
   And now from thee with naught to terrify
   I have all favor; ruled I here alone
   Much must I do perforce against my will.
   How then should any crown appear to me
   Sweeter than royal privilege secure?
   Not yet am I so foolish as to seek
   For other goal than honor linked with gain.
   Now all men greet me, all men wish me well
   And those that would reach thee, bespeak my ear
   Since there alone lies prospect of success.
   Why then should I abandoning the sure
   Advantage that is mine, seek other where?
   No mind that harbors wisdom can be false.
   And I have neither loved folly myself
   Nor could I join another in such act.
   Wherefore send now to Pytho for the proof
   Of these my words: find out the oracle:
   Ask if I told it true. And furthermore
   If thou canst prove that with Tiresias
   I ever have connived, then not with one
   But with a twofold vote, thine own and mine,
   Take me and slay me. Only charge me not
   In secret with dark counsels. Justice ne'er
   Lightly deems bad men good or good men bad.
   To cast away a faithful friend I deem
   No wiser than to fling aside one's life.
   This truth in time thou'lt learn, since time alone
   Reveals the just. A single passing day
   Amply suffices to disclose the base.

Chorus.
　　Wise words, my lord, for one that would not slip;
　　The swift in counsel rarely counsel best.
Oedipus.
　　When he who plots in secret moves apace
　　I too must counsel swiftly. Else my ends,
　　The while I linger sleeping foolishly,
　　Are lost forever, his forever gained.
Kreon.
　　What wilt thou then? Wouldst drive me from the land?
Oedipus.
　　That least of all: my will is death not flight,
　　Proclaiming to the world base envy's power.
Kreon.
　　These are the words of stubborn unbelief.
Oedipus.
　　Thou hast not acted to inspire belief.
Kreon.
　　Thou seemst not sane. *Oedipus.* Yet am in my affairs.
Kreon.
　　Thou shouldst be so in mine. *Oedipus.* But thou art base.
Kreon.
　　What if thou knowest naught? *Oedipus.* Yet must I rule.
Kreon.
　　Not if thy rule be wrong. *Oedipus.* O city mine!
Kreon.
　　Not thine alone—for Thebes is mine as well.
Chorus.
　　Desist, my lords. Most happily for you
　　I see Iokaste coming from the house.
　　Her help should end this present quarreling.
Iokaste.
　　What foolish strife of words, all ill-advised,
　　Is this ye raise? Are ye not then ashamed,
　　Your country perishing, to air abroad
　　Your private wrongs? Nay, rather come within
　　Nor magnify your petty difference.
Kreon.
　　Nay sister, for thy husband Oedipus
　　Makes twofold threat against me—either death
　　By violence or exile from this land.
Oedipus.
　　'Tis so for, woman, with base treachery
　　I caught him plotting ill against my life.

Kreon.
>Never may joy be mine but death accursed
>If I am guilty of thy lightest charge.

Iokaste.
>Now by the gods believe him, Oedipus,
>For his oath's sake that he has sworn and for
>My sake as well and these that stand by thee.

KOMMOS

Chorus.
>Yield thee, my King, hearken I pray.

Oedipus.
>What is thy will?

Chorus.
>Grant him belief, wise hitherto, pledging his oath.

Oedipus.
>Knowest thou what thou wilt? *Chorus.* Aye. *Oedipus.* Then
>   declare it me.

Chorus.
>Never should friend by friend, sworn under oath,
>Lightly be thrust aside.

Oedipus.
>Know then assuredly asking of me this boon
>Exile for me or death
>Follows thy prayer.

Chorus.
>Nay by the god of light
>By Helios' self, first of the gods above,
>May I in misery
>Friendless of god and man
>Wretchedly die,
>If in my inmost breast lurks such desire.
>Yearns now my sorrowing heart
>Torn by my country's plight
>Mocked by thy strife.

Oedipus.
>Let him then go, even though it mean my death
>Or if dishonored into banishment
>I must depart. Thy words, not his, prevail.
>For him where'er he be my hate pursues.

Kreon.
>Grudging is thy surrender, arrogant
>Thy wrath. Natures like thine by Fate's decree
>Are ever to themselves hardest to bear.

Oedipus.
>Wilt thou not leave me and begone? *Kreon.* I go.
>Thou canst not comprehend—these know me just.

KOMMOS

Chorus.
>Why, o my Queen, why dost delay?
>Lead him within.

Iokaste.
>First I must know what hath entailed strife such as this.

Chorus.
>Groundless suspicion here: rankling injustice there.

Iokaste.
>Nurtured by both? *Chorus.* Aye. *Iokaste.* And the cause?

Chorus.
>More than enough to me
>Seems now the harm that's done, while yet my country bleeds.

Oedipus.
>Seest thou then thy zeal
>Whither it leads?

Chorus.
>Not only once, my King—
>I say again, fool should I be and worse
>Witless and reft of sense
>Should I be false to thee
>Thou that didst come
>Bringing new life to me, saving the state
>Tossed on a raging sea
>Aye and again to be
>Savior and guide.

Iokaste.
>Tell me, my lord, I charge thee by the gods,
>Whence came to thee this wrath unquenchable?

Oedipus.
>Thee will I tell—I love thee more than these—
>'Twas Kreon and his plots against my life.

Iokaste.
>Speak plainly if indeed thou hast plain cause.

Oedipus.
   He plainly names me Laius' murderer.
Iokaste.
   Speaking his own words or some other man's?
Oedipus.
   Making a bastard priest spokesman for him
   To keep unsoiled his own lips, craftily.
Iokaste.
   Then think no more of it—hearken to me
   And know that never yet hath mortal man
   Shared in prophetic art. I'll show to thee
   Sure proof of these my words. There came of old
   A prophecy to Laius, I say not
   From Phoebus' self but from his ministers,
   How death should come to him by his son's hand
   That should be born to Laius and to me.
   Yet—so the rumor hath it—Laius died
   Murdered by robbers—strangers—where forsooth
   The triple crossroads meet. That child of ours
   Not three days old, its ankles bound with thongs,
   By others' hands, Laius had left exposed
   Far on the trackless hillside. So, I ween,
   Apollo did not make of that poor child
   His father's murderer nor did fulfill
   The fears of Laius that his fate should come
   At his child's hand. So did the words of priests
   Foretell. Give them no heed. For what god needs
   He can himself most easily disclose.
Oedipus.
   What restless thoughts of terror, o my wife
   Hast thou engendered in my troubled mind?
Iokaste.
   What hath disturbed thee that thou speakest so?
Oedipus.
   Methought I heard thee say that Laius' death
   O'ertook him where the triple crossroads meet.
Iokaste.
   So ran the story and hath never ceased.
Oedipus.
   Where is the spot that saw the murder done?
Iokaste.
   Phokis the land is called—a branching road
   Leads there from Delphi and from Daulia.

Oedipus.
   How long the time from that event till now?
Iokaste.
   'Twas just before thy coming that the word
   Was brought to us—ere thou wast King of Thebes.
Oedipus.
   O Zeus, what is thy will to do with me?
Iokaste.
   Why, Oedipus, should this so trouble thee?
Oedipus.
   Ask me not yet—but tell me this instead.
   Laius, what was his form, what years were his?
Iokaste.
   His stature tall, silver just streaked his hair,
   And in appearance not unlike to thee.
Oedipus.
   Woe, woe, is me: it seems that I have hurled,
   Unwitting, dreadful curses on myself.
Iokaste.
   How sayest; my lord, I tremble at thy word.
Oedipus.
   I fear in truth Tiresias still hath sight.
   But thou mayst show. Tell me this one thing more.
Iokaste.
   I tremble, yet I'll answer and thou wilt.
Oedipus.
   Did Laius go alone, or like a king,
   Surrounded by his spearmen royally?
Iokaste.
   Five men in all, a herald one, the King
   Rode in his chariot, the rest afoot.
Oedipus.
   Alas, 'tis all too clear. Who was the man
   That here returning made report to thee?
Iokaste.
   A servant that escaped, alone of all.
Oedipus.
   And now perchance is in the palace here?
Iokaste.
   Not so, for when he came to Thebes and found
   Thee on the throne, with Laius dead, he pled,
   Seizing my hand, to be dispatched far hence
   Into the fields, the pastures of our flocks,

That so he might not see the city more.
And I consented. Faithful service given
Deserved such favor, aye and greater too.
Oedipus.
Might someone bring him here without delay?
Iokaste.
'Tis possible. Why dost thou wish it so?
Oedipus.
I fear that I have spoken overmuch.
And for this reason I would see the man.
Iokaste.
The man shall come anon, yet o my lord,
I too deserve to know what troubles thee.
Oedipus.
Nor shalt thou be denied when such dread fear
Possesses me. For whither should I turn
If not to thee, fast in misfortune's clutch?
My father was King Polybus, the lord
Of Corinth, and my mother Merope.
Dorian she. And I was held the first
Of all the citizens, till there befell
A chance surprising yet not meriting
My great concern thereat. A banqueter
Befuddled with much wine, hurled in my face
The taunt that I was not my father's son.
Much angered, for that day I held my peace
Though hardly: on the next I questioned straight
My parents both who flamed with instant wrath
At him who spake the insult. From their scorn
I took some comfort, but anon the taunt
Rankled unceasing, while the rumor spread.
Wherefore without their knowledge I betook
Myself to Pytho. Whence, touching the quest
That brought me thither, Phoebus caring naught
Sent me away unanswered, yet himself
Vouchsafing other knowledge, bade me know
Dread horror past believing: 'twas my fate
By wedlock with my mother to beget
Offspring abhorrent in the eyes of all
Mankind and be besides the murderer
Of mine own father. When I heard these words
Guided by heaven's stars I fled apace
Corinth and all her land that so I might

Escape fulfilment of the oracle.
Making my way I came unto the spot
Where thou dost say this King of thine was slain.
The truth I'll tell thee, for thou art my wife:
Nearing this triple crossways as I went,
A herald met me and a traveler
Drawn in a carriage, as thou saidst, by colts.
Straightway the herald and the old man too
Were both for pushing me aside. I struck
In righteous anger at the charioteer
Who jostled me; the old man when he saw,
Watching the moment when I passed him close,
Reached from the car and with his two-pronged goad
Smote me upon the head. Unequally
He paid that debt, for with quick reckoning
Struck by the staff in this my hand, he plunged
Headlong from out the chariot. All the rest
I killed, forthwith. Now if there chanced to be
Twixt Laius and this stranger any bond
Of kinship who in all this wretched world
More wretched than myself? What man more cursed:
Whom not a soul may welcome in the home,
Stranger nor friend, nor speak a word to me
But all must thrust me out. No other man
Invoked this curse but I myself decreed
Such things against myself. The dead man's couch
I have polluted with the self-same hands
That slew him. Am I cursed in very truth?
Am I not all unholy? I must flee
And fleeing may not look upon my own
Nor tread the pathways of my fatherland,
Fearing that Fate foretold, that I should wed
My mother and become the murderer
Of Polybus my father who begat
And reared me. Surely one may well believe
'Tis from some cruel god that on my head
Such fate hath fallen. Never, o gods above
August and holy, never may I see
That day. Rather from sight of all mankind
May I be hidden far, nor e'er behold
The stain of such a doom clinging to me.

Chorus.
Dreadful to me, my lord, these things, yet till
Thou hearest from that witness, nurse thy hope.

Oedipus.
　So much of hope is all that's left me now:
　To await the herdsman and to hear his tale.
Iokaste.
　And when he comes, what wouldst thou hear from him?
Oedipus.
　I'll tell thee: if his story still remain
　Consistent with thine own, then I am cleared.
Iokaste.
　What word of mine hath so impressed thee then?
Oedipus.
　By thine account he said in telling thee
　Robbers killed Laius. If he still persist
　Nor change the number, then I killed him not.
　For one and many tally not; but if
　He now maintain 'twas but a single man
　Surely the deed can only be mine own.
Iokaste.
　Nay but he told it so, be well assured,
　Nor can deny it now, the city heard,
　Not I alone. And if he now deny
　Or change his story, he can never prove
　That Laius' murder came as prophesied.
　Since Loxias said that by his own son's hand
　Laius must die. And surely 'twas not he,
　That wretched child, that slew him. Nay, himself
　Did perish long before. Wherefore henceforth
　I'll look not here nor there for oracles.
Oedipus.
　Just is thy reasoning. Yet do not fail
　To give thine orders that the peasant come.
Iokaste.
　I'll send in haste, but let us go within—
　Naught would I do that fits not with thy will.

SECOND STASIMON

Come whensoe'er it will may Fate o'ertake me still
Guarding each word and act with reverent awe
For swift are the laws of Fate
That have fared from heaven's gate
And god on Olympus' height hath made each law.
No mortal brought them forth, no lethal breath
Awaits them: hall-marked with divinity they know not death.

But arrogance breeds force, swift on its course
When glutted full, proud arrogance climbs high,
Snatches the cornice—then, clutching foothold in vain
Plunges, far down on heartless crags to lie.
But the strife that leads to good I shall ever ask,
And to god who rules on high perform my task.

Whosoe'er in word or deed
Acts with arrogance
Whoso will not justice heed,
Godward looks askance,
Him may justice overtake
Him may Fate unhappy shake
If he get not gain with praise
If he keep not all his ways
Pure from stain of guilt.
Else why this offering here of love,
This worship of dance to the gods above?

Never again to Delphi's shrine
Shall I go with heart's desire,
Never again to Abbae's pine
Nor Olympus' altar fire,
If there be not here
Such music clear
As proveth divinity.
But o thou god if thou hearest aught,
Thou Zeus that rulest on high,
May our impious acts with evil wrought
Scape not thy watchful eye.
For the prophet's word
By our dead King heard,
With holy horror fraught,
Has vanished like air
And Apollo's care,
Is held as naught.

THIRD EPISODE

Iokaste.
    Lords of this land, my purpose is resolved
    To visit now the temples of the gods
    Bearing this wreath and gifts for sacrifice.
    For Oedipus' emotions run too high

> Beneath his sufferings. Not like a man
> Of wisdom doth he judge these new events
> By what is old, yielding to each new voice
> So be it speak of terrors. Therefore, since
> My counseling is vain, to thee I come,
> Lycian lord Apollo, suppliant,
> (For thou art nearest) to petition thee:
> Grant us release without defilement: now
> Terror possesses us as who behold
> Smitten with fear the captain of their ship.

Messenger.
> Strangers I fain would learn from you where dwells
> King Oedipus—or better, where is he?

Chorus.
> Here stands his palace and himself within.
> This is his wife, the mother of his brood.

Messenger.
> Happy be she forever, may she dwell
> Always in happiness, being his Queen.

Iokaste.
> Blessed be thy lot too whoe'er thou art
> For so thy words deserve. But speak: wherefore
> Dost thou now come: what news wouldst thou impart?

Messenger.
> Good news unto this house and to the King.

Iokaste.
> What is it and from whom thine embassy?

Messenger.
> From Corinth, and the word that I shall speak
> Shall bring thee happiness, and grief as well.

Iokaste.
> What word is that that hath such twofold power?

Messenger.
> The dwellers of the Isthmian land will make
> Him King of Corinth, so the rumor ran.

Iokaste.
> How so? Is not old Polybus their king?

Messenger.
> Nay, for Death holds him fast within the tomb.

Iokaste.
> How sayest thou? Is Polybus then dead?

Messenger.
> If I speak not the truth then let me die.

Iokaste.
>Maiden, run swift and tell thy master this.
>Where are ye then, ye oracles of god?
>This was the man that, long since, Oedipus
>Feared and avoided lest he be constrained
>To murder him, and now the self-same King
>Lies dead, outdone by Fate and not by him.

Oedipus.
>O dearest wife, Iokaste, why, I pray
>Hast thou now summoned me from out the house?

Iokaste.
>Hearken to this man's word, then judge thyself
>The outcome of the dreaded oracles.

Oedipus.
>Who is the man? What would he say to me?

Iokaste.
>Coming from Corinth he brings messages
>Of Polybus thy father, and his death.

Oedipus.
>How sayest thou stranger, speak now for thyself.

Messenger.
>If this must be my first report then know
>That he has gone indeed the way of Death.

Oedipus.
>By violence, or died he by disease?

Messenger.
>Slight matters turn the scale when one is old.

Oedipus.
>Illness it was then that hath brought him low.

Messenger.
>Aye, and the long long tale of passing years.

Oedipus.
>Alas, alas, why therefore O my wife
>Should one look ever to the Pythian shrine
>Or hearken to the cry of birds? 'Twas they
>That would have made me murderer of him
>My father, yet it seems he now is dead
>While here I stand unarmed and innocent—
>Unless he died of longing for his son:
>So only could one blame me. And in truth
>Polybus lies in Hades and hath swept
>With him the oracles and proved them naught.

Iokaste.
>And said I not long since it would be so?

OEDIPUS OF SOPHOCLES

Oedipus.
   Thou didst, and yet by fear I was misled.
Iokaste.
   Now therefore give them not a single thought.
Oedipus.
   Surely I still must fear my mother's couch.
Iokaste.
     What fear should be for mortal man whose life
     Fate rules supreme, nor can he aught foresee?
     Better to live by chance as best ye may.
     Nor shouldst thou fear this wedlock horrible
     With thine own mother: many men there be
     That in their dreams have done this act. He best
     Supports his life who counts these things as naught.
Oedipus.
     Well spoken were thy words save that she lives
     Who bore me: since she lives she still compels
     Terror in me, fair though thy counselings.
Iokaste.
     And yet thy father's death should give thee pause.
Oedipus.
   'Tis true I grant thee, but my mother lives.
Messenger.
   What woman is it whom thou fearest so?
Oedipus.
   Merope, who was wife to Polybus.
Messenger.
   And what the fear that she inspires in thee?
Oedipus.
   An oracle that came, stranger, from god.
Messenger.
   Mayst tell it, or must others know it not?
Oedipus.
     Truly I may. Loxias spoke of old
     How I must marry with my mother, then
     Shed with these hands of mine, my father's blood.
     Corinth and I have therefore been long since
     Strangers and happily too save that it's sweet
     To look on those who brought us to the light.
Messenger.
   Such was the fear that wrought thy banishment?
Oedipus.
   Aye, that I might not work my father's death.

Messenger.
    How then have I not freed thee from thy fear
    Coming, my lord, with welcome messages?
Oedipus.
    And truly thou shalt have thy just reward.
Messenger.
    I will confess that was my secret hope
    That I might profit by thy coming home.
Oedipus.
    Home will I never come while she yet lives.
Messenger.
    My son, 'tis clear thou knowest not what thou dost.
Oedipus.
    How so, old man? Tell me now by the gods.
Messenger.
    If for this cause thou wilt not now return.
Oedipus.
    'Tis cause enough, lest Phoebus prove his word.
Messenger.
    And from thy parents thou incur some guilt?
Oedipus.
    Just so, for that shall always be my fear.
Messenger.
    Dost know, then, that thy fears are all for naught?
Oedipus.
    How can that be and I a child of theirs?
Messenger.
    For Polybus was never kin of thine.
Oedipus.
    What sayest thou? Polybus not my sire?
Messenger.
    No more than I myself, as much, no more.
Oedipus.
    Why match thyself with him who caused my birth?
Messenger.
    Nay, he begat thee not, nor he nor I.
Oedipus.
    Wherefore if this be so, called he me son?
Messenger.
    Delivered by these hands, a gift thou wert.
Oedipus.
    And could he love me so when gotten thus?

Messenger.
He could by virtue of long childlessness.
Oedipus.
Thou, hadst thou bought me or didst find this gift?
Messenger.
I found thee in Kithaeron's wooded glades.
Oedipus.
Purposing what didst wander to this land?
Messenger.
In charge of flocks that ranged these mountainsides.
Oedipus.
Thou wert a shepherd and a hireling then?
Messenger.
My son, I was thy savior in those days.
Oedipus.
How so, what suffering didst thou save me from?
Messenger.
Whereof thine ankles give thee evidence.
Oedipus.
Alas, why call to mind that ancient woe?
Messenger.
I loosed thine ankles fastened with a thong.
Oedipus.
An outrage from my days in swaddling clothes.
Messenger.
And from that outrage thou hast still thy name.
Oedipus.
Speak, by the gods; was that a parent's deed?
Messenger.
I know not, he knows best that gave thee me.
Oedipus.
Thou didst not find me? I was given thee?
Messenger.
Another shepherd placed thee in my hands.
Oedipus.
What man is that? Dost know? Canst point him out?
Messenger.
'Twas one of Laius' shepherds, so 'twas said.
Oedipus.
His who was King in Thebes in days gone by?
Messenger.
Aye his indeed, a herdsman of that King.

Oedipus.
>Lives the man still that I might look on him?

Messenger.
>Ye men of Thebes should know that best of all.

Oedipus.
>Knows any man of you of whom he speaks
>Or have ye seen this shepherd in the town
>Or on the upland pastures? Let such speak.
>The time is come that these things be revealed.

Chorus.
>Methinks it is no other than the man
>Thou hast desired to see. Iokaste now
>Surely might best reveal to thee the truth.

Oedipus.
>O wife and Queen, knowest thou whom but now
>We summoned hither? Speaks he of the same?

Iokaste.
>What matters whom he mentioned? Give no thought
>To what he said, for all such thoughts are vain.

Oedipus.
>It may not be. With such proofs in my grasp
>I must discover now my lineage.

Iokaste.
>No by the gods, if thou hast any care
>For thine own life, ask not. My woe's enough.

Oedipus.
>Fear not, for though from triple servitude
>I find my line thou shalt not so be base.

Iokaste.
>Believe me none the less: touch not this thing.

Oedipus.
>I may not so believe thee, I must learn.

Iokaste.
>For thine own sake I speak and counsel well.

Oedipus.
>These counselings have long since vexed my soul.

Iokaste.
>O hapless man, god grant thee ignorance.

Oedipus.
>Let someone bring this shepherd to me straight:
>This woman, let her boast her royal line.

Iokaste.
>Alas, most wretched man; for this one word
>I speak thee now, none else forevermore.

OEDIPUS OF SOPHOCLES

Chorus.
>Why has she gone, thy Queen, o Oedipus,
>In frenzied grief? I fear that from this deep
>Silence of hers misfortune shall break forth.

Oedipus.
>Let come what will. Low though my lineage
>Be proven, yet I'll know it. She perchance
>Womanlike in her pride may fear in shame
>To face mine origin. I hold myself
>Own child of Fortune; she beneficent
>Shall never cause me shame. Her child am I
>Brother of all the months whose passing course
>Made me now small now great and being such
>In parentage pray god I never prove
>False to that mother Fortune nor desert
>The search that shall yet prove my lineage.

THIRD STASIMON

STROPHE

>Now by Olympus high
>If aught of prophecy
> Or wisdom lie
> Within this breast
>Tomorrow's moon shall see
> Our Oedipus stand confessed
>Thy countryman, Kithaeron, and thy son,
> This dance a duty done
>   In loyalty.
>Lord god, Apollo, let these our deeds be blessed.

ANTISTROPHE

>Whose was the goddess' womb
>That unto Pan bore thee
> Through wooded coomb
> And grass grown run
>Pursued relentlessly?
> Or art thou Apollo's son?
>For dear to him is every upland way.
> Or Hermes'—who shall say?
>   Or was it he
>Great Bacchus loved of the nymphs on Helikon?

FOURTH EPISODE

Oedipus.
   Sir, if I too who never met the man,
   May yet venture a guess, yonder, methinks
   I see the herdsman whom we seek. In years
   He matches well this stranger and besides
   Servants they are of mine conducting him.
   Yet better is thy knowledge than mine own
   Since thou hast seen the fellow ere today.
Chorus.
   I know him, have no doubt, of Laius' men
   Shepherd of all most faithful to the King.
Oedipus.
   Thee first I question; didst thou mean this man,
   Stranger from Corinth? *Messenger.* Aye, the man thou seest.
Oedipus.
   Thou too old man, look hither, answer me
   My question: wast thou ever Laius' man?
Herdsman.
   I was, a house born slave, no market prize.
Oedipus.
   What task was thine? How didst thou spend thy life?
Herdsman.
   The larger part in following the herds.
Oedipus.
   What were the regions thou didst most frequent?
Herdsman.
   Kithaeron mostly and its neighborhood.
Oedipus.
   This fellow here, hast ever seen him there?
Herdsman.
   What doing, sir, and what man dost thou mean?
Oedipus.
   Who stands before thee: hast met him before?
Herdsman.
   Not so that I might say at once from memory.
Messenger.
   Nor any wonder. Yet, my lord, I can
   Clearly recall what now he has forgot.
   I doubt not he remembers well the time
   When for three summers clear from spring until
   Arcturus' rising we together roamed

These stretches of Kithaeron, he with two
Herds while I tended one. When winter came
I drove my flocks to Corinth home, he his
To Laius' folds. Is this the truth I speak
Or do I tell of things that never were?
Herdsman.
The truth indeed, and yet 'twas long ago.
Messenger.
Come tell me then, canst thou recall how once
Thou gavest me a child to rear as mine?
Herdsman.
How now? Why dost thou question me of that?
Messenger.
For this is he who was a baby then.
Herdsman.
Destruction take thee, wilt thou hold thy tongue?
Oedipus.
Old man, revile him not, thy words not his
Seem most to need amendment, chide him not.
Herdsman.
And what, good master, have I done amiss?
Oedipus.
Refusing thus to answer what he asks.
Herdsman.
He asks in ignorance, and all in vain.
Oedipus.
Thou speak not freely, thou shalt speak in pain.
Herdsman.
By all the gods, force not an aged man.
Oedipus.
Will someone quickly bind the fellow's hands?
Herdsman.
Ah wretched me, for what, what wouldst thou know?
Oedipus.
The child, didst give it to him as he says?
Herdsman.
I did, and would to god I had died then.
Oedipus.
Thou shalt die now and thou speak not the truth.
Herdsman.
And if I do, more surely shall I die.
Oedipus.
The fellow seems determined to delay.

Herdsman.
　Not I, I told you that I gave the child.
Oedipus.
　Whence had thou it, was't thine or someone's else?
Herdsman.
　'Twas not mine own, I had it from a man.
Oedipus.
　A Theban? One of these? And from what home?
Herdsman.
　No, by the gods, my lord, ask me no more.
Oedipus.
　Thou art a dead man if I ask again.
Herdsman.
　Well then it was a child of Laius' house.
Oedipus.
　A slave, or one free born of his own race?
Herdsman.
　Alas I tremble on the brink of speech.
Oedipus.
　And I of hearing, yet perforce, I must.
Herdsman.
　His own the child was called. The Queen within
　Thy wife may best confirm to thee the fact.
Oedipus.
　Was it she gave the child?　*Herdsman.* 'Twas she, my lord.
Oedipus.
　What was her purpose?　*Herdsman.* I should kill the child.
Oedipus.
　Unnatural mother.　*Herdsman.* Oracles she feared.
Oedipus.
　What?　*Herdsman.* He should kill his parent, so 'twas said.
Oedipus.
　How then didst thou bestow him on this man?
Herdsman.
　In pity, sire, thinking that he would take
　The child to his own country, yet it seems
　He saved him to misfortune. If thou art
　The man he says, then dreadful is thy doom.
Oedipus.
　Alas, alas. It must then all be true.
　O light of day, may I ne'er look on thee
　Again, who now am found cursed at my birth,
　Wedded in incest, steeped in mine own blood.

OEDIPUS OF SOPHOCLES

FOURTH STASIMON

FIRST STROPHE

Alas, alas for the years of mortality:
    I count ye as naught.
  Who is he that hath ever found
  More than a vision of empty sound
    By fancy wrought?
And ever the vision ends in calamity.
    For now, my King, soul wracked and sore distressed,
    Thy fate do I behold
      Woes manifold
  And I count no mortal blessed.

FIRST ANTISTROPHE

Beyond man's skill did he speed his unerring shaft
    And won to his goal
  Fortune's prize of prosperity
  Slaying the Sphinx with her mystery
    And stopped the toll
Of that death she levied: foully she wrought and laughed
    Till thou didst come, champion and tower of might.
    Henceforth all conquering
      Art hailed as king
  In this land of god's delight.

SECOND STROPHE

And now on the lips of all
  Whose fate so black?
While the Furies of madness in hungry pack
  Cry for thy fall.
For into a harbor strange thou hast sailed
Where the deathless laws of the gods have failed,
Where the same unhallowed love prevailed
On sire and son in the self-same hall.
  What god bestowed
This poisonous boon, this fatal goad
  To sow where his father sowed?

SECOND ANTISTROPHE

But time that is never blind
  Hath now disclosed

What the dwellers of earth, to the light exposed,
    Shudder to find.
Seed of begetter and him begot
In the self-same furrow that sensed them not
And I would to god thy thrice-cursed lot
Were hidden darkly from all mankind.
    I mourn thy plight
That unto me brought sudden light
    To end in eternal night.

EXODUS

Exaggelos.
    Ye ever-honored most in Thebes what deeds
    Shall smite your ears, what sights shall ye behold
    What grief is yours if to tradition true
    Ye still revere the house of Labdakus.
    Waters of Ister, streams of Phasis ne'er
    Can cleanse this dwelling, such the dreadful deed,
    It hides but shall disclose, no deed of chance
    But wittingly contrived. Always those griefs
    Hurt most whose choice the world shall mark our own.
Chorus.
    Already we have witnessed here such deeds
    As might call forth such cry; what hast thou more?
Exaggelos.
    To take the shortest course for him who speaks
    And him who hears: the Queen Iokaste is dead.
Chorus.
    O lady of ill fortune, by what means?
Exaggelos.
    By her own hand. The part most horrible,
    The sight of it, is spared thee. What remains
    Of all her woe within my memory
    Straight shalt thou hear. Frantic with mad despair
    She came within the ante chamber. Then
    Rushed to the wedding couch, with both her hands
    Tearing her hair, dashed shut the doors behind
    Invoking Laius, dead these many years,
    And called to mind that son that he begot
    So long ago by whom he died and left
    Her that had borne him wretched to produce

Offspring to share with his. She cried against
That marriage which to her misfortune raised
A double brood, husband by husband got
And children by her child. How after that
She perished I know not, for Oedipus
Burst in with shouting who allowed us not
Further to look upon her misery
Since on his frenzy rested all our eyes.
Madly he raged, asking of us a sword
And calling for the wife that was no wife
The mother's womb that bore alike himself
And his own children. In his madness some
Divinity did guide him for 'twas none
Of us poor mortals who were standing by.
Then with a dreadful shout, as beckoned on
He hurled himself upon the double doors—
Back from their sockets bent the yielding bolts—
And rushed within. There we beheld his wife
Hanged by a twisted cord still swaying there.
And when he saw her, with a mighty cry
He loosed the rope that held her. As she lay
Stretched on the ground, followed a gruesome sight.
For from her dress he tore the golden brooch
That held it. Raising it aloft he smote
Full on his eyeballs shouting as he struck
That they should nevermore behold what he
Had suffered nor the evil he had wrought.
Darkened forever they might never look
Again on what they had no right to see,
Failing to recognize what most they ought.
And with such imprecations 'twas not once
But many times he beat upon his eyes.
The bloody eyeballs burst upon his beard
Not in slow drops of blood but in one black
Down-rushing stream of blood, like shower of hail.
Such are the woes that issue from these twain,
Husband and wife commingled. What was once
Their happy lot, and happiness in truth,
This day is turned to wailing, madness, death
And all the woes that are, are theirs today.
Chorus.
Hath now the wretched man some rest from pain?

Exaggelos.
>He shouts aloud that some one draw the bolts
>And show to all in Thebes the murderer
>Of his own father and his mother too.
>With blasphemies that I may not repeat
>He swears to hurl himself forth from this land
>Nor still remain a curse unto the house,
>>Under the curse he spoke. Yet someone's strength
>>And guidance too he needs, his agony
>>Is more than human strength can bear. Thou too
>>Shalt see, for now the unbolted palace gates
>>Open to show a sight that can but win
>>Thy fierce abhorrence but thy pity too.

Chorus.
>O agony too sore for sight
>Beyond the utmost range
>Of human agony.
>What madness, hapless man, assailed thy soul?
>What angered god
>O'erleaping space
>Struck down thine ill-starred Fortune?
>Woe is me,
>Much as I fain would learn,
>Frozen with horror, impotent,
>I dare not ask nor look but overwhelmed
>Shudder and hold my peace.

Oedipus.
>Woe, woe is mine.
>Where in mine agony
>Shall I be borne?
>Fluttering words are naught.
>Where, god, the end?

Chorus.
>Where there is no relief for ear or eye.

Oedipus.
>O cloud of the nether night,
>Abhorrent, unspeakable,
>Wafted on following breezes fraught with death
>Alas the goad of memory strikes
>Piercing my heart
>Cruelly joined in one with the stabs
>Of the golden brooch.

OEDIPUS OF SOPHOCLES

Chorus.
   No wonder in thy plight there comes to thee
   A double grief, a twofold pain to bear.
Oedipus.
   O friend that art steadfast still
   Thou only art left to me.
   Pity for suffering blindness makes thee kind.
   Alas thy presence speaks to me
   Blind though I am.
   Darkness like death is mine, yet I know
   Thou hast left me not.
Chorus.
   O doer of dread deeds, how couldst thou dare
   Destroy thine eyes? What god compelled that act?
Oedipus.
   Lord of the Delphian shrine,
   Apollo, god of the taut strong bow,
   Wrought for me woe on woe:
   His was the curse
   But the hand that struck was mine;
   Mine was the blow.
   God! Would I see again
   Whose opened eyes
   Could naught behold that held not memory's curse?
Chorus.
   True is that word of thine.
Oedipus.
   What should I see? Shall I ever know
   Love or a welcoming word?
   Banish me ere ye too
   Fall neath the blight that clings
   Round me accursed
   Hated of god, damned through eternity.
Chorus.
   Twofold thy misery: for, being damned,
   Thou still canst feel. Would god I knew thee not.
Oedipus.
   Cursed forever be
   The hand that loosed from my feet the thong
   Striking the shackles off
   Giving me life
   When I lay a helpless babe.

Graceless the deed;
Better were death for me
Than live a curse
To mine own self and all that touches me.
Chorus.
Better were death indeed.
Oedipus.
Then had I not with the curse of god
Drenched in my father's blood
Mounted the couch of her,
Mother and queen to me.
Outlaw from earth
Outlaw from heaven, woe beyond woe is mine.
Chorus.
I cannot say thy counsel was the best
For death would be to thee a very boon.
Oedipus.
Instruct me not that all is evilly
Contrived. I cannot bear more counseling
For had I now my sight could I endure
To face my father in the halls of hell,
To look upon my mother? I have wrought
Such wrongs against those two as would make death
By hanging seem as nothing. Can ye think
Beside that sight of mine own progeny
Begotten as they were could give me joy?
Not in mine eyes at least. Not Thebes herself,
Not all her parapets, her sculptured gods
Seeing that I of all her citizens
Fairest of promise, now accursed, have won
The doom of seeing these no more, myself
The spokesman of the curse bidding men thrust
Forth from the city the unholy one,
Disclosed by god of Laius' royal line.
Could I with such a brand upon me look
Upon my fellow citizens? Not I,
And were there means to dam the fountain head
Of hearing, I had not withheld to close
This wretched body fast that neither sight
Nor sound should penetrate. Our thoughts should dwell
Beyond the reach of evil, o Kithaeron, why
Didst thou accept my life? Why didst thou not
Slay me at once? So had I never shown

OEDIPUS OF SOPHOCLES

Myself unto the world and whence I sprang.
O Polybus and Corinth and that home
Once called mine own, how fair the object seemed
Of thy kind nurture, and how foul beneath
Proven at last both base and basely born.
O triple crossroads and that hidden glade
Narrowing through the oak trees where those three
Roads met that drank mine own blood by my hand
Drawn from my father's veins, do ye then still
Remember me, the deed I showed you there
And coming hither wrought again? O rites
Of wedlock, ye that brought me forth and gave
Harvest to me sown in the self-same field
Confounding name of father, brother, son,
Of mother, bride, and wife to consummate
All that is held most shameful of mankind.
Yet what is foul to do is foul to speak.
Wherefore by all the gods with utmost speed
Hide me in some far hiding place or slay
Outright or cast me in the sea where none
May e'er behold me more. Come, scruple not
To touch this wretched man. Ye need not fear.
No mortal but myself may bear this guilt.

Chorus.
Lo at thy words comes Kreon who may best
Grant thy request or counsel thee for he
Alone is left our guardian in thy place.

Oedipus.
Alas what word is left for me to speak
To him? What truth shall he behold in me
Who proved myself to him in all things false?

Kreon.
I am not come to mock thee, Oedipus,
Nor speak reproaches for thy evil past.
But if ye here respect no more the race
Of man at least show reverence to the flame
All nourishing of Helios nor expose
Pollution such as this which neither light
Of day, nor earth, nor rains of heaven may bear.
With all your speed lead him within. The woes
Of kindred they alone should see and hear
To whom the bonds of kinship give the right.

Oedipus.
> Nay, by the gods, since thou hast quelled my fear
> Coming thus nobly to a man so base
> Grant me one boon. For thine own sake I'll speak.

Kreon.
> What favor dost thou ask so eagerly?

Oedipus.
> Cast me forth swiftly from this land, where I
> May share no more in human intercourse.

Kreon.
> That had I done, be well assured, save that
> I would be taught of god what's best to do.

Oedipus.
> God hath already spoken bidding us
> Destroy the unholy man that slew his sire.

Kreon.
> Such was his word yet seeing where we stand
> 'Tis best to learn anew our proper course.

Oedipus.
> Wilt ask advice about one so accursed?

Kreon.
> Aye for thyself wilt now believe god's word.

Oedipus.
> One charge I lay on thee, one last request.
> To her that lies within give burial
> As seemeth best to thee. So shalt thou give
> Last rites unto thine own. But never doom
> This city of my fathers to receive
> Me as a citizen to dwell therein.
> Nay send me forth to live where rises steep
> Kithaeron, called mine own, the living tomb
> My father and my mother gave to me:
> Thus at their hands who willed it I may die.
> Yet this I know. Never shall dread disease
> Nor human ill destroy me. I was snatched
> From death, to serve some stranger will of god.
> For me let Fate lead where it will. And more
> I ask no favor, Kreon, for my sons.
> They are now men and wheresoe'er they are
> Shall win their livelihood. I crave thy care
> For my two daughters. Piteous is their lot
> Who know no table but mine own, have shared
> All things with me. Grant too, most noble lord,

That I may touch them once again and mourn
With them this evil plight. Could I but place
My hands on them methinks I could believe
That they were mine as when I saw them here.
O god what shall I say? Do I not hear
Their weeping voices? Hast thou pitied me
And brought my daughters, Kreon? Is it so?

Kreon.
'Tis so. 'Twas I that brought them, knowing well
From thy past joy what comfort they might give.

Oedipus.
God give thee blessing and a happier fate
Than mine for this good act. Where are ye there,
My children? Hither, hither come and take
These hands that are in truth a brother's hands.
Hands which wrought havoc with your father's eyes
That saw so clearly once. Yet seeing naught
Nor gaining wisdom's light, he gave you life
By his own mother. 'Tis for you I weep
Whom now I may not see. But I perceive
What bitterness of life amongst mankind
Henceforth is yours. What friendly gatherings
Will you attend, what feasts whose end for you
Shall not be weeping in the place of joy?
And when you reach the years of womanhood
With thoughts of marriage, who will then assume
Reproaches that must ever fall alike
On my descendants and on yours? What woe
Exists that is not ours? Your father slew
His sire, quickened the womb that gave him life
To bring you forth. Such is your heritage.
Who then shall wed you? There is none that lives.
Unwedden, barren, 'tis your doom to die.
But o Menoekeus' son, since thou alone
Art left to father these—for she and I
That brought them to the light are lost indeed—
Suffer them not—thy kin—to wander lone
Beggared and husbandless nor make them one
With this my misery. Nay pity them
Seeing their youth deprived of everything
Save what may come from thee. Take thou this hand
And grant my wish. To you my children much
I should bequeath of counsel were thy minds

Mature. Now let this be your constant prayer
That wheresoe'er chance place your lot, ye live
With happier fate than was your father's share.

Kreon.

All sufficient now thy mourning. Thou must go within the house.

Oedipus.

Yield I must, though yield I would not. *Kreon.* Aye, for all things have their time.

Oedipus.

Knowest how I might go freely? *Kreon.* If thou sayest I shall know.

Oedipus.

If thou wouldst but grant me exile. *Kreon.* That lies on the knees of god.

Oedipus.

Yet to god am I most hateful. *Kreon.* Hence may win thy wish perchance.

Oedipus.

Thou dost will it? *Kreon.* Nay, 'tis never mine to speak what I mean not.

Oedipus.

Send me then within the palace. *Kreon.* Go, but leave thy children here.

Oedipus.

Rob me not of them I pray thee. *Kreon.* Seek not to prevail in all.
For the power thou once hast wielded has not followed to the end.

Chorus.

Ye that dwell in Thebes behold him. Oedipus thy King is this,
He who solved the far-famed riddle, mightiest in all Thebes was he.
On his fortune who that dwelt here gazed not once with envious eye?
Now behold what surge of evil hath encompassed him about.
So the while we wait the outcome of the fateful final day
We may call no mortal happy till his course of life is done
And he reach the goal of darkness, find his heaven free from pain.

OEDIPUS REX of SENECA

PROLOGUE

Oedipus.
　　Banishing night, the uncertain sun returns,
　　The dawn creeps up by squalid clouds oppressed:
　　And, with a baleful light of ominous flame,
　　It shall behold homes swept by greedy pest
　　As day shall show destruction wrought by night.
　　Joys any man in power? O treacherous boon,
　　What ills with what fair seeming thou dost hide!
　　Even as the loftiest peaks ever receive
　　The tempests' blasts or as the surging sea
　　Howsoe'er mild lashes the cliff that cleaves
　　With rocky front the mighty deeps, so power
　　Exalted lies exposed to Destiny.
　　How wise I fled the throne of Polybus
　　My sire. An exile fearless, wandering
　　From care set free, by gods and heaven I swear,
　　I stumbled upon power. And now I cherish
　　A fear unspeakable that by my hand
　　My father die: so warn the Delphic laurels
　　And yet a greater crime beside they tell.
　　Is there then fouler than a father's murder?
　　O wretched filial love (I blush to speak
　　The fated word), marriage incestuous,
　　A bridal couch by son and mother shared
　　With impious torches Phoebus prophesies:
　　Such fear now spurs me from my father's realm.
　　No driven exile I, forth from my hearth,
　　But, trusting not myself, for safety's sake
　　I yielded, mighty Nature, to thy sway.
　　When fearsome terror rules thee thou must dread
　　Even what thou still believest impossible:
　　I fear all things nor trust me to myself.
　　　Now, now for me the Fates prepare some blow.
　　Else how am I to think this pestilence
　　That slays the race of Cadmus far and wide
　　Spares me alone? For what am I reserved?
　　Amidst the city's ruins and the deaths
　　Wept ever by new tears, the holocaust
　　Of a whole folk I stand apart untouched,

OUR SENECA

Victim I ween of Phoebus. Could'st believe
A realm so prosperous abandoned so
To such dire crimes? We have stained heaven with guilt.
   No tender breeze with cooling draught revives
The hearts that breathe forth flames, no Zephyrs light
Blow now, but Titan multiplies the fires
Of burning Dog Star, pressing hard behind
The Nemean lion. Moisture leaves the rivers,
Color the grass; Dirce is dry, within
A tenuous stream Ismenus flows and scarce
Moistens the shallows with its failing flood.
Darkened, from heaven Phoebus' sister slips,
The world ensaddened pales 'neath clouded day.
No star shines forth in any night serene
But black and heavy vapor broods o'er earth.
The counterfeit of hell has deep disguised
The strongholds of the gods, the homes on high.
Ceres, long pregnant, will not bring to birth
But trembles yellowing on the lofty stalks.
In withering shoots the sterile harvest dies.
Nowhere is safety from destruction: each
Sex and all ages fall alike, old men
And youth, fathers and sons the pestilence
Unites in fatal bond, the wedding torch
Kindles the couch of death and funeral trains
Know neither sounds of weeping nor lament.
Persistent death in such catastrophe
Has drained the eyes, the customary tears
Are dead. Here to the funeral flames a sire,
Dying himself, carries his son and there
A mother maddened carries one child, in haste
To seek another for the self-same bier.
Nay, from each grief another grief upsprings
And round the pyre gather new obsequies.
Bodies of dear ones burn with alien fires
Stolen by force: such misery knows no shame.
The cherished bones have not their separate tombs.
Enough to burn them—yet how much of all
Departs to ashes?—earth for the burial mounds
Is wanting and the wood for funeral pyres.
No prayers, no skill avail the stricken, those
Fall that give aid. The pest filches the cure.
   Prone at the altar stretch I suppliant hands

Craving swift death that I may anticipate
My falling country nor when all are gone
Die last to be my kingdom's final loss.
O gods too cruel, bitter Fate! To me
Alone of this great multitude is death,
So prompt at hand, denied? Then fly these realms
Infected with a fatal touch, desert
These tears, these deaths, stains that contaminate
The heaven, stains that thou broughtest with thee here.
Ill-fated guest, flee with all speed, begone
Even to thy parents.

Iokaste.
     What avails my lord
To augment with such complaint these evils sore?
This is the role of kings methinks, to accept
Misfortunes, and, the more in doubt thy state,
The while the might of crumbling empire fails,
With foot more firmly planted brave to stand.
'Tis not the hero's part to flee from Fate.

Oedipus.
No fault is mine of cowardice or shame;
My valor knows not timid fear. If now
Drawn weapons should confront me or the dread
Power of Mars—against fierce giant hosts
Boldly I'd raise contending hands: not I
Did flee the Sphinx, weaving in riddling wise
Her words, but dared to face the bloody jaws
Of that foul prophetess, the scattered bones
That whitened all the ground, and when upon
Her lofty cliff, scenting the prey, she reared
Her wings, lashing her tail and lionlike
Threatening destruction, I did ask her test.
Above me then with dreadful din she roared,
Her jaws snapped and, impatient of delay,
She clawed the cliffside as she hoped to claw
My vitals. But the words involved wherein
She hid her prophecy, the blind deceit,
The treacherous riddle of the beast, I solved.

Iokaste.
Why now in madness pray too late for death?
Thou might'st have died. Yet here is thy reward:
The scepter that repays the Sphinx destroyed.

Oedipus.
    There, there is that which fights against us now,
    The fatal ashes of that clever beast.
    She now in death is Thebes' destroying pest.
    One safety, only one, remains for us
    If Phoebus show us yet the way to life.

CHORUS

Scion of Cadmus' home
Fallen art thou,
Thou and thy state alike;
Reft is thy land of men,
Desolate Thebes.
Bacchus, to death a prey
Falls now thy soldiery—
Host that to farthest Ind
Followed thy call,
Riding the eastern waste,
Planting thy standards where
Earth at her farthest stretch
Greets the new light;
Looked on the Arab tribes
Dwelling in spicy groves,
Faced the false Parthian shaft
Flung in retreat;
Traversed the Red Sea shore
Whence on his rising course
Phoebus with nearer flame
Paints with a darker hue
Savage of Ind.

We of unconquered stock
Perish in headlong fate
While unto death still ride
Panoplies new;
Down to the shades beneath
Hastens our endless line
Till for the countless throng
Thebes with her seven gates
Offers no way.
Falters the long slow line,
Death makes delay for death.

Ready to strike the blow
Stood with uplifted hand
Priest of high god.
But ere he struck, the bull,
Bending his gilded horns
Halted before him;
Swift fell the axe, the wound,
Gaping unsightly wide,
Stainless the weapon left;
Stumbled and fell the beast
Helpless before him.

First hath the pestilence
Stricken the feeble sheep
Cropping in vain the grass,
Then as they fail,
Fail too the cattle strong.
While midst the dying herds
Shepherds lie dying,
Flocks unattended stray
Into the meadows.
No more the timid deer
Flee from the ravening wolf;
Lions their roaring cease,
Bears lose their sullen wrath,
Serpents forget their sting,
Reft of their poison.

No more do the leafy groves
Spread shade on the mountainside,
No more are the meadows green
Or the vines bowed down with grapes:
All things have tasted our woe.
From the depths of hell have burst
The Furies with torch aflame,
While Phlegethon changes his course
And Styx is loosed from its banks.
Black death spreads her greedy jaws
And stretches o'er earth her wings,
While the aged ferryman plies
His barque with a wearied arm—
His barque that carries the dead
Across the benighted stream—
And ever returns for more.

And the hound of hell is loosed
From his bonds to roam the earth.
The deserts are filled with groans
And through the sacred groves
Go wandering shades of the dead.
The Cadmeian grove is torn
With hail and Dirce's stream
Runs blood: in the silent night
Go howling the dogs of the dead.

O death that is worse than death!
Dull languor seizes the limbs:
Comes a flush on the sickly skin
That is spotted and seared in death.
A breath like a fire consumes
The seat of this mortal life,
Till the cheeks are aflame with blood
And the eyes are glazed and stiff,
Till the eardrums roar and the nose
Drops blood that is black and bursts
The veins till they stand agape.
Incessant the entrails groan
As the fever feeds on the flesh.
In vain do they seize apace
The chill of the cold gray stone.
The happier sons of wealth
Seek springs to assuage their thirst;
The rest at the altar base
Beg death and the ready gods
Grant this as their only boon.
For now the shrines are sought
With never a thought of a vow
But only to sate the gods.

EPISODE 1

Oedipus.
Who seeks the palace there with hurrying step?
Is Kreon come, famous in birth and deeds,
Or does my sickened mind blend false and true?
Chorus.
Kreon is come, sought by our common prayers.

OEDIPUS OF SENECA

Oedipus.
With dread I tremble fearful whither Fate
May lead, my fluttering heart fails me distraught
By twin emotions: when ambiguous
Joys come commingled with calamity
The uncertain mind, though eager, fears to know.
Brother of mine own wife, if aught of help
Thou bringest to the weary, speak with haste.
Kreon.
Doubtful the oracle and puzzling sore.
Oedipus.
Who gives but doubtful aid in woe gives none.
Kreon.
The Delphic god is wont with riddling turns
To hide his secrets. *Oedipus.* Speak; though the riddle's dark,
Oedipus only has the gift to solve.
Kreon.
That royal murder must be expiated
And Laius' death by exile be avenged,
The god decrees. Not sooner shall the day
Through heaven course serenely nor produce
Safe draughts of ether uncontaminate.
Oedipus.
Who was the slayer of that famous King?
Whom Phoebus hints at, name, that he may pay
The penalty. *Kreon.* I pray that safely I
May speak things terrible to see or hear.
Dull torpor wraps my limbs, my blood congeals.
For when with suppliant foot at Phoebus' shrine
I entered duly raising reverent hands
In prayer unto the god, an ominous roar
Burst from Parnassus' twofold citadel,
Snow clad, and Phoebus' laurel pendant there
Trembled and shook its leaves while suddenly
Castalia's sacred stream stood motionless.
Straightway the Letoan prophetess began
To shake her dreadful locks, in frenzy caught,
To receive Apollo. Ere she had reached the cave
Burst forth these words in more than human voice:
"Kindlier stars shall come to Cadmeian Thebes
If thou, o exile stranger, shalt depart
From Dirce, guilty of a monarch's death,

Known as thou art to Phoebus from thy birth.
For thee no lengthy joys remain from that
Slaughter most foul: nay, wars with thine own self
Thou shalt engage, and to thy sons beside
Leave other shameful wars when thou has turned
Back in thy course to thy nativity."

Oedipus.
What now at heaven's behest I contemplate
Is fitting tribute to a monarch slain
That none by craft may assail true royalty.
A king should guard the safety of a king:
No man reveres when dead whom safe he fears.

Kreon.
A greater fear expelled our reverence.

Oedipus.
Could any fear prevent the pious task?

Kreon.
The Sphinx and her fierce threats of baneful song.

Oedipus.
Now shall this crime by order of the gods
Be expiated. Of the immortal host
Whoever looks appeased upon our realm,
Thou in whose hands reside the eternal laws
Of swift revolving heaven, and thou the lord
Supreme of this bright universe that dost
With swift revolving wheel unfold the slow
Centuries, thou, too, sister to the sun
That keepest with thy brother constant tryst,
Night wandering Phoebe, thou that rulest the winds,
Driving thy dark blue chariot o'er the deep,
And thou that lordst it in the realms of night:
Hearken ye all: by whoso's violence
Laius fell dead, him may no peaceful home,
No faithful hearth, no kindly welcoming land,
Receive in exile. Sorrowing let him mourn
His shameful wedlock and the fruit thereof;
By his own hand may he his father slay
And (what more dreadful can be prayed) commit
All that I fled—no hope for pardon then.
By this my realm I swear which now I rule,
By that I left, by all my household gods,
By thee, o father Neptune, that dost wash
On either side mine ancient heritage

With twin floods swift recurring: come thou too
As witness to my words, thou that dost stir
The pregnant words of Cirrha's prophetess:
So may old age be sweet for me, my sire
Pass his last day in rich security
Upon his lofty throne and Merope
Conceive no wedlock but with Polybus,
As I spare not through favor him that slew.
    But tell me now, where was the impious act
Committed, was it war or treachery?

Kreon.

Faring to chaste Castalia's shady grove,
He trod a road with thickets dense beset
Where to the open fields a threefold way
Divides itself: while one road intersects
The land of Phocis, dear to Bacchus' heart,
Whence rising from the plain, soaring aloft
Parnassus rears its double head to heaven,
The second leads to where two oceans guard
The land of Sisyphus; and still a third
Winds through a hollowed valley to attain
The Olenian meadows, skirts the wandering stream,
Crossing at last fair Elis' chilling flood.
There as he passed secure, all unobserved,
A robber band wrought suddenly the deed.
    Now at our time of need, roused by the word
Of Phoebus, comes with slow and trembling step
The blind Tiresias led by Manto's hand.

Oedipus.

Honored of gods, second to Phoebus' self,
Expound this word: name him whom Justice seeks.

Tiresias.

That slow my tongue is, seeking some delay,
Thou with thy generous heart canst understand.
Great share of truth lies hidden from the blind.
But where my country calls and Phoebus too
I follow: let the facts be brought to light:
If still within my veins the blood ran hot
With lusty vigor, I should welcome god
Himself within this breast. Now to the shrine
Drive ye a bullock with a whitened back,
Likewise a heifer knowing not the yoke.
Thou, daughter, that dost teach my unseeing eyes,
Recount the unfailing signs of augury.

Manto.
   At the dread altar stands the victim rich.
Tiresias.
   Call thou the gods solemnly to our rites,
   Strewing the altar's top with frankincense.
Manto.
   Already incense burns on the gods' hearth.
Tiresias.
   What of the flame? Doth it burn copiously?
Manto.
   Quickly it blazes bright and quickly dies.
Tiresias.
   And is the firelight clear, does it rise pure,
   Rearing its head untarnished to the sky
   To wave its fiery locks to heaven's breeze?
   Or creeps it low about the altar's sides
   Uncertainly bedimmed in circling smoke?
Manto.
   Not one the fashion of the flickering flame,
   But, like the rainbow when the showers fall,
   It takes on varying hues: where to high heaven
   Its arch heralds the rain with painted bow
   Till doubt assails what colors fail and what
   Are there. The blue of heaven is intertwined
   With saffron hues, these with blood red until
   All ends in darkness; lo the battling flame
   Divides and ashes of one sacrifice
   Are made twofold; father I dread to look;
   Blood takes the place of Bacchus' offering
   And round the King's head rolls a darkening smoke
   Settling more dense around his countenance
   And hides in one thick cloud the murky light;
   The meaning, father, speak.
Tiresias.
                    What can I speak,
   Lost in the tumult of a mind distraught?
   What shall I say? 'Tis evil, dire but dark.
   The gods are wont to show their anger clear;
   What may it be that so they would reveal,
   Then would not, but conceal their dreadful wrath?
   There is that shames the gods. Bring hither swift
   The salted meal and on the victims' necks
   Sprinkle it now. Do they with peaceful mien
   Endure the sacred rites, the hands that touch?

Manto.
>The bullock rears aloft his head, his face,
>Turned to the rising sun, avoids the light
>And trembling looks away, shunning its rays.

Tiresias.
>And do they fall to earth each at one blow?

Manto.
>The heifer yields to the sword: at the first stroke
>She falls; the bull, struck for the second time,
>Blunders now here now there till weariness
>At length extorts his last reluctant breath.

Tiresias.
>Spurts forth the blood from out a narrow wound
>Or flows more sluggish from a deeper source?

Manto.
>Forth from the heifer's breast an abundant stream
>Pours rushing out, the bullock's mightier wounds
>Are stained with lesser stream, but, turning back,
>The blood flows amply through the mouth and eyes.

Tiresias.
>These portents dire augur some mighty fear.
>But tell me now the entrails' certain signs.

Manto.
>My lord, how now? Not in accustomed wise
>Tremble the entrails; mightily they shake
>And from the veins there leaps a fount of blood.
>The heart is shriveled, hides far out of sight;
>The veins show livid; sinews that should be here
>Are not, the rotting liver seethes with black gall
>And lo, an omen dread to tyrant's reign,
>Two heads appear rising on equal trunks
>Until a slender membrane hides them both:
>The side unfriendly, granting no hiding place
>To secret members, rises in its might
>Displaying seven veins that in their turn
>Are thwarted by the border set aslant.
>Nature and nature's order are reversed:
>No single organ holds its rightful place:
>All are reversed—the lungs, that cannot hold
>The breath, lie bloody on the right, the heart
>Has vanished from the left, the bowels give
>No passage to the body's excrements,
>Nature herself is changed: no natural law
>Controls this womb. Come, let us find the cause

That makes these entrails stiffen as they lie;
What impious horror here? An embryo calf
Within the unwedded womb, nor holds its place
Therein but fills its mother's body, groans
And weakly moves its legs that stiffly shake;
The livid blood besmears the sinews black,
The empty body rears itself and strikes
With budding horn the sacrificing slaves.
The vitals slip from out my hand. That sound
That startles thee is not the lowing herd;
The cattle make no sound: the altar fire
It is that groans and tremblings seize the hearth.

Oedipus.
What mean these omens of the fearful rite?
Expound; I hearken with no timid ear.

Tiresias.
You will be angry at the signs you seek.

Oedipus.
Tell me that one thing that the gods would tell,
What man with royal murder stained his hands.

Tiresias.
Nor birds that fly high heaven on pinions light
Nor vitals torn from living breasts can tell
That name: we must explore another way.
The King himself from shades of nether night
Must be called forth from Erebus to speak
His murderer's name. Earth must be reft in twain,
Dis the implacable invoked and all the host
Of Styx infernal summoned to our sight.
Name one to act for thee: who reigns in might
May not behold the dead.

Oedipus.
                      Kreon to thee
This labor falls who art second in this realm.

Tiresias.
While we unloose the bolts of lowest Styx
Let all the host give voice to Bacchus' praise.

CHORUS

With nodding ivy wreathe your disheveled locks:
Seize ye the thyrsus—seek the Corycian rocks.

Thou light of heaven, come.
Thy suppliant band,
Here in thy Theban home,
Summon thee, Bacchus, from thy native land.

Hither in festive dance
Turn thy clear virgin glance
And with the starry light
Of thy bright countenance
Scatter the clouds of night,
The threats of Erebus
And Fate omnivorous.

Flowers of spring are thine to wear,
And, to crown thy ambrosial hair,
Tyrian miter is for thee
And the clinging briony.
Tresses flung to the wanton wind
Or with a serpent clasp confined.

So, in the fear of Juno's hate,
Thou didst grow in virgin state,
And maiden figure counterfeit
To thy saffron robe commit.
Thence thy soft luxurious ways,
Trailing robes and roundelays,
Thus, in golden chariot drawn,
Lions swept thee toward the dawn
Where the Ganges' waters flow
And Araxes clothed with snow.

On humble ass Silenus follows thee,
Aged, his swelling temples garlanded,
While wanton followers bear the mysteries.

Following thee a maenad train
Scorned the lowlands and the plain,
Trod in joy Pangaeus' height,
O'er Thracian Pindus took their flight.

Thence to Thebes the maenad band
Led our Bacchus. Cadmus' land
Welcomed with its frenzied horde
India's fair Ogygian lord.

Matrons of the Theban state,
Girt with fawn skins dedicate
To Bacchus, thyrsus wielding
Blindly to his madness yielding.

Limb from limb the thyiad band
Tore the monarch of the land;
Then from Bacchic frenzy freed
Saw and knew not whose the deed.

O'er Ocean, Bacchus' foster mother reigns,
Cadmeian Ino, trailed of Nereids,
And Bacchus' youthful kinsman o'er the waves
Shares sway, Palaemon clothed with deity.

Thee a child the Tuscan band
Stole away till Nereus power
Stilled the waves; his mighty hand
Made the salty sea ways flower.

Plane trees burst to vernal green;
Laurel loved of Delphi's lord
Flashes twixt the branches seen;
Birds break forth with one accord;

Ivy twines about the oars,
Ivy to the masthead soars,
Indian tigers roam the stern,
By the bow a lion roars;

Pirates filled with strange alarms
Plunge beyond the ivied rail,
Rise transformed, their vanished arms
Shrunk to fins, a crescent tail

Cleaves the waves behind a back
Curved and shiny. Where before,
Pirates ranged o'er Neptune's track,
Dolphins follow evermore.

Thee Pactolus, Lydia's golden stream
Bore on its wealthy waters twixt hot banks
While the blood drinking Massegete foreswore
His Getic arrows and his unstrung bow.

Bacchus is lord; the realm Lycurgus wrought
With fierce axe-wielding hands,

The savage lands
Where range wild Dacian bands
Call Bacchus lord; the roaming races caught
By cold Maeotis flowing past;
Tribes frozen fast
By Boreas' nearer blast
Call Bacchus lord; hoardes that the years have taught
To seek on high
Where zenith crowns the sky
The wagons twain, the Arcadian galaxy.
Bacchus is lord.

Victor he o'er tribes Gelonian,
O'er the warriors Amazonian:
Squadrons from the Thermodon,
Steeds abandoned, arrows gone,
Maenads tread the rites Edonian.

For him Kithaeron's sacred earth,
   Crimsoned with stain
   Of Pentheus slain,
And Proetus' daughter reft of mirth
   Fled to his wood;
   While Juno helpless stood,
Argos bowed down to his miraculous birth.

To him the sea girt Nasian isle
Gave for a bride the Cretan maid
Abandoned by Athenian wile
To join with godhead unafraid.
Then from the barren stone,
Not in one stream alone,
Burst brooks of wine,
But fountains sprang apace
Down grassy slopes to race,
Fruit of the vine,
Thyme scented and withal
The milky streams of liquor mystical.

All heaven above
To bind that love
Followed the new made bride,
While Phoebus sang
The age-old nuptial song,

Adown whose shoulders hang
The curling locks ambrosial, wondrous long;
Twin Cupids waving torches by his side
Light the procession.
And Jupiter, his fiery terror shed,
Disowns the thunderbolt for Bacchus wed.

So while the stars of heaven shall run their course
Or Ocean with his ambient stream enclose
The imprisoned earth; while the full moon shall still
Collect her scattered fires and Lucifer
Proclaim returning dawn; until the Bear
Leave heaven above to plunge in Nereus' flood,
We shall do homage to the Lycean lord.

EPISODE 2.

Oedipus.
   Albeit thy face bespeaks a sad report,
   Tell me whose life shall pacify the gods.
Kreon.
   Thou bidst me speak what fear would bid me hide.
Oedipus.
   If crumbling Thebes move thee not, yet regard
   The slipping scepter of a kindred house.
Kreon.
   Thou'lt pray to know not what thou seekst to know.
Oedipus.
   A futile cure for ills is ignorance:
   Wouldst thou then hide the way to public weal?
Kreon.
   When medicine is foul, one shuns the cure.
Oedipus.
   Speak what thou knowest or prepare to know
   What ill can follow from an angry king.
Kreon.
   Kings hate the words they order men to speak.
Oedipus.
   Thyself shalt go a scapegoat unto hell
   And thou speak not thy secret utterly.
Kreon.
   Would that I might be silent. Can a king
   Be asked a lesser liberty than that?

Oedipus.
   Mute liberty is oft a greater bane
   To king and kingdom than the spoken word.
Kreon.
   When silence is forbidden what is left?
Oedipus.
   He nullifies the law who will not speak.
Kreon.
   I pray thee hear in peace words that are forced.
Oedipus.
   Was ever penalty when force made speech?
Kreon.
   Far from the city wall there lies a grove,
   Dark with thick ilex, Dirce's is the spot
   Within a well-washed valley. Stately woods
   Are guarded by a cypress and an oak,
   The one forever green, the aged oak
   Spreading wide crooked branches dry with age;
   One side consuming time has stripped away,
   The other, tearing loose its rotted roots,
   Leans on its neighbor. Laurel trees are there
   With bitter berries, quivering lindens too
   And Paphian myrtle, ash that presently
   Shall drive its branches through the unending sea,
   And pines whose branches battle Zephyrus,
   Defying Phoebus. In the very midst
   Rises a mighty tree whose shade widespread
   Covers the lesser woods, with far-flung branch
   Above, it stands defender of the grove.
   Darkling beneath, bereft of Phoebus' light,
   The unmoving waters sense eternal chill,
   A stagnant swamp that rims a sluggish spring.
     Hither the aged priest guided his step
   Nor hesitated; for the spot itself
   Bred night. Into a trench new dug were hurled
   Torches snatched up from funeral pyres. Himself
   The priest wrapped in his garb funereal
   Brandished his wand. Down to his very feet
   Fell his black robe and round his hoary head
   A wreath of blackest yew. So he advanced
   A downcast aged man in squalor clad.
   Black sheep and oxen black within the trench
   Are driven till on their living flesh the flame

Feeds as they tremble. Thence he summons forth
The shades and thee the ruler of the shades
And him who guards the dark Lethean Lake.
Magic he chants and with inspired voice
And threatening mien recites whatever words
Have power to appease or force the shades. He pours
Blood on the hearth the while he burns the beasts,
Making the trench run blood, then pours above,
Snow white, great streams of milk, with the left hand
Bacchus-made wine; his eyes upon the ground
A second time he chants with louder voice
Of Frenzy, calls upon the shades to come.
Then howled the host of Hecate and thrice
The hollow vales reëchoed mournfully.
Earth shook to her foundations till he cried
"They hear my words well spoken. Chaos black
Is burst asunder: to the hosts of hell
A passage opens to the upper air."
The woods drew back yet reared their foliage
In horror, mighty oaks were split, the earth
Retreated groaning as afraid to see
The piercing of the depths of Acheron,
Or as perforce, its framework wrecked, itself
Giving passage to the dead resoundingly.
Perchance 'twas Cerberus with triple head
That in his anger shook his mighty chains.
For suddenly earth yawned and opened wide.
I saw myself the sluggish lakes that lie
Amongst the shades, I saw the ghostly gods
And veritable night; the blood within
My veins stood frozen. Forth in ranks there leaped
Full armed the serpent host, the serried ranks
Of brothers, harvest of the dragon's teeth,
Baleful Erinys shrieked and Madness blind,
Horror and all the hidden brood produced
In the eternal darkness: Grief that tore
Her locks, Disease with weary sinking head,
Old Age that hates itself, uncertain Fear
And Pestilence the greedy scourge of Thebes.
Our spirits failed us: even she who knew
The old man's art and ritual, stood dumb.
Her sire unterrified, bold, by his curse
Summoned the bloodless troupe of dreadful Dis.

Straightway like fleecy clouds flitting they come
To breathe heaven's freedom. Eryx scatters not
So many falling leaves, innumerable
They come as flowers on Hybla in the spring
Where gather swarms of bees, more countless they
Than waves that shatter on the Ionian sea
Or birds in winter flying from the wrath
Of Strymon's bitter cold cleaving the sky
To exchange the Arctic snows for the warm Nile.
So thronged the shades to hear the prophet's voice.
Eager the trembling spirits hasten toward
The darkling grove; first from the earth emerged,
With right hand seizing by the horns a fierce
High-spirited bull, Zethus, and after him
Amphion, lyre in hand, charming the rocks
With dulcet tones; safe in her arrogance
Amongst her sons, head bowed, comes Tantalis
Counting the shades. More dread than Tantalis,
Agave, fury tossed, followed by all
The band that tore to shreds their wretched king:
And after them Pentheus himself who still,
A mutilated Bacchant, breathed forth threats.
Then last of all, invoked incessantly,
Hanging his head in shame, cringing apart,
Seeking concealment while the priestess calls
Unceasing and repeats her Stygian prayers,
Until he shows at length his features veiled,
Comes Laius—terror seizes me to speak:
His limbs still smeared with his own blood, his hair
Squalid with dreadful filth he stands and speaks
In frenzied tones: "O cruel house of Cadmus,
Ever delighting in the blood of kin,
Shake high the thyrses and with hands inspired
By god tear limb from limb thy sons—at Thebes
The crime that tops all crime is mother's love.
O country mine, no anger of the gods
But thine own guilt destroys thee. Pestilence
That comes with Auster's leaden breath nor drought,
When earth under a burning blast receives
No rainfall—these are not thy bane but he,
That bloodstained king who holds the scepter as
The prize of cruel murder, occupies
Impiously the couch that was his sire's,

Sowing where he himself was sown, to breed
Offspring unholy in his mother's womb
And, daring what wild beasts would spurn, beget
Brothers unto himself—sin so involved
So monstrous as to shame the very Sphinx.
A hateful progeny, yet not so cursed
The son as his own sire who bears the guilt
Of that twice outraged womb. 'Tis thou, 'tis thou,
The bloody scepter in thine hand, 'tis thou
That I, thy father unavenged, pursue,
Thou and thy city bringing in my train
The Fury, fit attendant o'er thy couch.
Her far resounding blows follow me where
I shall o'erthrow this house accursed and so
With impious war obliterate its gods.
Hence from your borders drive in haste your king
An exile wheresoe'er his guilty steps
Shall lead him; let him flee the land for then,
Bursting to green with spring fair flowering,
It shall repair its herbage and the air
Produce once more pure breezes and the woods
Regain their ancient glory: Pestilence,
Wasting and Death, Disease and Toil and Grief
Shall fare with him, companions suitable.
Yet, though he flee our land with hurrying step,
I shall make slow his feet, holding him back,
The while he creeps uncertain of the road
Testing each cruel step with aged staff:
Take ye his earth from him: I'll hide his heaven."

Oedipus.
Through all my frame, aye to the very bones
Pierces a chilling terror. All that I feared
To do is charged as done—yet Merope
Refutes the impious charge of lawless love,
Wedded to Polybus, and Polybus
Living acquits my hands: both parents give
The lie to charge of incest or of death.
What circumstance of blame remains? Before
I e'er set foot upon Boeotian soil
Thebes had long mourned her sovereign Laius slain.
Doth then the old man lie or is the god
Angered at Thebes? Nay, but I see the wiles,
The treacherous plot: to hide his deviltry

OEDIPUS OF SENECA

The prophet, making pretext of god's will,
Invents these lies to win for you my power.
Kreon.
Would I expel my sister from the throne?
Did not the sacred faith of kindred hearth
Hold me contented in mine own estate?
Fortune herself, beset with constant care,
Would fright me from such action: couldst thyself
Cast off unscathed this load intolerable
Thou shouldst be safer in a lesser sphere.
Oedipus.
Dost counsel me willingly to resign
Such royal power? *Kreon.* Counsel it, yes—to such
As still are free to make unfettered choice:
Thou of necessity must bear thy fate.
Oedipus.
The surest path for him who seeks a throne
Is praise of moderation, quietude:
The turbulent soul oft counterfeits repose.
Kreon.
Does such long loyalty avail me naught?
Oedipus.
Loyalty gives the traitorous soul its chance.
Kreon.
Free from encumbering care, I share the fruit
Of royal power; my home is ever filled
With citizens; and each returning day
Sees favors from the throne heaped lavishly
Upon my hearth: rich vestments, ample feasts,
And succor by my favor richly given:
What may I dream is lacking in such lot?
Oedipus.
That which indeed is lacking: second place
Knows never satisfaction. *Kreon.* Shall I then
Fall as though guilty with my case unheard?
Oedipus.
Did ye give reasons when ye sought my life?
Did even Tiresias hear my case? And yet
Ye deem me guilty: yours the precedent
I follow. *Kreon.* If I then be innocent?
Oedipus.
Kings must fear doubts as certainties. *Kreon.* Who fears
Vain terrors earns the real. *Oedipus.* He who's at fault
And is forgiven, hates: let doubt be done.

Kreon.
 Even so are hatreds born. *Oedipus.* Who dreads too much
Such hatreds knows not royal power: for fear
Guards kingdoms. *Kreon.* Whoso wields with tyranny
The scepter fears even the fearful: dread
Returns against its author. *Oedipus.* Guard him well—
For he is guilty—in some rock-bound cave.
Myself will hie me to my palace home.

CHORUS

Not thou the cause of ills
So great. Never from thee
Found Fate excuse to attack
Labdakus' sons.
Nay, 'tis an ancient wrath
Nursed by the gods.
Time was Castalian shade
Sheltered Sidonian guests;
Settlers from Tyre bathed
In Dirce's stream,
When first Agenor's son
Wearily searching
Jove's victim came at last
Weary and worn to Thebes;
Sat 'neath our sacred tree,
Bowed there in prayer,
Heard from Apollo's self
Bidding divine;
Followed the wandering heifer's track,
Heifer untouched of plough
Or curving share;
Ceasing at last his flight
Gave to our land a name
From that same heifer's plight.

Ever since that ill day
New marvels haunt our land:
The serpent monster reared
In lowly vale to rise
Hissing beyond the height
Of oak and pine.
O'er the Chaonian heath
It reared its head
Its body spread beneath.

Anon an armèd host arose
From earth; the trumpet sang
Untaught, the curving brass
Sounded its infant note
In battle line.
Lines of embattled kin
Swarmed o'er the plain,
Worthy the dragon seed,
Spanning in single day
A lifetime whole.
Born when the stars had set,
Dead before evening star.
The Tyrian stranger feared
Monsters of such surprise
Dreaded to war with such
Till youth in combat fell
With cruel youth and earth
Received again in death her progeny.
So civil strife spread wide
And Herculaean Thebes
Learned fratricide.

Hence came the fate untoward
Of Cadmus' scion when,
Horns decked his head and, now
A stag, transformed he fled
From his own dogs.
Swift through the hilly woods
Actaeon fled
With agile leaps through rocky glades,
Fearing the traps
Himself had set,
Till in the limpid stream
He saw his horn-crowned head,
Himself a wild beast,
Where once the goddess that tradition hymns
Of too stern chastity,
Had bathed in perfect peace her virgin limbs.

EPISODE 3.

Oedipus.
My heart renews its cares, renews its fears.
The gods of heaven and hell are joined to prove
My guilt—'twas I slew Laius: but my heart,

Nearer to me than any god, protests
And knows its innocence. Memory traces still
The story of a man too proud, too old,
That in his chariot drove me from the road.
I, in the flush of youth, struck with my staff
And sent him on the way to Dis. 'Twas on
The triple road of Phocis, far from Thebes.

Wife of my heart, tell me what I would know:
Was Laius broken in age or still a youth?
Iokaste.
Twixt youth and age but nearer age than youth.
Oedipus.
And were there many followers with the King?
Iokaste.
The most had lost their way, a faithful few
Still followed constant by his chariot wheel.
Oedipus.
Did any perish sharing the King's fate?
Iokaste.
One man whose faith and courage held him true.
Oedipus.
I see it clear: the number fits, the place—
But when was this?
Iokaste.
Ten years have passed since then.
Senex.
The host of Corinth summon you to take
Your father's throne, Polybus sleeps in peace.
Oedipus.
How cruel Fate attacks me everywhere.
Speak more and tell me how my father died.
Senex.
In peaceful sleep of age he breathed his last.
Oedipus.
My father dead and by no murderous act!
Bear witness all, I now may raise to heaven
Hands pure of guilt nor fearing any crime.
And yet Fate's greater part remains to fear.
Senex.
Thy father's throne will banish every fear.
Oedipus.
I'll seek that throne; but no, I fear my mother.

Senex.
   Thou fearest her who waits impatient there
   Thy coming? *Oedipus.* Piety forbids me thence.
Senex.
   Wouldst leave her then bereft? *Oedipus.* There lies my fear.
Senex.
   Speak out; what hidden fear burdens thy mind?
Oedipus.
   A mother's couch, that Delphi prophesied.
Senex.
   Then cease to dread vain shadows; put aside
   Base fear; thy mother was not Merope.
Oedipus.
   What profit sought she then from such pretense?
Senex.
   Children bring pride of confidence to kings.
Oedipus.
   Speak out: how knowest thou secrets of her couch?
Senex.
   These hands bestowed thee as a babe on them.
Oedipus.
   Thou gavest the babe to them: who gave it thee?
Senex.
   A shepherd on Kithaeron's snowy ridge.
Oedipus.
   What chance brought thee unto Kithaeron's groves?
Senex.
   Upon that mountain side I watched my herds.
Oedipus.
   Tell me beside, what marks prove me that babe?
Senex.
   Thou wert already pierced by the iron goad
   And from thy swollen feet didst get thy name.
Oedipus.
   And who was he that of my body made
   A gift to thee? *Senex.* He kept the royal herds,
   And under him the lesser shepherds served.
Oedipus.
   Tell me his name. *Senex.* I cannot, memory
   Slips first away beneath the weight of age.
Oedipus.
   Couldst recognize the man by face and form?

Senex.
>Perchance I might; often some trifling thing
>Recalls a memory clouded long by time.

Oedipus.
>Unto the altars drive the royal herds,
>Their shepherds with them: go ye slaves and call
>Those who are masters of the royal herds.

Senex.
>Whether intent or Fortune hid these things
>Let what is hidden be forever dark.
>Truth oft brings ill to her discoverer.

Oedipus.
>Is there aught worse to fear than what we know?

Senex.
>Be sure what must be greatly sought is great.
>Here stands the public safety, here the king's,
>Full weighty both: keep thou an even hand;
>Stir not—and Fate will manifest itself.

Oedipus.
>To disturb a happy state availeth naught;
>Safe is't to unsettle one in extremity.

Senex.
>Dost seek some nobler state than royalty?
>Beware lest found thy father cause thee shame.

Oedipus.
>I shall search out my lineage though low
>It be, if I may surely learn. And see,
>The aged guardian of the royal herd,
>Phorbas. Dost know the old man's name or face?

Senex.
>His presence stirs my mind. Not wholly known
>Nor yet unknown his countenance to me.

Oedipus.
>When Laius reigned wert thou his slave to tend
>His lordly herds upon Kithaeron's slope?

Phorbas.
>Kithaeron ever with green pasturage
>In summertime welcomed our roving herd.

Senex.
>Dost know me? *Phorbas.* Nay, my memory hesitates.

Oedipus.
>Was once a child given to him by thee?
>Speak. Dost thou falter? Why that paling cheek?
>What wouldst thou say? Truth cannot brook delay.

Phorbas.
  Thou stirrest matters hidden long by time.
Oedipus.
  Confess or pain shall wring the truth from thee.
Phorbas.
  Useless the gift on him by me bestowed.
  That child could never live to enjoy the light.
Senex.
  May god avert the omen. Live he does.
Oedipus.
  Why sayest thou the infant could not live?
Phorbas.
  The iron driven through had pierced both feet
  And bound his limbs. The wound quick festering
  Consumed with fever all his childish frame.
Oedipus.
  Why question further? Fate approaches near.
  Tell the child's name. *Phorbas.* My loyalty forbids.
Oedipus.
  Bring fire ye slaves. The flame shall force thy faith.
Phorbas.
  Shall truth be sought through bloody means like this?
  Forgive I pray. *Oedipus.* If cruel I seem to thee,
  Tyrannical, thy vengeance lies at hand.
  Speak out the truth. Who was he, who his sire?
  Who gave him birth? *Phorbas.* He was thine own wife's son.
Oedipus.
  Yawn earth, and thou great monarch of the dark,
  Thou ruler of the shades, to lowest hell
  Receive a scion worthy of its stock;
  Ye citizens upon this guilty head
  Heap rocks; slay me with weapons; with the sword
  Let every father seek my life, each son
  Worthy the name; let husbands arm themselves
  Against me, brothers too and let the sick
  Pest-ridden populace from funeral pyres
  Seize brands to hurl at me. I am become
  The guilty curse of all our age, a thing
  Detestable to gods and ruinous
  To all that's sacred; on that very day
  Whereon I breathed the first crude breath of life,
  Worthy of death. Up, rouse thy courage now,
  Dare again something worthy of thy crimes.
  Begone and swiftly seek the palace there,
  Congratulate thy mother on her brood.

CHORUS

If Fate were mine to guide
As I should choose,
Only to Zephyr's breeze
My sails I'd loose,
Lest 'neath the sterner gale
The sheets should fail.

Ever may gentle airs
That mildly float
Nor threaten ill, conduct
My unfearing boat.
From life's safe middle way
I would not stray.

Fearing the Cretan king,
In mad career
Seeking a starry course,
With new found arts
Striving to emulate
Birds of the air,
Trusting too much to wings
Fashioned by craft,
Icarus to the sea
Gave his lost name.

Daedalus warily,
Finding his way
Through the more lowly clouds
Midway to heaven,
Like an old hawk his brood,
Watched for his son
Till from the sea he saw
Hands stretched for help:
All that betrays excess
Stands insecure.

But what is this? The door
Creaks and a royal slave
Downcast with shaking head
Comes forth.
Tell us what news thou hast.

EPISODE 4.

Messenger.
When Oedipus had learned the will of fate
And his own origin and had condemned
Himself guilty of crime unspeakable,
Seeking the palace furious he came
With hastened step within that hated home,
Like Libyan lion raging o'er the plain
Shaking its tawny mane with threatening head.
His face was grim with fury; flashing his eyes,
With a deep roar he groaned and down his limbs
The cold sweat ran, foam flecked his lips, he breathed
Dire threats, his mighty passion overflowed.
In rage he plans some great catastrophe
Fit for his fate. "Why hesitate," he shouts.
"Let whoso will pierce with the sword this breast
Dishonored or with kindled flame or rock
O'erwhelm me. Is there no cruel tigress then
Or bird ill-omened that shall feast upon
My vitals? Thou Kithaeron that dost hold
Crimes all uncounted, send thy cruel beasts
Against me, send thy maddened hounds, let come
Once more Agave. Soul, dost fear to die?
Death only saves the innocent from Fate."
So did he speak and put his impious hand
Swift to the hilt and drew his sword. "Is't so?
Canst pay such short-lived penalty for crimes
So mighty? Thou shalt die and satisfy
Thy father, what of thy mother then and what
Of thy most ill-begotten children, what
Sufficient ruin to requite thyself
And thy great guilt; what of thy country's wrong?
Thou canst not pay: Nature that ratified
New laws for Oedipus, devising strange
And unknown ways of birth, shall be herself
Deviser of his punishment: were I
To live and die again, by constant birth
To pay fresh penalty—come wretched soul,
Bestir thy mind; what may not be but once
May be protracted; seek some lingering death.
Find out some means whereby, though not yet dead,
Thou yet mayst linger here bereft of life.

Die must thou but beyond thy father's realm.
Dost hesitate, my soul?" A sudden storm
Of tears drenched both his cheeks. "Is it enough,
To weep," he cried; "Is such an innocent flood
Enough? Nay, let my battered eyes themselves
Follow these tears: ye gods of married love,
Is this enough? I'll gouge these eyes." He spake
And raged in fury, cheeks aflame with fire
And eyes that scarce retained their wonted seat.
His face transformed with anger, like one mad,
He groaned and with a roar assailed his eyes,
While they in turn flashing with fell intent
Leaped forth to meet the hand that wounded them—
Hands like to talons that laid hold of them
And tore them pitiless from their very roots.
Then impotent explored the hollow space
Tearing the sockets where the eyes had been
And raged incontinent in fury vain.

  At last he tried the light, raising his head,
And from his empty hollows searched the sky
Finding but night. The last mangled remains
Of what were eyes he sweeps aside and shouts
Victorious to the gods: "Spare ye, I pray,
My Fatherland; I have made good the debt
Of punishment and for my marriage couch
Found worthy night." The foul descending flood
Watered his face, the wounded head belched forth
From severed vein abundant streams of gore.

CHORUS

By Fate we are compelled—yield ye to Fate:
No anxious thought
Can change the fabric wrought
Upon the loom of Fate;
All that befalls this race of mortal man,
All that we do began
Within the clouded past.
For Lachesis with hand that may not stay
Without regret
Preserves the pattern set.
As all things move by Fate's predestined way,
So Earth's first revolution fixed the last.
Not god himself may turn

From its appointed course
Aught that by precept stern
Must hold to the order of its ancient source.
Many in futile hate
Have wrecked their lives—or soon or late
Seeking to outwit destiny have met their fate.

The doors are opening—lo, the King himself
Sightless, abandoned, makes his way alone.

EXODUS

Oedipus.
'Tis well, 'tis finished, unto my father's spirit
I have performed the rites decreed. This dark
Delights me. Pray what god at length appeased
Spreads o'er my head this cloud of blackness. Who
Gives recompense to crime— I have escaped
The witness of the day—yet, parricide,
Thou owest naught to thy right hand—the light
Fled thee—that face disfigured suits thee well.
Chorus.
Look you, Iokaste comes with maddened heart
And maddened leaping step like that bemused
And frenzied mother of the Cadmeian house
When she had torn away her own son's head—
And knew what she had done. She would address
The sufferer; she halts in fear; till shame
Overcomes sorrow. Yet the words half formed
Stumble upon her lips.
Iokaste.
                    What shall I call thee?
Son? For thou art my son. Dost hesitate
In shame before that name? Nay speak,
My son, even against thy wishes. Why
Avert thy head, that empty countenance?
Oedipus.
Who now forbids me to enjoy the dark?
Giving me back my eyes? My mother's voice.
All, all in vain. We may no longer meet.
Our impious selves let the deep sea divide,
The depths of earth or if beneath our earth
There be another facing other stars
And wandering sun—let it take one of us.

Iokaste.
    Fate's is the blame: no man can sin by Fate.
Oedipus.
    Ah mother, spare these words and spare mine ears,
    I beg you by this body's torn remains,
    And by the ill-omened issue of my blood,
    By all that's foul or noble in our name.
Iokaste.
    Why dost thou sleep, my soul, why dost refuse
    To pay the common penalty of crime?
    Through thee, incestuous, all humanity
    Hath lost its honor. Die thou then, destroy
    Thy guilty life. Not if the omnipotent
    Father of all the gods himself should hurl
    Through shaken universe his thunderbolt,
    Would he exact from me full punishment
    To fit my crimes, foul mother that I am.
    Death is my will, now find the way of death.
    Come, and thou art a parricide, now give
    Thy hand to help thy mother; only this
    Is left for thy fulfilment. Seize the sword.
    By that blade fell my husband; nay not so:
    The father of my husband. Shall I plunge
    The blade into my breast or sheathe it deep,
    Deep in my throat? Thou canst not choose the place?
    Hither right hand, strike here the ample womb
    That bare my husband and my husband's sons.
Chorus.
    She lies there dead. Within the very wound
    Her hand succumbs; the gushing flow of blood
    Spews out the knife.
Oedipus.
                O, god of prophecy,
    God of the shrine of Truth, to thee I speak.
    My father only did the Fates demand:
    Twice parricide, more guilty than I feared,
    I killed my mother too: 'tis by my crime
    That she is dead. O lying god of light,
    I have outdone the impious Fates foredoomed.
    Trembling my step, I follow darkling ways;
    And with uncertain foot and quavering hand
    Master the unseeing night. Go wanderer,
    Hasten thy steps unsure, begone—Yet stay:

Step not upon thy mother.
                    All that be
Weary in body, with disease oppressed,
Disheartened unto death—behold I go.
Lift up your heads: a kindlier heaven shows
Behind me as I flee. Let whosoe'er
Clings to a failing life breath, draw again
Deep draughts that vivify. Go bear to those
Abandoned unto death some timely aid.
The ills of all the world I take with me.
Ye Fates of Violence, fell Pestilence,
Wasting and frenzied Grief and dread Disease:
Come ye with me, with me. Such be my guides.